*On Being Nonprofit*

# On Being Nonprofit

*A Conceptual and Policy Primer*

Peter Frumkin

HARVARD UNIVERSITY PRESS

Cambridge, Massachusetts

London, England

*For my parents,*
*Allan and Jean*

First Harvard University Press paperback edition, 2005

*Library of Congress Cataloging-in-Publication Data*

Frumkin, Peter.
    On being nonprofit: conceptual and policy primer / Peter Frumkin.
      p. cm.
    Includes bibliographical references and index.
    ISBN 0-674-00768-9 (cloth)
    ISBN 0-674-01835-4 (paper)
    1. Nonprofit organizations.   I. Title.

  HD2769.15 .F78 2002
  361.7'63—dc21       2002017227

# Preface

In recent years, the study of nonprofit and voluntary organizations has been a growth field, a fact that is apparent in the proliferation of nonprofit degree and certificate programs in schools of business and public affairs, the founding of new independent centers devoted to nonprofit research, and the steady increase in scholarship concerned with nonprofit organizations. To date, however, the study of nonprofit organizations has yet to find a home in any single discipline. And this may well be for the best. Our understanding of nonprofit organizations has benefited from the attention of economists, political scientists, sociologists, psychologists, historians, and management scholars. In writing this book, I have endeavored to bring together some of the most significant and contentious ideas about the nonprofit and voluntary sector and to integrate at least some elements of the competing disciplinary perspectives that have emerged. This is, after all, a book about the nonprofit and voluntary sector written by an organizational sociologist who teaches strategic management in a public policy school. It is my sincere hope that this book will cross disciplinary bounds and that it will serve as a useful and clarifying overview of the pressing conceptual and policy problems facing nonprofit organizations today.

Dividing nonprofit action into four broad functions, this book examines how nonprofit organizations promote civic and political engagement, deliver critical services within communities, provide an institutional vehicle for social entrepreneurship, and allow the expression of values and faith. The core of the book explores the tensions and problems that have arisen in each of these functional realms and the boundary disputes that have broken out as nonprofit organizations have been drawn into competition and collaboration with government and business. In exploring the multiple roles of nonprofit organizations, I argue that the long-term health and viability of nonprofit organizations depend on the achievement of balance among the four functions, so that no one function is allowed to dominate the other three. This has not always been achieved in recent years and the results have been painfully clear: charges of politicization, vendorism, commercialism, and particularism have plagued nonprofit organizations. The argument developed here is that only when nonprofits achieve important successes in each of their functions will they receive and sustain the financial support and public acceptance that they need to continue to grow. In tackling these broad and complex issues, I have aimed to provide a perspective on nonprofit activity that will be relevant to scholars and students approaching the topic from a wide array of backgrounds and levels of familiarity.

The intellectual debts I have accumulated over the years are very large. From the very first moment I joined the faculty of Harvard University's Kennedy School of Government and began to work on this book, I have benefited greatly from the good counsel and insightful criticisms of Mark Moore and Christine Letts, who together helped launch the Hauser Center for Nonprofit Organizations, where I have been a faculty affiliate. I am grateful to both of them for creating a place where it is possible to do serious work within a community of scholars and students. My faculty colleagues at the Hauser Center and within the broader Kennedy School of Government have all contributed directly or indirectly to the completion of this book. Through numerous seminar presentations, e-mail exchanges, and hallway discussions over the years, their active—sometimes aggressive—questioning has led me to sharpen and improve my arguments. I owe a special debt to Peter Dobkin Hall, who read and commented on the entire manuscript and generously shared with me his encyclopedic knowledge of all things nonprofit. My understanding of the nonprofit sector has been substantially enriched by friendships, conversations, and collaborations over the years with Joseph Galaskiewicz, Paul Light, Steven Rathgeb Smith, Brint Milward, Barry Karl, Ellen Condliffe Lagemann, Marion Fremont-Smith, Allen Grossman, Elizabeth Keating, Donald Haider, David Reingold, and William Ryan.

One of the real pleasures of working at the Kennedy School of Government has been the opportunity to teach and work with a group of superb doctoral students, including especially Alice Andre-Clark, Gabriel Kaplan, and Mark Kim. For several years, Kennedy School students in my class on the nonprofit sector patiently listened and questioned me as the ideas in this book were formed and developed. From the start,

Shawn Bohen has expertly managed the Hauser Center's work and growth and, with great humor and patience, helped me navigate the serpentine world of Harvard rules, regulations, and budgets, while also providing the kind of advice and help that was necessary for seeing many projects to completion. Jennifer Johnson provided wonderful research assistance throughout the writing of the book and helped bring the manuscript to final form. Michael Aronson at Harvard University Press guided this book from an idea to a manuscript, arranged helpful reviews, patiently explained the publishing process to me, and made the whole process appear less mysterious.

Behind the scenes of much of my research, a group of generous supporters have allowed me to pursue ideas wherever they led. It is a pleasure to thank the Hauser Center for Nonprofit Organizations, Claude Rosenberg of NewTithing Group, Patricia Brown of the Burton G. Bettingen Corporation, Ted Halstead of New America Foundation, and Mark Abramson of the PriceWaterhouseCoopers Endowment for the Business of Government, all of whom supplied critical financial support for elements of my broader research agenda. Within the Kennedy School, Alan Altshuler, Ron Heifetz, and Fred Schauer furthered the project at critical stages, and I am grateful for their help.

Finally, my greatest debt is to my wife, Elizabeth, who encouraged me from my first day of graduate school and through all my subsequent research. Her unstinting support has made everything seem possible.

# Contents

# The Idea of a Nonprofit and Voluntary Sector

The nonprofit and voluntary sector is the contested arena between the state and the market where public and private concerns meet and where individual and social efforts are united. Nonprofit and voluntary action expresses a complex and at times conflicting desire to defend the pursuit of private individual aspirations, while at the same time affirming the idea of a public sphere shaped by shared goals and values. For this difficult balancing act to work, participation in the sector demands a commitment to, among other things, expression, engagement, entrepreneurship, and service. Constituted by both legally chartered nonprofit organizations and myriad informal groups and voluntary associations, this sector occupies an increasingly critical and visible position in our political, social, and economic life.[1] Yet despite its size and perceived influence, there is considerable uncertainty and confusion about its boundaries. The lines delimiting the sector have frequently been subject to challenge and revision, as funds and responsibilities have shifted back and forth among business, nonprofit, and government organizations. Reaching consensus on the very definition of the nonprofit and voluntary sector is difficult because many of the core features and activities of nonprofits increasingly overlap and compete with those of business and government.

Thus, the nonprofit and voluntary sector is at once a visible and compelling force in society and an elusive mass of contradictions. On the one hand, the rise of nonprofits is thought to have contributed to democratization around the world, opening up societies and giving people a voice and a mode of collective expression that has in too many cases been suppressed.[2] In the United States, nonprofit and voluntary organizations are seen as playing a central role in generating, organizing, and emboldening political opposition, working through national networks and building international linkages. Nonprofit and voluntary organizations have also acted as practical vehicles for the delivery of a broad spectrum of community services, ranging from affordable housing to theater performances to vocational training to health care. The nonprofit sector appears, therefore, to be a real and identifiable group of tax-exempt organizations that encourage political engagement and produce services. The sector is in fact a documented economic powerhouse that employs millions of people and accounts for a significant portion of the nation's gross domestic product. All of which makes the nonprofit sector a strong and compelling concept that appears grounded in economic, political, and legal reality.

On the other hand, the nonprofit and voluntary sector is home to such a wide range of organizations that grouping them together into one entity is highly problematic. From the largest hospitals and universities (which fund their operations by collecting fees or tuition) to small mentoring programs and avant-garde arts organizations (which survive on charitable contributions), nonprofits span a tremendous range of organizational forms. Many of these forms are stable and lasting, while others are fragile and transient. Some of the organizations that are considered part of the nonprofit sector, such as religious congregations and private membership organizations, operate without government funding. Other nonprofit organizations, particularly those that service the elderly and poor, could not survive without the steady flow of funds from federal, state, and local government. Beyond differences in funding, the organizations within the sector are balkanized by legal status, level of professionalization, and underlying purpose.

Thus, any exploration of the nonprofit and voluntary sector would do well to begin by acknowledging its fundamentally contested nature. This chapter reviews the difficulties in defining the central characteristics of nonprofit and voluntary organizations, the conflicting nature of the words we use to describe this part of our world, and the evolving place the sector occupies in America's fragmented and polarized political sphere. Throughout, the tensions inherent in the very idea of organizations operating between the state and the market emerge again and again. All of which leads to the analytic framework that guides this book in its exploration of the overarching functions of the nonprofit and voluntary sector.

## Three Features of Nonprofit and Voluntary Organizations

Attempting to define the fundamental features of the disparate entities that constitute the nonprofit and voluntary sector is a complex and daunting task. Yet there are at least three features that connect these widely divergent entities: (1) they do not coerce participation; (2) they operate without distributing profits to stakeholders; and (3) they exist without simple and clear lines of ownership and accountability. Taken together, these three features might make nonprofit and voluntary organizations appear weak, inefficient, and directionless, but nothing could be further from the truth. In reality, these structural features give these entities a set of unique advantages that position them to perform important societal functions neither government nor the market is able to match.

Perhaps the most fundamental of the three features is the sector's noncoercive nature. Citizens cannot be compelled by nonprofit organizations to give their time or money in support of any collective goal. This means that, in principle at least, nonprofits must draw on a large reservoir of good will. This noncoercive character is also what most starkly differentiates the sector from government, which can levy taxes, imprison violators of the law, and regulate behavior in myriad ways. The power of coercion that the public sector possesses is a powerful tool for moving collectivities toward common ends, but it is also a source of strife and contention. Trust in government is now low,[3] making the effective use of state power more and more difficult as its legitimacy fades. For nonprofit and voluntary organizations, these issues do not arise. Free choice is the coin of the realm: donors give because they choose to do so. Volunteers work of their own volition. Staff actively seek employment in these organizations, often at lower wages than they might secure elsewhere. Clients make up their own minds that these organizations have something valuable to offer. Though they stand ready to receive, nonprofit and voluntary organizations *demand* nothing. As a consequence, nonprofits occupy a moral high ground of sorts when compared to public sector organizations that have the ability to compel action and coerce those who resist.

In some ways, the noncoercive character of the nonprofit and voluntary sector situates it closer to the market than to government. Business depends on the free choice of consumers in a competitive market where alternatives are often plentiful and where no firm has the capacity to compel anyone to purchase its goods or services. Similarly, nonprofit organizations cannot coerce participation or consumption of their services. The sector makes choices available, rather than deciding for others. When it comes to the mobilization of funds, the parallel between business and nonprofits is equally clear. Just as no one forces anyone to buy shares or invest in enterprises, no one forces anyone to give or volunteer in the nonprofit world. The flow of resources to a nonprofit depends entirely on the quality and relevance of its mission and its capacity to deliver value. To the extent that a business firm or a nonprofit organization is performing well, investors and donors will be attracted to it. Should things take a turn for the worse, investment funds and philanthropic funds usually seek out other options quickly.

The second feature of nonprofit and voluntary organizations sharply differentiates them from business firms, however. While corporations are able to distribute earnings to shareholders, nonprofit and voluntary organizations cannot make such distributions to outside parties. Rather, they must use all residual funds for the advancement of the organization's mission.[4] By retaining residuals rather than passing them on to investors, nonprofit organizations seek to reassure clients and donors that their mission takes precedence over the financial remuneration of any interested parties. The nondistribution constraint has been seen as a tool that nonprofits can use to capitalize on failures in the market. Since there are certain services, such as child care and health care, that some consumers feel uncomfortable receiving if the provider is profit driven, nonprofits are able to step in and meet this demand by promising that no investors will benefit by cutting corners or by delivering unnecessary services.

While the noncoercive feature of nonprofits brings nonprofits closer to business and separates them from government, the nondistribution constraint pushes nonprofits closer to the public sector and away from the private sector. Government's inability to pay out profits from the sale of goods or services is related to its need to be perceived as impartial and equitable.[5] With nonprofits, the nondistribution constraint also builds legitimacy and public confidence, though this does not mean that special powers are vested in these organizations. In both sectors, the non-distribution constraint strongly reinforces the perception that these entities are acting for the good of the public.

The third feature of nonprofit and voluntary organizations is that they have unclear lines of ownership and accountability.[6] This trait separates these entities from both business and government. Businesses must meet the expectations of shareholders or they risk financial ruin. The ownership question in the business sector is clear and unambiguous: shareholders own larger or smaller amounts of equity in companies depending on the number of shares held. Similarly, government is tethered to a well-identified group of individuals, namely voters. Executive and legislative bodies—and the public agencies they supervise at the federal, state, and local levels—must heed the will of the electorate if they are to pursue public purposes effectively and retain the support and legitimacy needed to govern. There is also a long tradition in the United States of conceiving government as "belonging" to citizens, though the ways in which this ownership claim can be exercised are severely limited. In the nonprofit sector, clear lines of ownership and accountability are absent.[7]

Nonprofit and voluntary organizations must serve many masters, none of which is ultimately able to exert complete control over these organizations. Donors, clients, board members, workers, and local communities all have stakes, claims, or interests in nonprofit and voluntary organizations. Yet none of these parties can be clearly identified as the key ownership group. The relative strength of these ownership claims depends on how an organization is funded and on its chosen mission.[8] Nonprofit organizations that depend heavily on charitable contributions are often held closely accountable by their donors, some of whom believe that as social investors they have a real stake in the organizations to which they contribute. Nonprofits that are largely driven by service fees or commercial revenues are in a different position. While these more commercial organizations do not have donors asserting claims over them, social entrepreneurs and professional staff may view themselves as the key stakeholders in these more businesslike organizations.

Often, however, the lines of ownership and accountability are rendered more complex by the fact that many nonprofit organizations combine funding from multiple sources—foundations, corporations, and government—with earned income, making it hard to point to any particular party as the key stakeholder to whom these special institutions must answer.[9] One might be tempted to point out that nonprofit and voluntary organizations are almost always governed by boards, and to propose this as a solution to the ownership and accountability issue. Unfortunately, board members are not owners. They are stewards who are held responsible for the actions of their organization. In the end, nonprofit and voluntary organizations are authorized to act in the public interest by the communities in which they operate, though the lines of accountability are weaker than those in the public sector and the lines of ownership far more obscure than in the business sector.

These three features of nonprofit organizations are not without controversy and contention. In fact, each has been called into question in recent years. First, the noncoercive nature of the sector has been challenged by the growing tendency to mandate community service or volunteer work. In the case of welfare reform, many states have required aid recipients to complete a community service requirement in order to continue receiving their monthly support payments.[10] A growing number of high schools now make volunteering with a local organization a condition for graduation. In addition, there have long been parts of the nonprofit landscape where strong norms are enforced on those who have committed to membership. Within professional associations, licenses to practice medicine, law, and other callings are granted and denied by nonprofit entities.[11] Within many religions, the behavior of adherents is severely constrained by doctrine. In some neighborhoods, independent community groups have been granted the power to plan and constrain future development by residents. The exercise of power may be subtle in some cases. For example, many private funders exercise considerable influence over the recipients of their grants. This influence can take the form of a gentle suggestion or a condition of support that programs be revamped.[12] Although the constraints imposed in each case follow a decision to participate and join, the power of some nonprofits over groups of individuals is considerable. In each and all such instances,[13] the noncoercive character of these organizations is called into question.

Second, the nondistribution constraint of nonprofit organizations has likewise been under assault from a number of different directions. In recent years, increased scrutiny of the high salary levels of many nonprofit executives has led some to ask whether the "profits"—or, more accurately, the increased program revenues—are not in fact being routinely distributed to staff in the form of generous compensation and benefit packages.[14] In the area of capitalization, large nonprofit organizations have been aggressive in raising funds through bond offerings, which do not offer investors the ownership stake that stock offerings do, but which have the effect of opening up major capital flows into the non-profit sector. The accumulation of capital in the form of large endow-ments has also called into question the boundary between business and nonprofit organizations: endowment funds, by their nature, are not used to fulfill an organization's immediate needs. Instead, they are invested in stocks, real estate, and other speculative investments designed in the long run to maximize financial return. This is a strategic move that some have characterized as contrary to the public purposes of nonprofit orga-nizations.[15] Making the boundary between nonprofits and business firms even more opaque, at least one study has argued that the nondistri-bution constraint does not significantly increase consumer confidence in the trustworthiness of nonprofits compared to business firms.[16]

Third, the ownerless character of nonprofit and voluntary organiza-tions has come under fire as the legal claims of nonprofit stakeholders have evolved. The courts have held that only members (in the case of a membership organization), trustees or directors, and the attorney gen-eral in the state where the nonprofit is located have legal standing to contest the action of a charitable corporation. Over the years, however, the power of trustees and directors has grown substantially, not to the point where they can claim ownership of the assets of a nonprofit, but to the point where boards now have tremendous leeway in the way they operate a charitable organization.[17] While these claims have rarely come to equal those of ownership, the lines of accountability have been drawn more sharply, particularly as questions about the transfer of assets have come up when nonprofit organizations have attempted to convert to for-profit status.[18]

The ultimate result of these debates and trends is that the defining fea-tures of nonprofit organizations are evolving and are the subject of con-siderable debate. The notion that there is some simple and unambiguous test that can be developed to decide what sector an organization belongs to is no longer reasonable. While the Internal Revenue Service (IRS) and the states have developed statutes and rules that define and regulate these special institutions, a different and far more complex reality has emerged. The legal code is often of limited value in the effort to deter-mine which organizations are really nonprofit and voluntary in their operation.

## Composition of the Nonprofit and Voluntary Sector

In the United States today, there are more than one and a half million registered nonprofit organizations, as well as several million informally organized community groups. The formally registered organizations fall into two broad and porous categories: those that serve the public and those that serve members. The public-serving organizations, classified under section 501(c)3 of the IRS code, operate in almost every imaginable field of human endeavor, and include, among countless others, social service agencies helping children, the elderly, and the poor; independent schools and private colleges; community clinics and hospitals; think tanks; environmental organizations; cultural groups such as museums, theaters, and historical societies; and a range of international assistance organizations. They are the most visible and recognizable part of this organizational universe. But substantial resources are concentrated in the member-serving or mutual benefit organizations, which include credit unions, business leagues, service clubs, veterans' organizations, and trade associations. They tackle problems ranging from the most complex issues of business policy to the most prosaic challenges of small-town life. Also included in the sector (though not filing forms annually with the IRS) is a vast array of churches, synagogues, and mosques that form the foundation of the nation's religious life. While we tend to think of congregations as membership organizations, they are treated differently by government and are not subject to the same forms of oversight as other member-serving nonprofits.

While the largest and better-financed nonprofit organizations receive the bulk of public attention, important work is done by the army of less visible associations, clubs, networks, and groups through which communities come together and act.[19] There is considerable dispute as to whether the legally chartered nonprofit organizations share enough traits with informal voluntary associations to justify including both groups in one sector.[20] However, leaving these grassroots associations out of the picture grants far too much deference to the tax treatment of nonprofits and ignores the fact that informal associations and formal nonprofits both eschew the distribution of profits, are noncoercive, and have no owners.

Public awareness of the sector is rapidly increasing, though surprisingly little is known about the underlying purposes and values that animate nonprofit and voluntary action or the vehicles through which these values and purposes are channeled. In part, this is because these activities reflect a sometimes confusing agglomeration of strongly held private values, as well as a set of complex public purposes. The sector can thus be conceived as a tent covering public-serving charities, member-serving organizations, and a range of informal organizations, including voluntary and grassroots associations (see Figure 1.1).

This diverse and at times contradictory group of entities comprises organizations and associations that are neither part of the state nor fully engaged in the market. The sector's solutions to community and public problems at times represent a conscious disavowal of commercial markets and a realization that some exchanges are simply better conducted under terms of mutuality and trust than under the strict dictate of *caveat emptor.*[21] Using charitable contributions, many nonprofit and voluntary organizations can deliver services to clients who are unable to pay. At other times, nonprofit and voluntary action represents an attempt to move beyond government action to find solutions to public problems that a majority of citizens are unable or unwilling to support. Nonprofits

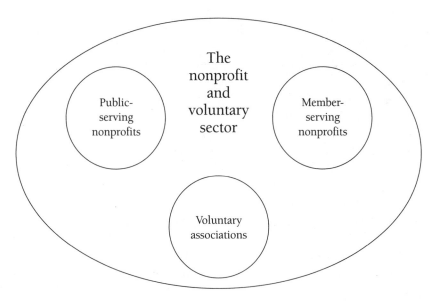

1.1 Elements of the nonprofit and voluntary sector.

can and do speak to community needs that lie outside the priorities of the median voter. But the position of this group of organizations in relation to the market and the state is far more complex and changeable than these simple claims of differentiation might lead one to believe. In some fields of activity within the sector, intense commercialism has eroded the moral high ground of these organizations and transformed nonprofits into shadow businesses that compete actively for clients able to pay for the services they offer. In other fields, nonprofits have lost their autonomy from government and have come to serve as dutiful implementers of public sector programs and priorities. The lack of clarity in the identity of nonprofit and voluntary organizations in relation to business and government becomes ever more evident as soon as one considers the range of names used to speak about these entities.

## What's in a Name?

The process of arriving at a single term to designate this sphere of activity has been long and conflicted. Although the term "nonprofit and voluntary sector" is common today, many other terms have been devised over the years. The long-standing confusion over terminology can be traced to the diversity of activities that need to be covered by whatever term is chosen.[22] Programs are delivered through both formal and informal organizations, carried out by both salaried and volunteer staff, and supported through donations, contracts, and commercial revenues. As a consequence, the formal organizations that constitute the sector have at various times and for various reasons been called "the tax-exempt sector," "the nongovernmental sector," "the independent sector," "the third sector," "the civil society sector," "the commons," "the charitable sector," "the voluntary sector," "the nonproprietary sector," and "the nonprofit sector." The terminological debate continues today. Each of the many terms that has emerged over time has had its own historical and political baggage. A brief review of these terms will illustrate the scope of the sector, even if a definitive defense of any particular term is impossible.

One of the earliest names attached to these organizations was in some ways the narrowest and the most descriptively accurate: "tax-exempt." After the ratification of the Sixteenth Amendment to the Constitution and the establishment of the national income tax in 1913, Congress granted tax-exempt status to those organizations that were specifically "organized and operated exclusively for charitable, scientific, and educational purposes." Later additions included a long series of very specific purposes, including "prevention of cruelty to children or animals" (1918), "community chest, fund, or foundation" (1921), and "testing for public safety" (1954). The categories of tax-exemption have shifted over time; today there are more than twenty different specific categories of tax-exempt organizations delineated under the Internal Revenue Code. The arbitrariness of these narrow categories can best be seen today in the fact that international sports organizations are specifically recognized, whereas health organizations are not. But this is of little consequence, since the vast majority of public-serving nonprofits file today under the catch-all category 501(c)(3). For a time, the moniker "tax-exempt organizations" was widely used inside government and within the legal community because it pointed—or at least appeared to point—to the black letter of government regulation. Yet because this approach did not capture the huge number of clubs, associations, and groups that have never been formally registered with the IRS, it fell out of favor and was replaced with others.

In the 1970s, efforts to find a broader and more inclusive term led to a whole series of names that aimed at positioning the sector in opposition to government. Today, the term "nongovernmental organization" (NGO) remains popular around the world. It is used to denote the array of organizations that pursue public purposes through largely private means. It covers both indigenous organizations working within particular countries overseas and international organizations that work around the world. While not specifically limited to a particular field of activity, when the term "nongovernmental organization" is used today, it usually denotes an organization that works to promote such things as rural development, education, environmental quality, and community health. What is interesting about the term "nongovernmental" is that it defines these independent organizations in opposition to government, rather than in opposition to business firms. One possible explanation for the popularity of this term internationally is the power and dominance that the state enjoys in many developing countries and the relative absence of organized opposition. The sector is thus defined as that which is not part of the state, rather than that which is not oriented toward profit-making. This choice also implicitly reflects the oppositional role of local nongovernmental organizations, which do in fact challenge governments and hold them accountable. In some countries, small, informal organizations within the broader NGO sector are at times termed "people's organizations" and "community-based organizations," as a way of differentiating them from larger, more formal institutions. The label "nongovernmental" remains firmly entrenched in current usage, particularly when Americans seek to distinguish between American nonprofit organizations and international NGOs.

The term "independent sector" came into popular usage in the 1980s and can be traced to a particular event—namely, the founding of Independent Sector, the national trade association representing both grant-making and grant-receiving organizations.[23] Founded in 1979, the group consolidated two existing associations and sought to unify the motley world of foundations and nonprofit organizations. By advancing the use of the term "independent sector," organizers of the association wanted to emphasize the capacity of these organizations to devise solutions free from the market and political pressures. The only problem with this term is that over time it became increasingly obvious that nonprofits were neither independent from government nor free from the pressures of the marketplace. As government funding for social service and health nonprofits has risen sharply, many have come to view nonprofit organizations as engaged in important collaborative relationships with government. Independence from government has come to be seen as more of a wish than a reality. Similarly, the idea that nonprofit organizations operate independently from the market has been called into question by the growing number of cross-sector partnerships, joint marketing agreements, and nonprofit commercial ventures.

At times, the term "third sector" has been in vogue. Popularized by several early researchers in the field of nonprofit and voluntary action,[24] this term had the advantage of covering both formally constituted nonprofit organizations and the countless informal grassroots organizations that populate the sector. The idea that nonprofit and voluntary action was somehow third in line after government and business rubbed some people the wrong way, however. It seemed to imply a kind of inferiority and subsidiarity that few in the sector were willing to concede. While the term "third sector" is still sometimes used in the research community, the practitioner community rarely uses it. Like "nonprofit" and "nongovernmental," the term "third sector" seems to define these organizations in isolation from the other sectors.

The term "civil society" was coined by the classic writers of political theory, and has regained currency of late. The modern idea of civil society plays a prominent role in the work of Hobbes, Montesquieu, and Hegel, who used it to refer to the broad private realm outside the state. One of the problems with using the term today is that "civil society" traditionally encompassed everything from the family to the church to the business corporation. Still, the term is acquiring popularity both in the United States and internationally, and it has lately come to refer to something more concrete than the huge and abstract private realm outside the state. In practice, it has come to denote a set of voluntary mediating institutions that invite individuals to come together to pursue shared interests, values, and commitments. Over the past decade, "civil society organizations" has come to compete with "nongovernmental organizations" among people interested in indigenous social movements around the world, ranging from small local organizations to large international institutions.

More recently, yet another solution to the name game was proposed. Instead of a term that either defined the essential characteristic of these organizations or that situated these organizations in relation to government and the market, a new form of reference was proposed: "the commons." Advocates for the term argued that the vast landscape of nonprofit and voluntary action constitutes a special terrain of shared concerns.[25] "The commons" was intended to solve some of the problems associated with previous attempts at naming the sector. It denoted the vast array of relationships between benefactors, intermediaries, and beneficiaries that constitutes a space in which associative communities can operate freely. Linked to the Greek term *koinonia*, "the commons" emphasizes free participation, common purpose, shared goods, a sense of mutuality, and a commitment to fairness.[26] A critical part of what distinguishes "the commons" from other attempts to delineate the non-market and nonstate realm of activity is that the definition focuses not just on what kinds of purposes are accomplished, but also on the ways in which they are accomplished. By pointing to the features of *koinonia*, "the commons" defines the boundary of the sector in ethical terms.

In several European countries today, the dominant term is "the charitable sector," which captures the critical philanthropic character of these organizations and their activities. The very use of the term "charity," however, harks back to Victorian England, the settlement house movement, and the class elitism associated with "poor aid" and "alms giving." Because self-help and community empowerment have become rallying points for the sector, the idea of calling this part of society "charitable" offends some people because it puts the spotlight on the contributions of elite patrons and donors, not on the efforts of activists, caregivers, and clients. The term also implies that much of the work of the sector is funded through private gifts, when in reality government funding and earned income now fuel large parts of the sector.

"The voluntary sector" has been in use intermittently for decades, both in the United States and abroad. One clear advantage of the term is that it focuses on the vast landscape of formal and informal organizations that work for the public good. It is a way of including the millions of neighborhood-based groups that operate without legal recognition. Yet the name has been criticized at times for obscuring the growing professionalism of nonprofit activity, a subject of considerable sensitivity. As part of the process of receiving more and more funding from public sector agencies through contractual relationships, many nonprofit managers now take great pride in the fact that they have removed all vestiges of amateurism associated with volunteerism and have replaced it with the professional work of highly trained people.

Most recently, some people dissatisfied with the existing alternatives have begun using the term "nonproprietary organizations" in order to highlight the ownerless character of these entities. In contrast to business firms that are proprietary, nonproprietary organizations are not linked to a clear owner or ownership group. This alternative has been advanced because the term "nonprofit" obscures the fact that many "nonproprietaries" do in fact generate surplus revenue, though they do not directly distribute their earnings to shareholders or owners. While this term has the benefit of drawing a clear line between business firms and nonprofits, it does not resolve the question of what differentiates nonprofits from government agencies, which are also nonproprietary.

Of the many competing options, the term "nonprofit sector" has been the most widely used over time. Rather than defining these organizations in terms of the special privilege they enjoy of being free from taxation, the term points in a different and less contentious direction by emphasizing the benevolent character of the sector. Though there is some question as to when exactly the term "nonprofit sector" came into use, the consensus is that it is a product of the 1950s and 1960s. The term "nonprofit" focuses on one of the three defining features mentioned above—namely, that these organizations are not intended to generate profits and distribute them to investors. Since this term distinguishes nonprofit organizations from business corporations, some observers have argued that it was actually designed to confer a kind of legitimacy and trustworthiness.[27] In recent years, the substantial increase in commercial revenues and executive salaries within the nonprofit sector has led many to question just how unprofitable the sector truly is. Still, the label "nonprofit sector" has the benefit of currency and simplicity.

Because the sector comprises both legally chartered nonprofit organizations and countless informal groups and voluntary associations, I will use the somewhat cumbersome though descriptively accurate "nonprofit and voluntary sector" to denote the organizations occupying an increasingly critical and visible position in our political, social, and economic life. Though not perfect, the term points accurately to the target population of organizations that are emerging as critical actors even though they operate without coercion, profits, or owners. This is a compromise solution that many researchers working in this field use, though some fall back on "nonprofit sector" for brevity's sake. Though it does not please everyone, the term does meet the requirement of being broad enough to cover the range of organizations and groups that are acting privately for some collective good.

Underlying all the names that have been used to describe these entities is the fact that even when agreement is reached on a single appropriate name, it is not entirely clear that this complex and varied set of organizations constitutes a single coherent societal "sector."[28] In many ways, the word "sector" is just as problematic as "independent," "third," "nongovernmental," and all the terms that have preceded it. An important part of the problem is the lack of consistency across the organizations that are said to be part of this sector. After all, the sector includes organizations that cater to the narrow needs and desires of their memberships, as well as organizations that have broad public service missions.[29] The sector is also home to highly institutionalized organizations with millions of dollars in revenues and informally organized groups with little or no money. The sector includes political parties that exist to shape public policy and service delivery organizations that depend on the political process to deliver needed funds. The sector counts as its constituents both foundations that give away money[30] and a multitude of organizations that seek grants, as well as a growing number of organizations that depend on fees and commercial revenues. Thus, given the great diversity of formal and informal structures, the varieties of purposes pursued, and the range of financing systems used to support these organizations, the very use of the word "sector" is troublesome because it implies far more consistency than may be present. Some scholars of nonprofits thus maintain that the idea of a coherent sector may be an invention, which has begun to outlive its usefulness and now merely provides cover for a large and diverse group of organizations that have little in common.[31]

Yet, by defining a set of activities that are neither part of government nor part of the market,[32] we acknowledge that there is a sphere where coercion is not used, where profits are not the principal motive, and where lines of ownership are not clearly drawn. Why nonprofit and voluntary organizations exist and what functions they perform are among the central topics of this book. Before presenting a framework for thinking about these issues, it is important to recognize some of the political cleavages that the very idea of a nonprofit and voluntary sector creates.

## The Politics of the Nonprofit and Voluntary Sector

The nonprofit and voluntary sector occupies an ambiguous and at times contentious position in the current American political scene. Just as few people agree on the right name to use to describe these organizations, Americans are likewise engaged in heated debate about the sector's underlying politics. Today, for quite different reasons, nonprofit and voluntary organizations are embraced by both conservatives and liberals. How can this be? The answer lies in the fact that the sector comprises a great number of complex, multidimensional organizations that appeal simultaneously to many constituencies. The fact that both sides of the political spectrum applaud and see the potential of nonprofit and voluntary organizations, far from revealing some underlying weakness, ultimately reflects the sector's strength and enduring relevance.

For at least three reasons, nonprofit and voluntary organizations have, particularly from the 1960s forward, represented a tremendous resource and ally to liberals. First, a natural affinity between liberals and non-profit workers quickly became apparent, since those willing to toil in often low-paying or voluntary positions—and frequently in difficult circumstances—constitute a self-selected group of socially committed individuals dedicated to the idea of making a difference and initiating change. As membership in labor unions declined, thus eroding one of the traditional bases of the Democratic party, the rise of nonprofit social service agencies in the 1970s came at a very opportune moment. Not only could nonprofit organizations serve as new channels through which social programs could be delivered, but they also represented a new and important space in which potential supporters of progressive policies might well be located.[33]

The second reason liberals were attracted to the sector as a whole was more operational. Nonprofit organizations were seen as an ideal and untainted partner to government, one that could most effectively deliver needed services to the most disadvantaged populations. As concern over the impact of Great Society programs grew and as distrust of government increased, nonprofits came to be seen as neutral and legitimizing forces with the capacity to give large human service initiatives a more diverse, pluralistic face.[34] The funding crunch that most nonprofit organizations face on a continuing basis appeared to put government in a position to use its substantial resources, in the form of contracts and grants, to gain control over a whole new range of community actors and problems. At the same time, nonprofits represented an ideal "bottom-up" approach to implementation, one that empowered the grassroots level and that gave government tremendous leverage for each dollar spent.

Third and finally, liberals were attracted by the political activity of many nonprofits and their ability to mobilize groups around issues and concerns in a distinctive way. Unlike corporations, which are beholden to shareholders and the bottom line, and unlike government, which is bound by the limits of the Constitution and the pressures of public opinion, nonprofit organizations have a great deal more freedom to operate. This flexibility lends itself well, in principle, to the pursuit of progressive, alternative agendas. Moreover, since many advocacy nonprofits seek to give voice to populations that have long been excluded from the political debate, liberals continue to view the broader nonprofit sector as a means to exert pressure for social change and justice.[35]

Changes in the national political climate since the 1980s coincided with a very different set of ideas about the nonprofit sector. Instead of considering nonprofits a potential source of political and social change, conservatives were attracted by three completely different features of nonprofits. First, they believed that nonprofit organizations might well represent an appealing alternative to direct public expenditures on social programs that conservatives believed had not produced results.[36] Questions about whether the War on Poverty had failed were in the air, especially in the early 1980s. By encouraging private charities to take responsibility for local community needs, conservatives believed they could make an effective argument for shrinking government. After all, if churches and community groups were able to function with voluntary contributions of time and money, the need for an ever-growing number of public spending programs would surely be diminished. Compared to taxation and national spending, private charity and volunteerism were seen as preferred means of solving social problems because they permitted greater individual freedom and choice. A strong and vital nonprofit and voluntary sector fit well with the emerging ideas of both devolution and privatization, two mantras of the conservative movement. As government functions were pushed "down" from the federal level to the state and local levels, and transferred "out" of government to private providers through contracting, nonprofits were ideally situated to deliver services that once had been the province of "bureaucrats" in the nation's capital.[37]

Second, conservatives also argued that nonprofits, particularly faith-based nonprofits, were in a position to bring to social programs something that public entitlements had long lacked—namely, a moral or spiritual component.[38] Faith-based nonprofits were seen as willing to make demands on the recipients of charity and require a change of character and behavior in exchange for assistance. At the same time, given that many nonprofits are fueled by volunteer labor and private contributions, conservatives were attracted to the idea of nonprofits because they represented the ideal of self-help and independence. This was a powerful feature that, conservatives argued, was perilously missing from public assistance programs.[39] For those who believed that public entitlements bred dependence and complacency, the idea of delivering not just a check but a moral and spiritual message was a very strong attraction.

Finally, for conservatives, nonprofit organizations were also a potential wellspring of innovation, representing a plurality of local solutions to social problems and a powerful alternative to the ongoing search for uniform national solutions to public problems. Grounded in an ethos of self-help and respecting regional cultural variations, voluntary action fit well with a growing sense among conservatives that a broad range of alternatives to an expanding state needed to be actively cultivated. By giving local organizations a chance to try their hand at program implementation, conservatives believed that good ideas would percolate up from communities. Conservatives argued that expenditures on federal social welfare and education programs should not be increased. Instead, funds could be used most effectively and creatively when channeled through local groups that were more in touch with the diverse and changing needs of the people. Nonprofit organizations thus represented a way of breaking through the red tape of Washington to find new approaches to longstanding problems. Nonprofits, conservatives maintained, could serve as a battering ram for policy innovation.[40]

At first blush, it might appear that the capacity of nonprofit and voluntary organizations to speak to both liberals and conservatives implies either a split and conflicted identity or a simple lack of political scruples. In reality, the sector is a remarkably complex entity, one that is capable—like an inkblot—of evoking a broad range of reactions and interpretations. Because it simultaneously supports the autonomy of the private individual actor while affirming the importance of shared and public purposes, the politics of nonprofit and voluntary action can take on many different meanings. The ability to speak across, or rather above, traditional political boundaries has become one of the most powerful features of the sector, and this trait has led to its growth and popularity, particularly among young people.

## The Two Dimensions of Nonprofit and Voluntary Action

Given the confusion over what to call this sector and the complex and at times confused politics that have surrounded it, the goal of this small book is to help shape our understanding of the many different ways one can approach the core functions of these independent organizations. To make this task easier, I organize my exposition of the central functions of voluntary and nonprofit organizations along two broad conceptual distinctions. The first critical distinction concerns how the sector is explained; the question is whether nonprofit and voluntary activity is driven primarily by demand or by supply—that is, whether it can best be understood as a response to unmet demands or whether it is taken to be an important supply function that creates its own demand. The second distinction concerns how the sector is justified; here the issue is whether the value of nonprofit and voluntary action is seen as residing in the instrumental character of the outcomes that are generated for society or in the inherently expressive quality of the activities themselves that reward those who undertake them. These are complex and difficult distinctions, which will be discussed in turn and then brought together to form the conceptual framework for the analysis that constitutes the core of the book.

Starting with the distinction between demand and supply, it is easy to see nonprofit and voluntary action as responding to two quite different but important forces.[41] The demand-side perspective starts with the premise that the sector exists by virtue of the broader social context within which it is embedded and that its activities are responsive to the demands of the public or its members. Thus, nonprofits exist because they are able to meet important social needs. Urgent public problems such as illiteracy, drug addiction, and violence demand solutions, and the nonprofit sector exists to respond to the powerful pull of such issues. The demand-side approach to nonprofit activity has both descriptive and normative dimensions. Descriptive demand-side theories focus on patterns of nonprofit formation and growth. In the 1970s, researchers proposed detailed economic models and explanations for nonprofits' behavior,[42] most of which started with the assumption that nonprofits fulfill important demands that for one reason or another the market and government are unable or unwilling to meet. This led to the broad and popular belief that nonprofits were really gap-filling entities that historically have arisen when public needs were sufficiently strong.

On a more normative level, the demand-side approach to nonprofit organizations has spawned a literature focusing on the social and political responsibilities of nonprofit organizations—defined in relation to the demands of the neediest members of society. Starting with the claim that the tax exemption accorded these institutions conveys an obligation to help, many people have made the normative argument that nonprofit organizations should seek to assist the most disadvantaged and empower the most disenfranchised members of society. Accordingly, the success or failure of the sector can and should be judged by how well or how poorly it meets society's needs. The demand for nonprofit and voluntary action leads neatly to a set of prescribed activities, including greater advocacy work within the sector, and the empowerment and mobilization of those left out of the political process. The demand for nonprofit activity thus brings with it the expectation that these institutions will help give voice and opportunity to those who have been marginalized by the market economy and the political process.

The idea of a demand-driven nonprofit and voluntary sector dominates much of the research that is conducted in this field. Yet a central claim of this book is that the demand-side approach captures but one aspect of this broad social phenomenon. An alternative, supply-side position argues that the sector is impelled by the resources and ideas that flow into it—resources and ideas that come from social entrepreneurs, donors, and volunteers.[43] This is a more controversial perspective because it has led to some strong claims about how nonprofit organizations should be managed and operated. Rejecting many of the preceding arguments about the needs that pull on the sector, the supply-side perspective holds that nonprofit and voluntary organizations are really all about the people with resources and commitment who fire the engine of nonprofit and voluntary action. Drawn to the sector by visions and commitments, social entrepreneurs bring forward agendas that often operate independently of immediately obvious and enduring community needs. This supply-side theory of nonprofits, like the demand-side approach, has both descriptive and normative elements.

On the descriptive side, this approach emphasizes the entrepreneurial quality of nonprofit activity. Instead of starting with the demand of clients, positive supply-side theories of the nonprofit sector draw attention to the way various forms of entrepreneurship fuel innovation within the sector and how an emerging class of new social enterprises—increasingly led by a new generation of social entrepreneurs—is challenging old models of nonprofit management. Seen from the supply side, nonprofit organizations have a logic that is far more complex than a simple response to a gap in government service or the failure of the market to meet a particular demand. The entrepreneur, donor, and volunteer take on a much greater role in this model, since it is the supply of new ideas, charitable dollars, and volunteer commitments that is the real driving force behind the sector. This means that the task of explaining the emergence of nonprofit and voluntary organizations requires studying and developing typologies of social entrepreneurs who use the nonprofit form to pursue their private visions of the public good.

The supply-side approach has an important normative component, which holds that we must reassess the moral claims that needy clients have on nonprofit programs. Instead of asking that a nonprofit meet a test of moral stewardship that is ultimately decided by the level and quality of service provided to those in need, the supply-side approach advises that society should look to and protect the private interests and values of the critical actors who are fueling nonprofit and voluntary action, including philanthropic donors, volunteers, and social entrepreneurs. In order to ensure the continued flow of charitable inputs, the interests and values of these actors should be the first priority of those who seek an enlarged role for nonprofits. This means recognizing that the satisfaction of donors and the preservation of their intent constitute a critical normative task for the sector. Arguing that donors, volunteers, and social entrepreneurs should be the centerpiece of the sector is a controversial position because it unabashedly diminishes the claims that needy populations have on the charitable resources. Supply-siders counter this complaint with the argument that if one is truly committed to helping the needy, then constructing a sector that recognizes, protects, and encourages action by the private parties who control the resources should be an obvious priority.

Distinguishing between the demand and supply sides of the nonprofit and voluntary sector is a primary task when it comes to sorting through the arguments that have emerged in recent years. Yet we must also develop a second dimension for our conceptual framework. As soon as we begin to consider the broad number of important projects and causes to which the sector is dedicated, it becomes clear that nonprofit and voluntary organizations rest on two different ideas about what justifies and gives meaning to the work that is carried out in the sector.

First, nonprofit and voluntary action is an important *instrument* for the accomplishment of tasks that communities view as important. Nonprofit service agencies and volunteer helping organizations play an important role in the delivery of critical services in a broad array of fields. Nonprofits can be the principal means through which job training, arts education, shelter for the homeless, health care, neighborhood clean-ups, firefighting, crime patrols, and countless other functions are accomplished. When the sector works to accomplish popular social purposes, it acquires powerful instrumental value. It becomes a concrete tool to achieve some collective purpose that society considers important. The sector's instrumental value is measured in terms of its concrete outcomes. In the search for validation and learning, the programmatic outcomes of nonprofit and voluntary action are increasingly being measured and evaluated using metrics borrowed from the business and public sectors. The growing emphasis on performance has led to a vast new literature on nonprofit management, which is aimed at making these organizations more efficient and useful instruments for the accomplishment of public purposes.[44] The idea that nonprofit and voluntary organizations are valuable because they can be useful tools for the accomplishment of public purposes constitutes the core of what I will term the "instrumental dimension" of the nonprofit and voluntary sector.

Second, the sector can be seen as valuable because it allows individuals to *express* their values and commitment through work, volunteer activities, and donations. By committing to broad causes that are close to the heart or by giving to an effort that speaks directly to the needs of the community, nonprofit and voluntary action answers a powerful expressive urge. For donors, volunteers, and particularly staff, the very act of attempting to address a need or fight for a cause can be a satisfying end in itself, regardless of the ultimate outcome. The value that is created may be entirely psychic and may arise simply from the act of expressing commitment, caring, and belief. The expressive quality of the sector has led some to conclude that the narrow focus on the financial resources available to nonprofit organizations and on the level of services delivered has detracted from the deeper meaning of nonprofit and voluntary action, which derives from the fellowship and self-actualization experienced by those who give or volunteer. This is what I will refer to as the "expressive dimension" of nonprofit and voluntary action.[45]

The expressive and instrumental dimensions of nonprofit and voluntary action can compliment each other or they can create tensions. In the best cases, the moral energy that motivates those who deliver services can be harnessed to produce better and more effective programs. In some ways, this connection seems obvious: a committed volunteer or social entrepreneur is more likely to work hard to create value through his activities than someone who holds a job merely to earn a paycheck. In some cases, however, values and personal expression can be out of sync with instrumental goals and may lead to trouble. On the one hand, if strong expressive desires draw people to causes and community problems without adequate structure or planning, frustration can easily set in and group cohesion may be threatened. On the other hand, if too much focus is placed on improving a charitable organization's bottom line and maximizing the instrumental efficiency of its operations, an organization runs the risk of dimming the expressive flame of its staff, volunteers, and supporters. The managerial challenge, of course, is to bring the expressive and instrumental dimensions into alignment.

The contrast between the supply and demand sides and the opposition of the expressive and instrumental dimensions give us a basis for thinking systematically about the functions of nonprofit and voluntary action. We can construct a matrix that depicts, on one side, the nature of the value produced by the sector (instrumental versus expressive) and, on the other side, the underlying animus or force (demand versus supply). This book is organized around the four cells generated by this matrix (see Figure 1.2), which have come to represent the four underlying functions of the nonprofit and voluntary sector: encouraging civic and political engagement, delivering needed services, enacting private values and religious convictions, and providing a channel for social entrepreneurship.

The book works through and elaborates current debates relating to each of these four functions. Chapter 2 considers the role nonprofit organizations play in fostering civic and political engagement. Local nonprofits contribute in important ways to community cohesiveness, social solidarity, and what some call "social capital," which is constituted by the norms, networks, and forms of trust that make communities work. These ties prepare people to play an active role in civic life and democracy. Grassroots community organizations also have the capacity to harness this community spirit and generate social and political change.[46] Using the protection afforded by the First Amendment, these advocacy and organizing efforts are a critical ingredient in our national political life. In fields ranging from environmental protection to world peace, nonprofit and voluntary organizations have begun to exercise considerable political power. Nonprofits play a powerful role in setting the terms of many public debates, in mobilizing key constituencies, and in coordinating grassroots campaigns to effect change at the local, state, national, and transnational levels.

Chapter 3 considers how nonprofits represent an effective and powerful tool for responding to concrete public needs that the market and the state fail to meet. On the questions of why nonprofit organizations come into being and what role they play in society, a strong line of argument has emerged. Starting in the 1970s and continuing into the 1980s, theories about nonprofits focused heavily on the idea of government and market failure. Researchers proposed the idea that nonprofit provision of particular services arises when either government is unable to meet demand or when consumers are resistant to purchasing a given service in the for-profit marketplace. This positive theory of nonprofits embraced the subtle assumption that nonprofits were really just government's partners, charged with helping to deliver needed services. Since government and nonprofit organizations were thought to have the same basic goals and values, collaboration between sectors was seen as largely unproblematic. Some of the progenitors of this early, foundational per-

|  | Demand-side orientation | Supply-side orientation |
|---|---|---|
| Instrumental rationale | Service delivery <br><br> Provides needed services and responds to government and market failure | Social entrepreneurship <br><br> Provides a vehicle for entrepreneurship and creates social enterprises that combine commercial and charitable goals |
| Expressive rationale | Civic and political engagement <br><br> Mobilizes citizens for politics, advocates for causes, and builds social capital within communities | Values and faith <br><br> Allows volunteers, staff, and donors to express values, commitments, and faith through work |

1.2 The four functions of nonprofit and voluntary action.

spective argue that the future of the nonprofit sector lies in its capacity to cooperate and collaborate effectively with government, even though tensions between sectors appear to be rising. Chapter 3 presents the early models of nonprofit production, while raising new practical questions about the interaction of nonprofits with government and the market.

Chapter 4 considers the essentially private character of nonprofit and voluntary action that makes the sector an ideal vehicle for the expression of personal values and spiritual beliefs. Nonprofit and voluntary organizations are places where believers of all sorts are welcome, some of whom are motivated by faith, others by commitment to issues, and still others by strongly held private values and norms. The value component of nonprofit work—which goes beyond the rational, purposive function of that work—is part of what defines the sector and attracts donors, volunteers, and entrepreneurs to nonprofit and voluntary action. The values that animate nonprofit and voluntary action can often be important sources for innovation and experimentation, as private visions of the common good are tested and refined. The discussion covers the controversial normative position that has evolved in recent years from this positive analysis, which holds that the special visions of donors and entrepreneurs—not the growing demands of the recipient organizations and their clients—should define and shape nonprofit activity. It is important to note that when one shifts the focus of the normative analysis from recipients to donors, volunteers, and social entrepreneurs, the evaluative criteria for the sector change radically. Instead of measuring outputs and outcomes for clients, evaluation looks at the subjective experience of those funding and delivering the services. Because it flies in the face of the more progressive ideas that have dominated thinking about the sector, this particular part of the supply-side vision represents a way of seeing nonprofit and voluntary activity that challenges some of our comfortable assumptions about nonprofit organizations.

Chapter 5 tracks one of most important changes in the sector over the past two decades—namely, the growth of a new kind of social entrepreneurship and the rise of commercial activities as a way of financing aggressive growth agendas. Rather than waiting for donors to support initiatives with charitable dollars, more and more nonprofit managers are exposing their organizations to market forces. The rise of entrepreneurship in nonprofit organizations is manifest in many different ways, including the creation of new kinds of hybrid organizations, the influx of a generation of younger, more business-oriented managers, and a willingness to rethink the traditional boundaries between for-profit and not-for-profit enterprises. Many of the new entrepreneurial nonprofits explicitly start out with the intention of producing social innovations that will in turn create their own demand. This marks a major change from the traditional idea of delivering services for which there is already a demand. To finance this start-up strategy, some social entrepreneurs have developed funding plans that rely heavily on revenues from commercial ventures of all kinds, not just charitable contributions or government grants. Chapter 5 looks at both the theory and practice of nonprofit entrepreneurship.

After reviewing the four core functions of the sector, Chapter 6 explores emerging challenges connected to the sector's rapid growth and identifies a few significant consequences that flow from seeing the sector as a diverse and pluralistic realm. The chapter, and the book as a whole, advances a message connected to both the management of individual nonprofit organizations and the direction of the sector as a whole: each of the four functions of nonprofit activity is important in itself. But when pursued in isolation and in excess, any of the functions can lead to imbalance, at both the organizational level and the sectoral level. If individual nonprofits and the sector as a whole are seen as only engaging in political organizing and advocacy, charges of excessive politicization are likely to arise sooner or later. If the sole focus of nonprofit activity is the efficient delivery of publicly funded services, concerns about independence and vendorism will never be far away. If nonprofits do nothing but enact private values and interests, worries about particularism will almost certainly arise. If nonprofit activity comes to be focused too much on the creation of income-generating ventures, objections related to commercialism will be difficult to counter. Balance and a plurality of purposes thus turn out to be critical to sustaining nonprofit organizations and to the sector's continued growth and success.

At a time when nonprofit and voluntary activity has been the subject of increasing public attention and academic study, the breadth and depth of our understanding of this phenomenon has been severely constrained by the lack of a clear statement of the sector's core activities, rationales, and dimensions. This book strives to respond to this need by presenting four critical functions that the sector performs. While it does not pretend that these functions entirely exhaust the range of purposes and rationales that guide nonprofit and voluntary action, the book argues that many of the most essential conceptual and policy problems within the sector can be usefully captured with this framework. The normative argument of the book is simply that the sector cannot survive and garner financial, political, and volunteer support if it swings too far in the direction of any particular function. In the long run, balance, achieved through the fulfillment of a diversity of functions, is ultimately essential within the vast range of nonprofit organizations and across the sector as a whole.

Nonprofit and voluntary action can be a powerful force for good in society. Yet a good many myths have grown up around these private organizations that fulfill public purposes. In searching for the core functions of the nonprofit and voluntary sector, the book challenges some of these myths and suggests that the nonprofit and voluntary sector is an evolving and at times contradictory realm that now faces a number of significant challenges to its continued growth and legitimacy. Rather than attempting to smooth over and resolve these tensions, the exposition here deliberately brings them out in to the open. Ultimately, it is the diversity of purposes and rationales embodied in nonprofit and voluntary organizations that make them increasingly visible and exciting vehicles for the pursuit of common social goals. And it is the sector's diversity and flexibility that may well help nonprofit organizations to solve some of the pressing challenges they now confront.

# 2

# Civic and Political Engagement

Nonprofit and voluntary organizations respond to the deeply rooted need of individuals to be part of something bigger than themselves. As an antidote to atomistic individualism, nonprofit and voluntary activity at the local, state, national, and transnational levels brings people out of their isolation and puts them in touch with others who share their concerns and interests. The connections forged when people are drawn into civic space can be used to respond to community concerns, needs, and demands. By virtue of their emphasis on expressive, associational activity, nonprofits allow individuals and communities to transform their commitment into concrete collective action. When nonprofits speak directly to important public needs and lead collectivities to devise effective solutions to public problems, these diverse organizations—ranging from block clubs to national membership groups—help overcome some of the cynicism and distrust that stifle civic and political engagement. The special ability of nonprofit and voluntary activity to mobilize and connect individuals clearly has significant direct and indirect political implications.[1]

Nonprofit and voluntary organizations are linked with the political process in six different ways, which range in character from nonpartisan to very partisan. First, nonprofits build trust, cohesion and social capital in communities. Through church groups, veterans' clubs, PTAs, and many other kinds of organizations and associations, individuals find connections to one another and build a sense of community and solidarity that leads to greater enthusiasm for community life. This trust, or "social capital," represents a critical reservoir of good will and serves as a catalyst for civic and political engagement. Second, nonprofits promote civic engagement directly by offering individuals a door that opens onto the public square and a tool for demonstrating commitment to something greater than narrow self-interest. Civic engagement skills are learned and honed through nonprofit and voluntary action. Third, nonprofits translate trust and civic engagement into direct political action by organizing people at the grassroots around interests and causes, by registering voters and spurring them to get out the vote, and by organizing town hall meetings and a host of other participation and empowerment activities aimed at bringing the individual into the public sphere. Fourth, nonprofits are linked to politics through advocacy work. Organized around broad issues and concerns, nonprofits play an important role in informing and educating the public and policymakers. Advocacy efforts take place at the local, state, national, and transnational levels. Fifth, nonprofits engage in direct lobbying around specific legislative issues. Almost every time government moves forward with a decision, lobbying on both sides of the issue occurs. Different from advocacy in that it focuses on specific bills of legislation, lobbying is a way to translate public concerns into legislative action. Sixth, nonprofits figure prominently in our electoral system. Campaign fundraising organizations, political action committees, and a range of party institutions are all tax-exempt organizations. In recent years, cynicism about the role of moneyed interests in politics has raised some difficult questions about this particular function of nonprofits.

As they work to build cohesion in communities and as they speak out on issues, nonprofits enjoy freedom of association and speech under the First Amendment. While nonprofits have often had an adversarial relationship with government, the diverse forms of their political activity are still guaranteed government protection. No matter what causes they seek to advance, nonprofits do not risk the loss of their protected status as long as they follow a few basic rules when exerting their fundamental rights to speech and association. There is no test of reasonableness when it comes to the political views of nonprofits, nor are there prohibitions on coalitions' forming behind any peaceful cause imaginable. Of course, this has led to the advocacy of policies and agendas that have been controversial, often because they challenged majority positions. Still, law and public policy have affirmed that the role of nonprofit organizations in the political arena is a good in itself. Beyond protecting speech and association by enacting and enforcing laws, government also promotes this work by funding and supporting nonprofits that engage in all kinds of political work both at home and abroad.

Nonprofits have taken full advantage of the freedoms and protections afforded to them. Formal and informal groups of all kinds have played leading roles in a number of important social movements, including those for civil rights, women's rights, workplace safety, and environmental protection.[2] Nonprofits have also helped shape major shifts in the political landscape, including the move toward privatization, deregulation, and tax reform. Sometimes nonprofits have changed the political scene by mobilizing a large number of people and by making powerful moral arguments. Other times, nonprofits have influenced the political system by raising money to finance elections and by lobbying decisionmakers. No matter how change has been sought, from the grassroots up or from the decisionmakers down, fostering civic and political engagement is a critical function of the sector.

## Political Theories of Association

The modern American nonprofit organization is a relatively recent invention and a twentieth-century legal construct. Before there were nonprofit organizations, however, there were voluntary associations. For centuries, philosophers and social scientists have argued that associations are critical to creating and maintaining democratic political order. Within this long body of thought, voluntary associations, the pre-institutional manifestations of the impulse to form nonprofit organizations, have been seen as protectors of individual rights and personal freedoms within democratic states.[3] By offering an alternative means to accomplish social ends and by acting as a tool of social coordination, associations can counteract the power of the state. It is no surprise, therefore, that voluntary associations have also been viewed by nondemocratic governments as threats to be outlawed or severely restricted. In fact, the repression of voluntary associations has often been interpreted as one of the trademarks of totalitarian regimes.

The importance of nonprofit and voluntary organizations to democracy can be put this way: when individuals have alternative, nongovernmental means of accomplishing social ends, they are freer because their destiny is more closely linked to their own will. Instead of waiting for government to respond to pressure and provide needed services or hoping that business will meet the demand, individuals who are part of a society with a vital voluntary sector can take steps to meet their own needs. The sector can also serve as a laboratory for experimentation and risk taking, a place where new ideas are tested and evaluated. Often nonprofit and voluntary organizations attempt projects that government is either unwilling or unable to carry out for financial or political reasons. Yet it is not uncommon for programs designed and implemented in the nonprofit sector to be later imitated by government, especially when they have proven more successful than existing public sector programs.

This freedom to experiment is not, however, the only reason associations are critical ingredients in democratic societies. Associations can and do shape the values of individuals and produce a society that is able to move beyond narrow self-interest. By opening up new opportunities and options, associations also represent a powerful vehicle for expanding individual freedom. Associations have acted to bolster the power of individuals as members of democratic societies by giving them a sense of belonging to community, teaching them the importance of participation, and strengthening the ties that bind individuals together—all of which are crucial to maintaining the freedom of individuals against the state.

While many writers concerned with democracy have seen associations as a positive force, some have worried about the dangers of these private organizations. The view that private groups organized around community interests threaten the state was advanced early on by Thomas Hobbes.[4] Associations of individuals, Hobbes argues, exist not by virtue of some natural right but only because the sovereign allows them to exist. In Hobbes's world, the absolute sovereign has good reason to be suspicious of nongovernmental associations. By teaching organizational skills and by building a sense of community, associations can challenge the state's claim to power. Some scholars have suggested that Hobbes's concern with respect to associations was a direct reaction to an explosion of private clubs and groups in seventeenth-century England.[5] Beyond fostering solidarity, these clubs represented a first layer of space between the individual and the state, one that Hobbes saw as potentially dangerous. Looking ahead in English history, we see that Hobbes's worries were well founded, since associations did have a profound effect on the structure of many nations' social and political order.

Although Hobbes viewed private associations as potential challengers to the power of the sovereign, other political theorists have seen associations as both a right and a necessary element in democratic societies. The classical liberal tradition has always been concerned about individual rights, including the right of association.[6] John Locke, a central figure in this tradition, advanced one of the earliest defenses of associations when he noted that the right to associate was critically important because it was closely tied to freedom of religion. Even though Locke favored associations for religious reasons, it is possible nevertheless to see in his *Letter on Toleration* a more general defense of all forms of private associations.[7] Locke stresses that the right to associate is not contingent on the permission of the state or any other authority. In fact, he suggests that groups have rights which are derivative of the rights of their individual members and that these rights deserve protection against the power of government. Thus, for Locke, it is impossible to deny an individual the right to associate without undermining freedom.

In early deliberations by America's Founding Fathers, the role of associations and factions in democracy was a vital concern. In Federalist 10, Madison defined a faction as "a number of citizens, whether amounting to a majority or a minority of the whole, who are united and actuated by some common impulse of passion, or of interest, adversed to the right of other citizens, or to the permanent and aggregate interests of the community." Madison worried that the "zeal for different opinions" would lead to conflict and would make it hard for factions to cooperate in pursuit of the common good. While the cause of factions—the unequal distribution of property—might be clear, the solution could not lie in the eradication of the cause. Instead, Madison argued that the republican remedy gave the various factions enough room to express their views and a chance to influence government. Instead of the majority imposing its will on minorities, the multiple interests expressed in factions would negotiate their differences and arrive at a solution in which the majority would rule but adequate regard would be given to the views of minorities. In his "Farewell Address," George Washington also saw danger in groups devoted to shared interests and warned against "all combinations and associations, under whatever plausible character, with the real design to direct, control, counteract, or awe the regular deliberation and action of the Constituted authorities." Washington believed that associations were likely to "become potent engines, by which cunning, ambitious and unprincipled men will be enabled to subvert the Power of the People, and to usurp for themselves the reins of Government; destroying afterwards the very engines which have lifted them to unjust dominion."[8]

A more positive affirmation of the role of associations can be found in the work of John Stuart Mill. Instead of arguing that associations ought to be protected because they are among a number of rights that pertain to all individuals, Mill argued that voluntary associations deserve protection because they can actually build the character of the individual. In many cases, Mill argued, it was important for individuals acting through voluntary associations to achieve common purposes. Even if these private efforts were not as effective as those carried out by government, there was still value in private initiative. Mill believed that such efforts were a means by which people achieved "mental education—a mode of strengthening their active faculties, exercising their judgment, and giving them a familiar knowledge of the subjects with which they are thus left to deal. This is a principal though not the sole recommendation of the conduct of industrial and philanthropic enterprises by voluntary associations."[9] Mill went on to suggest that associations were important to individuals because they fostered debate within the marketplace of ideas, and because individuals could learn within associations the skills needed for a healthy political life.

Almost a century later, a different English liberal, A. D. Lindsay, focused on yet another important feature of associations: they protect the individual from the state and its growing bureaucracy. Voluntary organizations, according to Lindsay, bring individuals together, help them form bonds based on mutual interest, and give them the means to resist the domination of faceless public officials: "Within trade unions and perhaps as much in friendly societies, cooperative societies, and working men's clubs and institutes, the ordinary member of the rank and file has a chance to make his contribution, to have his work and particular gift recognized, to earn the personal respect of his fellows."[10] This ability to connect with others and build coalitions has significant political consequences: "The isolated individual is always powerless against great organizations. The ordinary man . . . must have his own discussion group if his personality is to hold out against the molder of mass opinion and the petty tyranny of officials."[11] Associations thus act as protective shields which defend individual identity.

The English admiration for associations is surpassed only by the enthusiasm for voluntary action shown by France's most famous visitor to America, Alexis de Tocqueville.[12] While *Democracy in America*[13] addresses a whole range of issues and topics, few could argue with the claim that one of the central questions of Tocqueville's study is: How can one account for the fact that America is truly a democratic nation? Tocqueville's famous answer starts with the unusual social condition of equality that he observed in America, a condition that made American democracy succeed where other attempts have failed. Tocqueville thus saw slavery as a profound threat to American democracy. For Tocqueville, the phenomena of democracy and equality were deeply intertwined. To be sure, equality is not the only determinant of democracy. Tocqueville did, in fact, point out the role that laws and fortunate circumstances played in allowing America to establish its democracy. But it is nevertheless the absolute equality of Americans, in terms of their education, intelligence, and abilities, that Tocqueville found most remarkable. The broad link between equality and democracy was crucial to the argument of *Democracy in America,* but Tocqueville elaborated far more than just a social theory of democracy. Indeed, much of Tocqueville's work was conducted at a much finer level of analysis, in that it focused on the moral character and personal traits of the average American citizen. Without looking into the heart of the individual to ascertain his values and commitments, Tocqueville found it difficult to understand and account for the broad social phenomena he observed in America. The nature of American mores flowed in great measure from the egalitarian social order that characterized the country in the nineteenth century. Additionally, American mores were congenial to democratic government in that they led men to participate in the election of representatives and to submit to the will of the majority. Mores, equality, and democracy were thus interrelated.

In examining the way Tocqueville structured his discussion of America's national character, it is clear that one of the features he found most striking was the orientation of the common man to getting things accomplished, be it in the realm of business, religion, community affairs, or politics. Tocqueville famously observed that individuals pursue ends through countless associations: "Americans of all ages, all stations of life, and all types of dispositions are forever forming associations. There are not only commercial and industrial associations in which all take part, but others of a thousand different types. . . . In every case, at the head of any new undertaking, where in France you would find the government, in the United States you are sure to find an association."[14] Civil associations were not the only way in which individuals united to get things accomplished. Tocqueville noted that the tendency of Americans to band together spilled over into the political arena, where associations also proliferated. These political associations were made possible in many ways by the "intellectual and moral associations" that allowed individuals with common values or goals to come together and talk. The importance of these associations was stressed by Tocqueville quite clearly. Since individuals in an egalitarian society have very limited personal power—especially in contrast to the power of European aristocrats—American citizens

> become powerless if they do not learn voluntarily to help one another. If men living in democratic countries had no right and no inclination to associate for political purposes, their independence would be in great jeopardy, whereas if they never acquired the habit of forming associations in ordinary life, civilization itself would be endangered. A people among whom individuals lost the power of achieving great things single-handed, without acquiring the means of producing them by united exertions, would soon lapse into barbarism.[15]

In one sense, it is possible to read *Democracy in America* as a handbook on the practical uses of associations for accomplishing a whole range of private and public purposes. In Chapter 7 of Book 11, Tocqueville argues that because Americans have civil associations, they are able to establish the political associations crucial for democratic government. Through a free press, ideas circulate beyond narrow civil associations and reach the ear of the public. This wide dissemination of ideas facilitates the formation of broad political associations aimed at accomplishing goals that are national in scope. Tocqueville describes an "inevitable connection" between the two types of associations and notes that civil associations teach people the power of combined effort. Civil associations are thus a kind of training ground for political associations. Tocqueville makes it clear that political associations could also strengthen the fiber of civic life: "Civil associations pave the way for political ones; but on the other hand, the art of political associations singularly develops and improves this technique for civil purposes."[16] In view of the connections he draws between equality and democracy, civil and political associations, and the mores of individual citizens, Tocqueville's theory can be seen as having three levels: an associational level links the individual to the broader social condition (see Figure 2.1).

Perhaps the most impressive aspect of Tocqueville's understanding of associations is that it draws a plausible link between his understanding of personal traits of individuals and the broad social phenomenon of democracy that he aims to explain. Instead of making the mistake of relying on the brute aggregation of individual acts to explain social reality, Tocqueville shows how associations are the crucible in which the individual mores of Americans are forged into a social state characterized by democracy. It should also be clear by now that if we wish to understand Tocqueville's classic analysis of the role associations play in promoting democratic values, we must begin with the condition of equal rights that makes associations possible in the first place. Tocqueville argues at great length that equal rights are more essential to democracy than even expansive individual rights. While citizens in a democracy may be willing to tolerate certain limits on the rights of the individual, they are usually unwilling to compromise one iota on the equality of those rights. Thus, Tocqueville's central point is that by putting all citizens on equal footing, America's social and political system created a situation in which individuals could—in unprecedented numbers—form associations and take charge of their own communities.

Although Tocqueville is quoted frequently and has become the surrogate father of American voluntarism, Peter Dobkin Hall has pointed out that William Ellery Channing actually recognized America's vibrant civil associations years before Tocqueville did. In 1829 Channing noted: "In

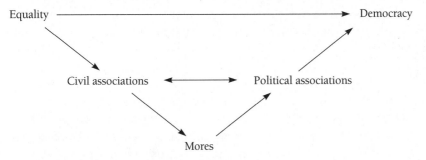

2.1 Tocqueville's theory of associations.

truth, one of the most remarkable circumstances or features of our age is the energy with which the principle of combination, or action by joint forces, by associated numbers, is manifesting itself. It may be said, without much exaggeration, that everything is done now by Societies." Yet in Channing's eyes, voluntary associations posed a potential danger: "A few are able to excite in the mass strong and bitter passions, and by these to obtain an immense ascendancy. . . . They are a kind of irregular government created within our constitutional government. Let them be watched carefully."[17] Rather than seeing private associations as the buttress of democracy, Channing perceived them as a possible source of instability and usurpation. Today, long after Tocqueville and Channing, the debate still rages over whether groups of citizens acting through associations contribute to or conflict with individual rights.

In recent years, progressives have begun to question the usefulness of clinging to Tocqueville's early observations about small local associations at a time when American voluntarism has become professionalized, nationalized, and institutionalized. Important questions have been raised about whether the kinds of linkages that Tocqueville and others saw between small-scale civil society and political commitment still hold true, given the balkanization of the country over race, class, and ideology. According to some liberal critics, the power inherent in small groups of citizens banding together to accomplish collective purposes has been romanticized by conservatives, who have latched onto Tocqueville's picture of America and faulted Great Society social programs for their abandonment of local self-help and charitable efforts. Progressives have rebelled against this proposition and against the idea that nonprofit and voluntary action can ever or should ever displace the state.[18] Beyond political differences, conflicting theories about the role of associations in American democracy have generated much research, which has revealed that nonprofit and voluntary organizations contain more than just the seeds of social organization and collective action. Associations have been described as the spawning ground for widespread participation in elections. In fact, a good deal of research has been conducted to test the "Tocqueville hypothesis" that strong nonprofit and voluntary organizations are necessary for strong democracies. Many of these studies have located a strong correlation between membership in nonprofit and voluntary organization and voting behavior within communities in the United States and around the world.[19]

As empirical research has developed, several American theorists, especially Robert Nisbet, have argued that associations are an integral part of all truly pluralistic societies.[20] In contrast to the liberal democratic tradition of Locke and Mill, the pluralist school conceives the role of associations somewhat differently. Instead of seeing the individual as the basic unit within society, the pluralists have argued that small groups are the fundamental building blocks of social and political order. Nisbet has suggested that focusing on the individual and his rights may obscure more crucial components of democracy: "The liberal values of autonomy and freedom of personal choice are indispensable to a genuinely free society, but we shall achieve and maintain these conditions only by vesting them in the conditions in which liberal democracy will thrive— diversity of culture, plurality of association, and division of authority."[21] The pluralist tradition in political theory has interpreted associations both as a training ground for participation in politics and as an informal school in which toleration and compromise are taught. When individuals work together voluntarily toward a shared goal, they are led to communicate and deal with one another, a process that fosters better community relations and understanding. In this way, associations can be seen not just as an efficient, nongovernmental means of accomplishing socially desirable ends, but also as a way of creating communities. The informal ties stemming from voluntary action are important because they ensure that no single issue or individual becomes dominant and that a plurality of voices is heard instead of one.

Not everyone has been convinced by the pluralist defense of associations. In America, a strong critique of pluralism emerged in the 1960s in the work of C. Wright Mills and other critics of "mass society." At the heart of this critique of the pluralist endorsement of associations was the belief that the formation of many competing groups within society would lead to a diffuse and ineffectual opposition to elite domination. That Mills saw America's penchant for collaboration as a weakness is not surprising, given his affinity for the work of Marx and his suspicion of any social phenomena that might distract individuals from class conflict.[22] Like Marx, Mills feared that association could placate the individual by giving him a false sense of participation and thereby divert him from his real task, which was to question the power of elites. In this radical critique, associations emerge not as engines of change but as cooling-off places, where collective energies are dissipated and refracted into many small ineffectual local movements.

The debate over the connection of voluntary associations to the well-being of democratic nations has continued to this day. In some ways, both the arguments favoring small groups and local civic life and the arguments advocating national movements and broad cohesion point toward the same conclusion. Whether associations are defined as a way to strengthen the pluralist tradition in public life or as an alternative method of organizing broad social movements, the research tradition on associations confirms at least the central element of Tocqueville's insight: if individuals are to be truly free, they must have ways to accomplish projects of their own invention and ways to join together with others to form strong communities.[23]

## Social Capital, Civic Engagement, and Political Participation

The idea that nonprofit and voluntary organizations are deeply connected to politics and democracy has been extended in an interesting new direction through the development of a body of research on the concept of social capital. Different from either human or financial capital, social capital comprises "features of social organization, such as networks, norms, and trust, that facilitate coordination and cooperation for mutual benefit."[24] The existence of social capital has important consequences for the quality of civic engagement and politics. Trust built through civic associations and community projects spills over into the political realm and creates enthusiasm for public life that is connected to more active political engagement and participation.[25]

Although the idea of trust is an old one, it has in recent years become a powerful organizing concept for researchers studying markets and politics. For those interested in what makes any organization function effectively, trust and strong personal relationships have become a focal point. After all, how can a complex organization carry out a mission if those within the organization do not share a common set of understandings and beliefs that makes cooperation possible? Trust, or social capital, is the reservoir of good will that organizations need when standard operating procedures do not provide an answer. Research related to trust and social capital within organizations has led to important insights about the importance of teamwork, shared decisionmaking, and flatter hierarchies. This research has also challenged traditional economic explanations of phenomena as diverse as stock trading, bank exchanges, and manufacturing networks, by showing that many market transactions are in fact embedded in complex social relationships where trust and confidence in others is critical.

Politics is the arena in which trust and social capital are most significant. It is also the arena in which the ideas of Tocqueville come back in their clearest and most influential way. An important recent return to Tocqueville's preoccupation with associational life began with a study of political life in regions across the Italian countryside. Robert Putnam's research in Italy found that in some areas government was inefficient, lethargic, and corrupt, while in other areas it was rife with initiatives and was satisfying constituents.[26] The most likely factors that might have explained this variation—income, ideology, and social stability—were not determinative. In accounting for these variations, Putnam found that social capital was a critical predictor of citizen satisfaction and government effectiveness. His study returned to and reinforced Tocqueville's argument that the quality of connections, civic engagement, and associational life is essential for strong democratic institutions.

Turning his attention to the American scene, Putnam has noted that the United States has experienced a precipitous decline in civic engagement in recent decades. When he measured involvement in clubs, PTAs, unions, and other forms of socializing, Putnam found that Americans over the past half-century have slowly withdrawn into increasingly isolated private lives. Putnam's most memorable image is that of the bowler who has chosen to do without the camaraderie of a league and instead simply bowls alone. While the decline of bowling leagues has significant economic consequences for bowling-lane proprietors, the real significance of this trend "lies in the social interaction and even civic conversations over beer and pizza that solo bowlers forgo."[27] In assessing the causes of this civic retreat, Putnam sorted through dozens of possible factors—including daily time pressures, economic hard times, residential mobility, suburbanization, the movement of women into the paid labor force, divorce, political disillusionment after Vietnam, the growth of the welfare state, the civil rights revolution—and eventually pointed to one culprit as perhaps the most likely of all: television and the information technology revolution. How might television work to undermine trust and networks of collaboration? Putnam discussed three possible ways. First, television, and the Internet more recently, take up large blocks of time that might otherwise be available for community activities. Second, television tends to increase cynicism and suspicion of the motives of others. Third, television has changed the patterns of social-ization among children, and this change has a long-term impact on ac-tivities that create social capital. The result is a nation that is losing its connectedness.[28]

This analysis has been challenged on several fronts. First, there are questions about how social capital is measured, and whether looking (as Putnam does) at large traditional membership organizations like the League of Women Voters, the Elks, the Shriners, and the Masons over a long period of time really gives an accurate picture of levels of social capital. After all, new forms of association are continually emerging. Al-though social and service clubs may have declined, other more political forms of associative activity have certainly spread. In areas such as envi-ronmental protection and human rights, large numbers of people have found new associative vehicles that speak to issues and causes close to their heart. By tracking membership in traditional service-oriented orga-nizations over time, Putnam may well have documented the organiza-tional life cycle of these entities from birth to growth to decline. Thus, while membership may have declined in some of these large organiza-tions, this might simply indicate a loss of relevance rather than a decline in social capital.

Second, new research has documented the transformation of social capital from old-line associations to new, smaller, local forms of connec-tions—the sort that Wuthnow has termed "loose connections."[29] These forms of interaction, including support groups, book clubs, and infor-mal community action groups, have allowed people across the country and within geographic communities to find each other. Wuthnow notes that some new forms of civic organizations may be meeting changing needs: "Instead of cultivating lifelong ties with their neighbors, or join-ing organizations that reward faithful long-term service, people are com-ing together around specific needs and to work on projects that have definite objectives."[30] These organizations give people a sense of em-powerment and involvement, allow them to share information, and enable them to build connections through networks increasingly consti-tuted by phone calls, faxes, e-mail, and web pages. These loose connec-tions are appealing because they fit well with the permeable and transi-tory institutions that populate the social landscape. Thus, in contrast to the claim that social capital is in decline, Wuthnow points to a different form of association, one that is not tracked by traditional surveys of organizational membership. Social capital thus may not be declining. It may simply be moving into more temporary vehicles that spring up and disappear faster than researchers are able to track and document them.

Whether social capital is declining or merely changing shape, we should recognize that the concept itself has been present in social science in a variety of forms for decades. In *The Death and Life of Great American Cities,* Jane Jacobs used the term in her analysis of the impact of social structure on city life—an analysis which focused attention on the economic benefits produced by social networks. Noting that "neighborhood networks are social capital," Jacobs pointed out that resources are critical to successful and vibrant cities.[31] Glenn C. Loury developed the social capital concept in the field of economics by examining neighborhood effects on the accumulation of human capital and intergenerational wealth distribution.[32] One of the most complete presentations of the social capital concept appeared in an early article by sociologist James S. Coleman.[33] Seeking to bridge sociology and economics, Coleman took an economic notion—that human behavior is rational and self-interested—and applied it to sociology's concern over community and social constraints. A key bridging concept was that of social capital, which he defined as an ephemeral element that facilitates action within social structures: "Social capital inheres in the structure of relations between actors and among actors. It is not lodged either in the actors themselves or in physical implements of production."[34] As examples of places where social capital is present, Coleman cited diamond markets, in which negotiations are conducted on the basis of trust and reputations developed over years; student "study circles" that hold political discussions in defiance of repressive regimes; and neighborhoods where children can play safely in public parks because of strong community ties and solidarity.

In recent years, social capital and trust have been subject to more formal analysis centered on the ties between individuals and the networks that result. One of the most interesting proponents of this approach is Mark S. Granovetter, who has advanced the idea that social structure is driven by the pattern of overlap in one-to-one interpersonal ties.[35] The strength of such ties depends on a combination of factors, including emotional intensity, mutual confiding, reciprocity, and the amount of time the two people spend together. The strength of a tie is also a function of the number of ties an individual has with other people.

Granovetter argues that the more time we spend building close friendships, the less time we will have to form broad social networks of contacts. If one assumes that there is indeed a zero-sum game at work in the building of networks (in other words, the more time we spend building strong ties, the less time we have to build an extensive though shallow network of weak ties), the question naturally arises as to where one's network-building efforts are best directed. Granovetter's argument is that weak ties and strong ties have very different functions and that in many situations—including gathering information, finding a job, and mobilizing a community to action—weak ties are more powerful tools for achieving social ends. Weak ties create broader sets of attachments that span geographic and interest communities. They create "bridging social capital," which exists *between* groups and is far more powerful than "bonding social capital," which exists *within* groups. Granovetter concludes: "Weak ties, often denounced as generative of alienation, are here seen as indispensable to individuals' opportunities and their integration into communities; strong ties, breeding local cohesion, lead to overall fragmentation."[36] Other research has pushed the idea of "the strength of weak ties" in other directions, showing that organizations may operate optimally when they achieve a mix of both strong and weak ties.

At one level, nonprofit and voluntary organizations are ideal vehicles for forging networks of weak ties that link people together. The very idea of associational life is one that is predicated on the idea of weak ties supplementing the strong ties of friendship and family. Weak ties take people out of their small inner circles and extend access and options. Nonprofit and voluntary organizations have a unique role to play in forging the ties that link people together so that they can accomplish collective tasks. When they meet to form a neighborhood crime patrol or when they volunteer at the local shelter, individuals make new acquaintances that can be useful for some time to come. These ties created by the pursuit of common purposes may seem rather pedestrian at the time they are being constructed. Efforts to raise money for a local school by holding a community rummage sale may seem unremarkable. Taking part in town meetings to set a budget for restoring historic buildings might seem insignificant. Going to a dinner dance that raises funds for the local chapter of war veterans may not sound like a big night out on the town. Yet these unremarkable activities forge linkages, as individuals see one another in the public arena and begin to match names and faces.

When it comes to enticing people outside their narrow networks of family and friends, nonprofit and voluntary activities at the community level can be powerful instruments for the forging of valuable weak ties, which may invigorate individuals' interest in public life. When nonprofits bring people together in a more structured and formal way—whether in a club, union, or business league—they can also foster bonds of reciprocity that carry over to other areas of public life. Small-business owners that take an active interest in the local chamber of commerce are also more likely to play an active role in local governance. In fact, research of all kinds has documented that the more engagement one sees both with voluntary associations and with formal membership organizations, the more likely it is that political engagement will follow.

It seems clear that nonprofit and voluntary action at the local level does connect people to one another and to the public sphere in important ways. These connections are often somewhat narrow and limited, however. Many nonprofit and voluntary organizations struggle to build extensive networks of weak ties that span the boundaries of income, race, and ideology. In small organizations, ranging from churches whose memberships consist of narrow demographic groups to PTAs that draw in only nearby suburban parents, individuals often associate with others who look, act, and think the way they do. Of course, the fact that social capital is often built among people who have much in common seems only natural. The impulse to associate and "bond" is one that is often driven by a desire to find others that share the same interests or concerns.

The natural contacts and operating methods of nonprofits tend to be focused on well-defined geographic communities or on issues that are of particular interest to self-selected groups and constituencies. This can be a significant shortcoming because bridging social capital is scarcer than bonding social capital. Many local nonprofit and voluntary organizations attempt to transcend narrow boundaries by linking up with national groups or even with international movements. Extending local ties into broader sets of relationships is a complex and demanding task, requiring significant resources. It also demands that persons drawn together at the local level find ways of building coalitions that are greater than the sum of their parts. Coalition building often entails reaching across traditional boundaries to find partners who are not the usual suspects, but who can advance a common agenda that bridges long-standing divides of nationality, race, class, and socioeconomic status.[37]

Why focus on trust and networks of affiliation in relation to politics? One reason is that public life has become atomized and alienating because of the success of narrow interest groups, which have separated citizens from politics by promising to act on their behalf. The failure of interest group pluralism to solve many lasting public problems is one reason that Americans have become interested again in the question of engagement and participation.[38] After all, it was long thought that a pluralistic approach was the best way to solve many public problems. Pluralism established an arena within which groups of farmers, manufacturers, real estate developers, environmentalists, senior citizens, gun owners, union members, and countless other groups could compete for resources and representation. For years, this epic battle of interest groups, each representing a small contingency of stakeholders, seemed like a promising way to find a solution for many of our public problems. Yet the system gradually began to weaken. Confidence in government is now at an all-time low. In a recent survey, only one-fourth of Americans reported that they trusted government to do the right thing, whereas fifty years ago this figure stood at three-fourths.[39] One of the great unfulfilled promises of pluralism was that it would give everyone representation and voice. Experience has taught us, however, that representation is not always a good substitute for participation. Thus, while nonprofits have emerged to speak for every interest group imaginable, this has not satisfied all our political needs, particularly the need to be engaged.

A critical issue in any democracy is the level of active citizen participation. Without adequate citizen involvement at all the different levels of political decisionmaking, there is a real risk that legitimacy and support for public decisions will erode. Nonprofit and voluntary action is central to democracy because it drives both civic engagement and political participation. The more closely people are connected to local groups and the greater their involvement in networks of civic voluntarism, the more likely they are to be engaged politically. How, when, and why individuals become active politically is a complex problem that has gained considerable attention from researchers over the years.[40]

One of the most recent and comprehensive surveys of American political participation was undertaken by Sidney Verba, Kay Schlozman, and Henry Brady, who surveyed over 15,000 people in an effort to understand the dynamics and drivers of different forms of political participation.[41] Their study considered not just voting activity but also work in electoral campaigns, contributions to campaigns and causes, informal activity in local communities, direct contact and communication with public officials, membership and affiliation in political organizations, attendance at demonstrations or protests, and service in local governing bodies.[42] Three critical factors explain variations in political participation: (1) resources, which include time to get involved, money to contribute, and the skills to use time and money effectively; (2) engagement, which encompasses interest in politics, belief that action can make a difference, and knowledge about the political process; and (3) recruitment, which is facilitated by social networks through which people are mobilized for political action. Socioeconomic status, educational level, and institutions play an important role in determining who has access to resources, who is engaged politically, and who is included in interpersonal networks. While most studies of political participation tend to focus on these political activities, Verba, Schlozman, and Brady also examined nonpolitical forms of voluntary participation because such activity "can enrich the stockpile of resources relevant to political action."[43] Like Putnam, they build on Tocqueville's insight that political engagement starts with civic engagement and attachment to community. Their findings, however, point to the fact that Americans are not participating in politics equally, because important inequalities in resources and opportunities persist. These inequalities raise difficult questions about the representativeness and responsiveness of democratic institutions.

In practice, nonprofit and voluntary organizations can play an important role in addressing some of these inequalities by stimulating political engagement—both directly, through efforts to mobilize citizens, and indirectly, by building broader interest in and capacity for civic engagement. The direct impact of nonprofits on political participation is most clearly seen in the activities of groups that organize voter registration drives, get-out-the-vote efforts on election day, demonstrations, petitions, ballot initiatives, and other forms of political participation. These activities are important ways of bringing the individual out into public life. They are usually successful when they are preceded by more indirect activities that simply build trust and enthusiasm within communities. Without a fairly robust stock of social capital, direct efforts to encourage political participation will inevitably struggle. Nonprofits can argue endlessly that individuals should be more politically engaged, but unless they can instill in citizens a desire to become active politically, even the most dedicated organizing and mobilizing work will not lead to substantial change.

Numerous models of community organizing have emerged,[44] particularly over the past three decades, to guide nonprofits in their mobilization work. One of the most prominent models is that of the Industrial Areas Foundation (IAF), a national and international organization that works with community groups to improve the effectiveness of political organizing at the grassroots level. Based on the ideas and practices of Saul Alinsky, a leading activist and organizer in the 1960s, this model of nonprofit political mobilization emphasizes the need for solid leadership and organizing around issues and interests that are critical to local communities.[45] Today, some fifty interfaith and interracial organizations across the country are executing a strategy geared toward empowering low-income Americans to shape decisions that affect their lives and communities. These efforts start by recruiting and developing local leaders who can identify common interests that bring together previously isolated groups, which then proceed on two tracks simultaneously. First, these groups pursue agreements and pacts with business and government leaders. By demanding negotiations with public and private sector institutions on issues such as better schools, more jobs, and higher wages, these coalitions have been able to achieve important breakthroughs. In Baltimore, for example, a coalition of churches and community groups called BUILD successfully negotiated a series of "commonwealth agreements" that helped secure company jobs for qualified high school graduates and that opened local colleges and universities to low-income children who did well in school.[46] Second, beyond negotiating such agreements, IAF models also often incorporate a range of empowerment activities that do not depend on outside agreements, including the founding of credit unions and the rehabilitation of housing. As important as these services are to neighborhoods, the greater significance of Alinsky's approach to change is that it stresses the formation and leadership of community organizations that connect the individual with the larger society.

While the invigoration of the grassroots through empowerment efforts is an important step in giving individuals the resources, commitment, and networks needed for active participation in public life, such efforts are often limited in size and scope. They also tend to be focused in urban areas, where the need for such programs is most acute. Sensing the need for broader solutions to the engagement program, state and local governments have at times supported efforts at comprehensive community development—programs that have sought to provide housing, education, and services to local communities as a first step toward bringing disenfranchised groups back into the public sphere. Over the years, the federal government has also experimented with programs designed to promote civic responsibility and engagement.

These efforts have raised two difficult questions: Is civic engagement really amenable to planning and policymaking by the state? If the state does have a role to play in enhancing civic and political participation, what concrete steps can policymakers take to stimulate civic commitment and participation? Since the United States has always had an abundance of associations, it might first appear strange that government should take an interest in promoting even greater levels of voluntary action. But when one considers the strong connection between civil associations and political participation that has been documented for over a century, and the worrisome fact that the most visible measure of participation—voting—has been declining in recent years, it is hardly surprising that government should take steps to encourage greater community service and voluntarism. Over the past half-century, a series of programs—including the Civilian Conservation Corps, Volunteers in Service to Action, ACTION, and others—have tried to build citizens' attachment to community and their commitment to service.[47]

The importance of voluntary, charitable, and religious activity was stressed throughout the "conservative revolution" inaugurated by Ronald Reagan's victory in the presidential campaign of 1980 and pursued in his subsequent budget reforms. Yet voluntary action received one of its most visible affirmations in 1988, when President George H.W. Bush described American society as "a thousand points of light"—a metaphor for the many private, voluntary efforts that occur in American society every day. Enthusiasm for volunteering, combined with shrinking federal resources, led to the idea of devising a public policy aimed at enlarging America's nonprofit and voluntary sector. As part of the process of implementing this policy, President Bush appointed a director of national service whose mission was to recognize and promote the work of voluntary groups and encourage the participation of citizens in these organizations. Reluctant to inject politics into community service, however, the Bush administration focused more on spotlighting and publicizing volunteer opportunities, rather than on creating and funding a program that would mobilize citizens in local communities.

During the administrations of President Bill Clinton, the effort to use government to promote voluntarism went one step further. In 1993 Congress passed the National and Community Service Trust Act, creating AmeriCorps, an organization that was hailed as a "domestic Peace Corps." AmeriCorps was designed to stimulate a sense of responsibility and caring in young people. To encourage volunteer service, the AmeriCorps program gave money to nonprofits that hosted corps members, enabling the organizations to pay these workers stipends. Though the payments were modest, they raised difficult questions: Was AmeriCorps really about public service and voluntarism? Or was it—like the other programs that had preceded it in the 1960s and 1970s—more about politics and patronage? Since AmeriCorps members received their stipends from the agencies where they worked, and since volunteers were able to volunteer only at nonprofit organizations approved by the government, the program proved vulnerable to charges of politicization. After all, with hundreds of millions of dollars at stake, the temptation to funnel stipend money to organizations working in key political regions or precincts was certainly great. These issues aside, early studies of AmeriCorps' effectiveness in promoting political engagement showed mixed results. This has not stopped some from calling for a massive expansion of community service directed at meeting the new homeland security needs of the nation.

While much of the recent debate about voluntarism has centered on what form government intervention in the area of civic engagement should take, other, more fundamental issues have never been fully addressed. First and foremost is whether voluntary action can ever—under any circumstances—be successfully promoted through a government program. It is significant that this issue never really arose in the public policy debate over voluntarism, even though so much was at stake: by bringing government into the nonprofit and voluntary sector, policymakers risked weakening the complex altruistic motive that it was attempting to promote. Overlooking the danger of subverting the autonomy of the nonprofit and voluntary sector, recent public policy has at times failed to take account of the need to shelter voluntary action, protect its ability to experiment without worrying about public opinion, and promote its ability to draw on local talent to meet the diverse needs of communities. In its efforts to place volunteers into nationally subsidized programs, government may well risk subverting part of the fragile voluntary impulse it seeks to foster.

Part of the process of forming a strong association is the difficult task of locating individuals who share common values and are committed to a common goal. This search can be an important process in itself, since it enables organizers to clarify and develop the mission and message behind the cause. When government takes hold of part of this process and attempts to manage this delicate coalescence through policies and programs, something important may be lost—namely, the personal commitment and local connection on which meaningful voluntary action depends.

## Advocacy, Lobbying, and Elections

Finding ways to move the individual into the public sphere is a laudable goal, especially when nonprofits undertake this task independently and with the goal of empowerment. Engagement is not, however, the only way that nonprofits can contribute to the process of improving the quality of politics. Many nonprofits actually approach their political work in an entirely different way. Rather than striving to mobilize people, a large number of nonprofit organizations take it upon themselves to speak on behalf of others. The expressive activity of nonprofit organizations is focused on the advocacy, lobbying, and political organizations that make up a large, if often misunderstood, part of the nonprofit and voluntary sector. These organizations take part in the political process by informing the public about issues, or by pushing for the passage of pieces of legislation, or by organizing the campaigns of candidates. Each of these three activities has different regulations and rules attached to it.

Nonprofit organizations have long been directly connected to politics through advocacy work, which starts with the premise that social change occurs through politics and that the power of the state can be moved to act on behalf of people.[48] Wishing to achieve results more quickly, some nonprofits do not start at the grassroots level or work to weave together disparate voices into one message. Instead, they proceed directly to articulate clear policy positions on behalf of citizens or interest groups, while simultaneously seeking to attract members and supporters. They direct their efforts at a range of audiences, including legislatures, executive offices, regulatory agencies, business firms, media organizations, international bodies, and public opinion. Such advocacy is carried out by many different kinds of nonprofits, including organizations that do nothing but advocate on behalf of a particular set of issues or interests, as well as organizations that pursue advocacy as part of a broader set of activities; the latter sorts of nonprofits include research institutes, universities, service agencies of all kinds, foundations, and community groups. What emerges is a complex set of initiatives and activities conducted by a broad spectrum of nonprofits, all seeking to use ideas and speech to shape the environment in which they operate.[49]

When it is successful, advocacy can indeed have a significant impact. One need only consider some of the work relating to consumer safety in the 1960s and 1970s, when progressive efforts to inform the public about automobile safety changed regulatory oversight and resulted in major shifts in public policy. During the 1980s, work by conservative policy research institutes produced many proposals that became part of the conservative policy revolution during the early years of the Reagan presidency.[50] The fact that advocacy efforts do not always lead to successful conclusions was, however, never more clear than during the ill-fated effort to overhaul the U.S. health care delivery system in 1993–1994, when advocacy work on both sides of the issue was undertaken by trade associations and consumer alliances. Whether such efforts are successful in the end or not, it is difficult to think of a major issue of national policy—from the protection of public forests and wetlands to the reform of welfare rules to the raising of the minimum wage—which has not evoked an outpouring of advocacy from all kinds of nonprofit groups.

How do nonprofits advocate? Nonprofits use their expressive capacity in a number of ways. First, they are good at identifying problems that have been neglected by the public and the media. Often, a focused advocacy effort can shine light on a problem or issue that has not previously attracted people's attention. Second, nonprofits are often skilled at developing new positions and policy alternatives that government actors have overlooked or ignored.[51] When significant legislative or regulatory decisions are being deliberated, nonprofits are often able to enlarge the debate so that a broader range of solutions and options are considered. Third, nonprofits can and do influence local priorities in ways that shape national priorities or challenge international conventions. Advocacy work can migrate upward through levels of government and shape priorities and decisions along the way.

Because it aims at shaping public priorities, some believe that advocacy work is a way of achieving substantial leverage or increased impact.[52] While direct service programs change the world one client at a time, advocacy efforts focus on broad changes in systems and policy. From this perspective, advocacy work looks like the wholesale part of the nonprofit sector, while service work might be viewed as the retail end of the operation. The reason advocacy appears to create leverage is simple: instead of converting nonprofit resources into units of service on a one-to-one basis, advocacy work takes a small number of resources and tries to multiply their impact by changing public priorities. This leverage is very attractive to supporters because many social problems are so broad and intractable that their solutions call for government action at a national level over a long period of time. Nonprofit activity may be useful in creating local models, but achieving scale and mobilizing resources are difficult tasks for a sector that does not have the state's enforcement power and that relies on voluntary action.

If advocacy work is built on a theory of leverage, questions remain about how effective this strategy is in achieving measurable change. When advocacy efforts are mounted, whether through public information campaigns, policy research, or lobbying, it is often difficult to ascertain the impact of such efforts. The causal link may be weak between what goes on in the advocacy world and the decisions that are ultimately reached. Of course, many of the groups representing narrow interests claim to have tremendous influence over the policy decisions that affect their constituents or members. Sometimes they are justified in their claims; other times, not. Still, public concern over the role of interest groups is rising, especially when their message is delivered through contributions to political campaigns or channeled through political action committees. In reality, however, links between public interest and issue advocacy efforts and political effects are difficult to establish, especially given that political bargaining, party politics, and many other factors within political institutions significantly shape decisions.

In order to get closer to a given public problem—and even to press for a specific solution—some nonprofits step beyond broad issue advocacy and engage in political lobbying. The main difference between the two activities lies in the nature of their connection to the legislative process. Lobbying involves activity on behalf of a *specific piece of legislation*.[53] Thus, when major bills are under consideration, nonprofits on all sides speak to Congress or state legislatures or city councils and work with elected officials and their staffs to influence the outcome. All kinds of nonprofit organizations can and do lobby, including business leagues, charitable organizations, social clubs, unions, and social welfare organizations.[54] While many trade associations lobby by means of paid professionals, large numbers of nonprofits work for the passage of legislation through networks of volunteers who are mobilized to write letters, make phone calls, send e-mails and faxes, and make office visits. Some nonprofits use staff members to work on lobbying projects, though resource limitations at smaller organizations often do not allow for full-time lobbying work. Critical to success in lobbying is knowledge of the issues and personal contacts with decisionmakers. Whether the group is a trade association representing the mining industry seeking access to public lands or an international relief organization seeking greater levels of foreign aid, lobbying requires knowledge about the legislative process, an understanding of the details of the bill and its effects on the legislators' constituents, and a strategy for communicating with concerned citizens at the grassroots level.[55]

The kind of lobbying effort undertaken is usually related to the type of organization carrying out the work. Private foundations are covered by rules that differ from those applicable to advocacy organizations, or 501(c)4 nonprofits, which in turn are different from those covering public charities, or 501(c)3 nonprofits (see Table 2.1). Public charities such as universities and hospitals are permitted to lobby, but they face some restrictions. They are required to be not simply bipartisan, but nonpartisan. They cannot take sides in elections by endorsing candidates, nor can they mobilize citizens behind or against any candidate. When it comes to political parties, charities need to maintain their distance by avoiding any contributions or transactions that appear to direct their re-

**Table 2.1.** Regulations governing nonprofit lobbying and political activities.

| Issue/question | Public charities 501(c)3 | Social welfare organizations 501(c)4 |
|---|---|---|
| Key tax rules | May receive deductible contributions. | Tax-exempt, but contributors do not receive a deduction. |
| General permitted activities | Charitable and educational activities, including public education and lobbying (for public charities). | May engage in any activity permitted a 501(c)3 organization, plus any activity that serves public purposes, such as lobbying and advocacy in the public interest. |
| Is lobbying allowed? | Yes, to a limited extent. But it may not be "substantial." | Yes; and lobbying may even be the organization's exclusive activity. |
| What campaign-related activities are allowed? | Nonpartisan voter registration, voter education, and get-out-the vote efforts. Campaign intervention is strictly prohibited. | May engage in nonpartisan activities permitted 501(c)3s. May engage in electioneering, so long as it is not the organization's primary activity and is not express advocacy. |
| What issue advocacy activities are allowed? | A wide range, including educational and lobbying activities. Tax laws limit issue advocacy that promotes or criticizes particular candidates, and they prohibit electioneering. | Neither election laws nor tax laws limit issue advocacy. |
| What disclosure is required? | No requirement to disclose donors to the public. | Most are not required to disclose donors to the public. |

*Source:* Adapted from Elizabeth T. Boris and C. Eugene Steuerle, eds., *Nonprofits and Government: Collaboration and Conflict* (Washington, D.C.: Urban Institute Press, 1999), p. 311 (article by E. Reid). Table originally developed by Elizabeth Sellers and Jane Gallagher of the law firm Caplin and Drusdale Chartered, Washington, D.C.

sources to elections. While this might seem limiting, it actually still leaves much room for expression. In particular, charities have the freedom to speak out about issues and to inform the public about problems or policies. Although they can lobby, there are restrictions on the amount of time and resources they can dedicate to lobbying while maintaining their 501(c)3 status and their ability to offer a charitable deduction to contributors. While some charities have significant lobbying power as a result of their leader's connections or reputation, most smaller organizations lobby on a modest level, particularly when it comes to funding that affects their organization. One factor which has limited the scope and impact of lobbying is that organizations are wary of running afoul of laws restricting the political activities of nonprofits that enjoy tax-deductible contributions. For public-serving nonprofits, a largely misunderstood rule limiting lobbying activity to a less than "substantial amount" of their time has caused some nonprofits to shy away from many allowable forms of political work.

Only a few nonprofits, such as the Christian Coalition, have actually found themselves under scrutiny for potential violations of the law, for distributing voter guides promoting Republican candidates. The Christian Coalition was eventually cleared of most of the charges leveled against it. Its leader, Pat Robertson, declared that a decisive victory had been won for churches: the coalition had dispelled the myth that organizations would lose their tax-exempt status if they became actively involved in elections.[56] Though the distribution of voter guides by the Christian Coalition was ultimately allowed, this high-profile case and a flurry of other cases connected to nonprofit advocacy work have done nothing to remove the chill on the overall advocacy work of public-serving nonprofits. This chill is due principally to an ongoing confusion over which political activities are allowed and which are not.

Beyond issue advocacy and lobbying, nonprofits are involved with politics in an even more direct way. Political parties, the campaigns of candidates, and the legion of political action committees that contribute to campaigns are all part of the nonprofit and voluntary sector. While they are the organizational backbone of American politics, this part of the sector has been blamed for a great deal of the public's cynicism and dissatisfaction with the entire political process. As money has become an ever-stronger force in elections, there is real concern that the quality and depth of our political life have been impoverished and that political institutions, instead of responding to the public interest, are increasingly tied to narrow and well-funded private interests. Many attempts to limit the way money enters campaigns have been tried, at both the state and the federal level—measures ranging from limits on contributions to the public financing of elections. To date, however, these efforts have met with resistance in the courts and have had limited effect as a result of the protections afforded by the First Amendment to political speech.

## Transnational Connections

The already complex political role of nonprofits is still evolving. As the traditional boundaries of nation-states become less and less significant, in view of the globalization of a number of important environmental, labor, and population problems, the character of advocacy and political work is also beginning to change. Efforts to build transnational alliances among nonprofits has led to important successes in fields such as women's rights, the control of greenhouse gases, and the banning of landmines. One of the clearest signs that transnational cooperation is changing the traditional operating principles of advocacy organizations appeared at the meeting of the World Trade Organization (WTO) in Seattle in November 1999. This important meeting was overshadowed by well-organized and at times violent demonstrations that aimed at attracting international media attention to labor and environmental issues that nonprofit activists believed were being overlooked by WTO representatives. This was a visible indication that nonprofits from countries around the world could work together to put pressure on political bodies in an attempt to shape policy and public opinion. Working across borders, nonprofits have sought to build consensus around solutions that affect large numbers of people, many of whom have been traditionally excluded from the political process. These success stories have given rise to great optimism about the future political role of nongovernmental actors in an increasingly connected and interdependent world.[57]

Nonprofit and voluntary organizations intervene in the international context in at least five different ways.[58] First, they identify problems and draw attention to issues that might otherwise go unnoticed. Working with the media, they shed light on government and business activities by publishing report cards and studies that are designed to awaken public opinion. Second, nonprofit and voluntary organizations help build international norms that can guide policy and practice. This often comes down to creating a culture and a set of expectations, designed to constrain and direct the behavior of governments and businesses. Third, these organizations help to enforce public policy and norms through public information campaigns and boycotts. This is especially true in countries where the state's will or power to act is limited. Fourth, transnational nonprofit and voluntary organizations work to resolve conflicts and mediate disputes. In many situations, a credible outside party is needed to resolve international tensions and disputes, and nonprofits have played this diplomatic role. Fifth, nonprofit and voluntary organizations have been able to mobilize people in great numbers to take action and become involved in global issues. Drawing on their local connections, they create linkages which give individuals access to people and organizations that otherwise would be inaccessible. The number of transnational nonprofits working in the most visible fields—including human rights, environmental protection, development, and gender justice—has gradually risen, from fewer than one hundred in the 1970s to more than three hundred in the 1990s (see Figure 2.2).

Yet amid the growing visibility and influence of large transnational nonprofits, important questions remain about the future independence of nonprofit and voluntary organizations in a globalizing world. Chief among these concerns is whether private, nongovernmental organizations will continue to serve as autonomous voices that generate a variety of contextually appropriate solutions to social problems. As globalization proceeds, as public and private funding sources around the world become increasingly connected, and as policy agendas spread ever more rapidly across national borders, important questions about how politically active nonprofits can maintain their *local* identities become ever more pressing.

In principle, the noncoercive, nondistributing, and ownerless character of nonprofit organizations positions these entities to be influential political actors in a globalized world. Nonprofits have in fact been powerful vehicles of democratic accountability because they appear to be independent voices for the public good. In countries where rights have been violated, the attraction of a form of collective endeavor that is completely voluntary and noncoercive is undeniably strong. At the same time, the nondistribution constraint also builds confidence and trust and allows these organizations to operate across traditional political and cultural boundaries and differences. While the motives and ethics of large corporations have frequently been questioned in light of their bottom-line orientation, nonprofit organizations do not labor under similar suspicions. Finally, their ownerless character puts them in a position of independence when it comes to navigating complex political environments.

Interestingly, many of the features of nonprofits that seem to be advantages turn out to create vulnerabilities. Nonprofit organizations are open to outside pressure by virtue of their limited ability to enforce agreements, their tight finances, and their often narrow focus and missions. Nonprofit and voluntary groups, particularly at the local level, tend to be closely aligned with the interests of the communities they represent, yet often obtain their funding from "outsiders," whether foundations, corporations, or government agencies. This can and does

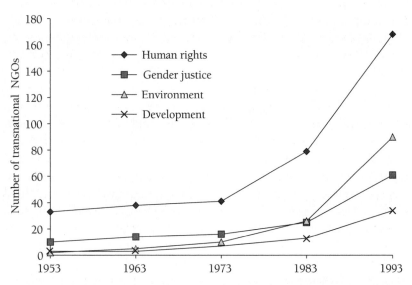

2.2  The growth of transnational nongovernmental organizations (NGOs). *Source:* Adapted from Kathryn Sikkink and Jackie Smith, "Infrastructure for Changes: Transnational Organizations, 1953–1993," in Sanjeev Khagram, James V. Riker, and Kathryn Sikkink, eds., *Restructuring World Politics: Transnational Social Movements, Networks, and Norms* (Minneapolis: University of Minnesota Press, 2002).

create difficult tensions that distract these organizations from their chosen missions. Compared to service delivery organizations, advocacy organizations must give even greater attention to the question of independence because their work is political in character and because their main products are ideas.

Globalization is changing the conduct and strategy of organizations at the grassroots and national levels in at least one other concrete way: the speed with which "successful models of political advocacy" are disseminated and replicated is fast accelerating. A successful intervention, whether achieved in New York or New Delhi, is documented, discussed, and disseminated through networks of communication and collaboration that operate within all fields of issue advocacy, ranging from community development to early childhood nutrition. A growing number of international nonprofit associations have created real and electronic forums where ideas and models are shared more widely and quickly then ever before. While professional networks have long been a part of the nonprofit world, the speed with which fads and trends develop in various nonprofit fields is quite new. Some of the new high-speed networks of model dissemination have been conceived and promoted by leading transnational nonprofits, which often play a coordinating and consulting role.

One clear example of the way in which transnational movements quickly bring order and models of political action to a field can be found in efforts to improve public integrity. In the field of corruption control, one transnational nonprofit, Transparency International, has taken a lead role in propagating both a model of government reform and a set of tools that can be used by groups within countries around the world. Included in these tools are model agreements that have been negotiated between local groups and government bodies and that aim to improve the management and openness of public sector institutions. From its headquarters in Europe, the group drafts materials designed to elicit the support and interest of local business leaders in corruption control. These materials are field-ready when they arrive at nonprofit organizations around the world. Beyond standardizing key programmatic elements in "partner" organizations in all parts of the world, Transparency International also serves as a communication point through which local parties come in contact with one another.

As fads and trends develop across many fields of nonprofit activity, a nagging question emerges about whether the anointed ideas and models in various fields truly represent the most effective means to the desired social end. The speed with which ideas and models come into fashion and are communicated across the world has made it harder to carry out meaningful evaluations that both measure impact and examine alternatives. After all, when important government agencies and private foundations back a particular idea on an ambitious scale, one wonders who will step forward to slow down these replication efforts, especially when more research may well be needed. The acceleration of the replication process has in some fields closed down important channels of communication between the "center" of the nonprofit world (funders and influential transnational nonprofits) and the "periphery" (small, local voluntary organizations).[59] This communication represents an important means by which new ideas enter the nonprofit world, as grassroots organizations are able to transfer local knowledge to national and international audiences. Today, too much of the "communication" that is taking place appears to be directed from the center to the periphery.

If nonprofit organizations wish to function as independent actors, political agitators, and agents of social change, they will need to take steps to protect their unique set of missions and messages. They will need to affirm the value of pluralism in issue agendas against demands for replication of "successful models" and increasing levels of coordination. This will entail arguing that nonprofit organizations exist precisely because society wants a motley crew of political actors speaking out on social problems from a multitude of different perspectives. Beyond holding on to their local agendas and visions, nonprofits may also need to resist and question the models that are handed down to them by funders and transnational organizations. The task of preserving their independence may actually entail taking a critical stance toward the models that have been selected, sometimes without a full search among competing alternatives or an understanding of local conditions and culture. Not all transnational nonprofit organizations will meet these tests. In fact, many organizations are currently falling short, and have been captured either by special interest groups or by funders wanting to shape the message and activities of these groups. Globalization will thus necessitate a broader discussion of the political work of nonprofit organizations and an appreciation of the sometimes precarious position in which organizations that are ownerless, voluntary, and unable to distribute profits find themselves, especially when they operate across national boundaries.

As the world around nonprofit and voluntary organizations changes, the role nonprofits play in connecting individuals to one another, to their local communities, to national politics, and to other organizations around the world will increase in importance. The political role of nonprofits lies at the heart of the sector's expressive rationale and allows these organizations to fight for change that meets the needs of their members, their constituents, and the broader public. Nonprofit and voluntary action can be directed toward building linkages at the local level that create trust and confidence, which have long been closely connected to civic engagement and political participation. Nonprofits can seek to promote greater levels of political participation by mobilizing citizens to vote and to make their voices heard in a variety of other ways. Nonprofits can speak directly and indirectly to the state on behalf of a group seeking to have its point of view heard. Nonprofits can also help organize and finance campaigns. Starting with this broad understanding of the political role of nonprofits, we can picture nonprofit activity as a spectrum of activities from social capital building all the way to campaign financing, ranging along a continuum from nonpartisan activities that are broadly supportive of politics to activities that are more explicitly partisan (see Figure 2.3).

The political work of nonprofits, no matter where it takes place along this continuum, fulfills an important expressive function. It allows these organizations to voice views on issues of public concern, whether they are speaking on behalf of a small group of interested parties or seeking to represent a broader conception of the public good.[60] While some of this speech may not always seem to be in the broadest definition of the public interest—particularly when the speech is connected to lobbying for

| Build social capital in communities | Encourage civic engagement | Support political participation | Advocate for causes | Lobby for legislation | Finance campaigns |

← Least partisan form of action →                     Most partisan form of action

2.3  Continuum showing the range of civic and political engagement.

narrow legislative provisions, or when it takes the form of the funding of political campaigns—democracy demands that one be extremely cautious when limiting this work. This political work affirms the value of diversity and pluralism. To the extent that nonprofits work or are seen as working exclusively or predominantly on the right-hand side of the continuum, public support for the sector may be increasingly difficult to sustain. This is why nonprofits of all kinds have begun to focus on the issue of civic and political engagement and are working to overcome some of the narrowness inherent in traditional interest group politics. When nonprofit and voluntary action builds social capital, encourages participation, advocates for issues, lobbies for legislation, *and* organizes campaigns, it takes an important step in supporting democratic principles and fulfills the first of its four critical functions.

# 3

# Service Delivery

One of the most visible and recognizable functions of the nonprofit and voluntary sector is as a provider of goods and services that fulfills the unmet demands of consumers and clients. Nonprofit organizations accomplish this service delivery role in an amazingly wide range of fields, and serve an equally broad array of clients and consumers. Needy families seeking affordable housing, middle-class teenagers seeking summer science programs, and wealthy patrons wanting high-quality artistic productions all turn to nonprofits for goods and services. The sector is able to respond to unmet demands by bringing together a mix of funds, including private contributions, earned income, and government grants, and by offering services that are not otherwise available or that are different from those that the market and the government offer.

The range of vehicles used to deliver services is immense. Volunteers work in communities around the country to deliver important services like mentoring and tutoring. Small community groups, such as the Inspiration Café in Chicago, operate pantries and restaurants that make food available to the elderly and poor. Large agencies, such as Catholic Charities, deliver a broad range of critical social services—including counseling, job training, and nursing services—in cities and towns. All these efforts to deliver services share a willingness to find a "third way" to provide. The scope of the sector's contribution to social provision has been the subject of considerable debate. Owing to a lack of precise data, at present we can only estimate its scope at somewhere between 5 and 10 percent of the U.S. gross national product. Still, few would argue with the proposition that nonprofits in the United States have taken on an important role in the delivery of all kinds of services.

## Two Theories of Nonprofit Production

Why does the nonprofit and voluntary sector produce anything in the first place? This question is important because there have long been two large and willing providers waiting to respond to citizen and consumer demand—namely, government and business. Government has stepped forward to offer programs aimed at pressing social problems and has worked to deliver public goods such as national defense and clean air, while also creating transfer programs like Medicaid and Food Stamps that are intended to help disadvantaged groups. For-profit firms have focused on providing private goods that consumers have expressed an interest in purchasing. These goods range from appliances, which promise to make life easier, to convertible cars, which symbolize freedom. In the context of an environment in which government and business provide both public and private goods and services, the question thus arises of how best to understand nonprofit provision.

The earliest attempts to explain the service delivery function of nonprofit organizations relied on basic economic logic. In the early 1970s, Burton Weisbrod set out to examine the provision of collective-consumption goods outside the government.[1] According to his analysis, government's failure to satisfy consumer-voters leads to "government market failure." This shortfall, or failure, shifts the provision of collective goods to private and nonprofit organizations. The nonprofit and voluntary sector develops as "an adjustment to the restricted capabilities of the other two sectors."[2] In this economic model of nonprofit activity, the level of government provision of goods is defined by the utility functions of "consumer-voters." In almost all situations involving social provision, whether it is a question of job training or affordable housing, some consumers will be dissatisfied with the level or cost of public output and will want either a lower price or higher level of output. Whenever such a disjunction occurs, dissatisfied consumers have several options they can pursue, including seeking recourse from lower levels of government, resorting to for-profit market alternatives, or turning to voluntary organizations for the production of the desired goods. In each case, Weisbrod argued, a process of equilibrium adjustment takes place.

Weisbrod's goal was to develop a theory of when and why provision shifts from the public sector to the other two sectors.[3] His argument was that forces of consumer preference lead the for-profit sector to supplement governmental output in the form of "substitutes" for the original collective goods. Collective goods such as lighthouses and clean air have been supplemented with private goods such as shipboard radar and air filters produced and sold by businesses. In cases where the unsatisfied demand is for essentially noncollective goods, the private sector responds well in producing these goods. Private substitutes for collective goods are often not socially optimal, however, even if these private alternatives may be personally optimal for some. All of which points to the opening that the nonprofit and voluntary sector exploits. In the "government market failure" model, nonprofit organizations develop because certain organizations are needed to serve as "extragovernmental providers of collective-consumption goods" which supplement government output and offer an alternative to private output.[4] There is no guarantee, however, that nonprofits will do a better job of delivering services than government or for-profit firms, especially since the free-rider problem (which occurs when people consume a service without paying for it) can be acute in the nonprofit and voluntary sector.

Because unsatisfied demand gives rise to the nonprofit and voluntary organizations, the number of entities operating in any particular industry or field is ultimately determined by the heterogeneity of population demands, which often reflects, but need not be a direct function of, the heterogeneity of the population itself. Hence Weisbrod's conclusion: "The larger the quantity of collective good demand that is undersatisfied at the tax price scheme used by government, the larger the expected size of the voluntary sector, ceteris paribus."[5] How, then, can one account for differences in nonprofit penetration across fields or industries? Weisbrod argued that a sector's industry share depends on the nature of the goods it provides. When the goods in question that are inadequately provided by government are essentially private or noncollective, the for-profit sector will be the principal source of supplemental delivery. When the goods in question are collective, the nonprofit and voluntary sector will play a leading role in supplementing delivery.[6] Beyond the collectivity or privacy of the goods, there are other factors that influence which sector will provide it, including the similarity of the private substitute to the governmental collective goods, and the relative production costs of each sector.

For all its clarity and rigor, the "government market failure" model does not help us answer the difficult question of how one might go about establishing the optimal level of production of a given good by any of the three sectors. In fact, it is entirely silent on almost all the normative issues raised by the nonprofit and voluntary sector's role in social provision. The model does, however, provide us with a clear argument in which "undersatisfied demanders [are] portrayed as the group that gives rise to the voluntary sector."[7] It is a model that directs our attention to the pull of demand on government, for-profit business, and the nonprofit and voluntary sector—a predictive model that explains the forces which drive nonprofit and voluntary action.

Almost a decade after Weisbrod's analysis first appeared, a second important theory about the rise of the nonprofit and voluntary sector emerged. Proposed by Henry Hansmann, it likewise took unsatisfied demand as its starting point but moved in a quite different direction. "Contract failure theory" aimed at explaining nonprofit provision by looking at the breakdown in trust between for-profit producers and consumers for certain goods.[8] Hansmann began by defining and categorizing nonprofit organizations. He argued that nonprofits were defined primarily by the nondistribution constraint, which prohibits those who control nonprofits from benefiting from or distributing earnings. Bound by this promise to use their resources to advance their missions rather than to benefit private parties, nonprofit organizations emerge as a solution to what Hansmann called "contract failure." People seek out nonprofits when they cannot control and police services using ordinary contractual devices, when trust and information are scarce, and when assessing the value of the services they receive for their money is difficult. The legally binding nondistribution constraint of nonprofit organizations provides a seemingly powerful contractual assurance that the consumer will not be taken advantage of or betrayed by producers for personal gain. The fact that profits cannot be distributed to shareholders or owners gives the consumer of services a certain confidence that the transaction will result in a fair exchange.

The nonprofit and voluntary sector's ability to respond to contract failure is not without its complications. Hansmann pointed out that the elimination of financial incentives by the nondistribution constraint can impair efficiency, and that the spirit of the constraint can be violated through high levels of staff compensation. Still, in cases where the consumer has little information and where the need to trust producers is important, the attraction of nonprofit and voluntary sector provision can be powerful.

Contract failure occurs in a wide variety of contexts and takes on a broad array of forms. The purchaser and the recipient of the service may be quite far apart geographically. With some charities, donors are unable to see the actual recipients of their money because they live some distance away or because it would be inappropriate to reveal the identity of service recipients. With overseas famine relief programs like CARE and Oxfam, for example, the donors that respond to appeals for contributions do so in part because they trust the charities to use their funds responsibly. It is unlikely that small donors living in the United States will be able to monitor closely the activities of a relief agency operating in Bangladesh and make judgments about how well or efficiently their funds were used. To be sure, some relief organizations have attempted to provide detailed information to donors about the people or children that are served, but for the most part emergency assistance is rendered with minimal client tracking. For donors, the fact that recipient organizations may be separated by great distances is not an insurmountable problem, because the agencies operate under the nondistribution constraint. Unlike employees in a for-profit business, the staff of relief organizations have no obvious incentive to maximize anything except the assistance they deliver to needy people.

Contract failure may also be a factor with certain public goods. These are goods that entail equal cost whether provided to one person or to many, or that are "nonexcludable": when one of these goods has been consumed by one person, other people cannot be prevented from consuming it. Examples of such nonexcludable public goods include air pollution control and public radio. Public goods naturally give rise to the free-rider problem because people can benefit from the goods without paying anything for them. Not surprisingly, only one in ten listeners to public radio makes a contribution to the local station, even though such stations depend on donations and do not carry traditional advertising. The problem is that radio signals cost no more to send to one person living in a given radius than to all, and nonpaying listeners cannot easily be excluded. Unlike contributors to relief organizations, the contributor to public radio is also the consumer of the goods. Thus, the problem of generating contributions does not stem from donors' inability to see if the services are ultimately delivered. It results from the indivisible nature of the services involved, which makes them public goods. Of course, there are many other conceivable ways of delivering commercial-free broadcasting, including contractual arrangements between listeners and broadcasters such as those that exist in the cable television field. These arrangements could be very elaborate and involve specifying a whole range of obligations that each side would be expected to carry out, perhaps including enforcement mechanisms to make sure these obligations are fulfilled. This does not often happen, since nonprofit organizations tend to be successful in providing some kinds of public goods precisely because they are able to streamline contracting and enforcement. The nondistribution constraint cuts through and simplifies contractual arrangements by providing a basis for trust. If absolutely necessary, donors to nonprofit organizations can rely on the state to enforce the legal contract of nondistribution, though this is rarely done. Yet there are strong normative constraints on profiteering that restrict the behavior of nonprofit managers and that help to maintain the bonds of trust.

For organizations that primarily serve members and that charge a fee for the services they render, the problem of contract failure is somewhat different. In commercial nonprofits, the person paying the fee is the consumer of the service. By contrast, in nonprofits where contributions support operations, the donor is most often not the beneficiary or client. Still, consumers of services often will seek out nonprofit organizations because they want to be able to trust the producers and grant them a great deal of discretion. It is therefore hardly surprising that nonprofit daycare centers enjoy broad popularity. By offering parents critical services that they themselves will benefit from, and by removing the profit motive, daycare centers are able to offer a complex service in a way that inspires confidence in the consumer. In some ways, fee-for-service arrangements make the contract failure problem more intense. The stakes rise when clients and consumers depend on nonprofits for services that are critical in their daily lives. Few people would dispute the fact that the safety of one's own children comes before worries about the effective use of relief funds to aid the needy overseas. Thus, while both contributors and consumers seek to overcome contract failure, it is the consumers of nonprofit services that most directly depend on nonprofits.

Hansmann detailed several other cases and causes of contract failure. Yet his central argument was consistent. We can understand the emergence of the nonprofit and voluntary sector by looking at the unsatisfied demand for certain kinds of goods. Contract failure provides an opportunity for the nonprofit and voluntary sector to capitalize on some of the shortcomings of for-profit firms. For Hansmann, the appearance and continued survival of nonprofit activity in a broad array of fields ultimately depend on the ability of these organizations to satisfy an unmet demand by inspiring trust.

The two earliest and most prominent theories about how and why nonprofit organizations deliver certain services were both analytic and descriptive in character. These theories did not ask whether the nonprofit and voluntary sector should deliver certain kinds of services. Instead, they attempted to explain why the nonprofit and voluntary sector operated the way it did. As positive theories, Weisbrod and Hansmann's approaches highlighted two important aspects of nonprofit provision. The first is that nonprofit action is the product of some failure on the part of government or business to meet demand. While there may be many reasons this unsatisfied demand arises, the critical point is that the nonprofit and voluntary sector responds to the need by offering services that are different—in terms of quality or price—from those available elsewhere. The second core feature of the nonprofit and voluntary sector that emerged from these arguments is that nonprofit organizations provide services within a legal context that consumers and clients understand is different from that of the other two sectors.

These features of the early work on nonprofits led to a criticism of the implications of these positive models—namely, that they consign the nonprofit and voluntary sector to a passive role: that of filling gaps in the service delivery system of government and the market. Instead of defining the nonprofit and voluntary sector as an active engine of change and innovation, the "failure models" depict nonprofit and voluntary action as a fallback position that consumers turn to when other parties drop the ball. Thus, the nonprofit and voluntary sector's service production is justified not by its quality or creativity, but rather by the inability of government and the market to meet citizen and consumer needs. These demand-side theories do not make it entirely clear why nonprofits have an advantage over government in the provision of certain services. After all, government likewise operates under a nondistribution constraint, while also reserving for itself the power to levy taxes to finance projects and services that otherwise would never be undertaken, either because of a lack of support or because of the free-rider problem. So where does the real strategic advantage of the nonprofit and voluntary sector lie? Surely not in the efficiency with which it delivers services. More likely in the quality and cost to clients of these services.

The idea that the nonprofit and voluntary sector can and does play a critical role in social provision has led to a set of difficult questions about the relationship of the nonprofit and voluntary sector to the state. Chief among these is who exactly should finance the services that non-profits have increasingly been called on to deliver. In this debate, many have advanced the idea of a public-nonprofit partnership—one in which government would play a central role in meeting the financial needs of nonprofit service delivery organizations.

## Service Delivery and the State

In the 1960s and 1970s, many nonprofit organizations working to deliver needed services began to derive a larger part of their income from government grants and contracts. As part of the Great Society's effort to create social programs aimed at the most needy, nonprofit organizations of all kinds became critical players in the implementation of human service programs. The idea of bringing nonprofits into the policy implementation process was appealing because it promised to move decision-making closer to the community. At the same time, resistance to "top-down" solutions made funding grassroots organizations very appealing. This trend toward government use of nonprofits as partners in co-production continued in the 1980s and 1990s, albeit under a different ideological flag. The dual move toward greater levels of devolution and privatization meant that many critical government functions would be pushed "down" from the federal level to the state and local levels, and "out" from government to for-profit business firms and nonprofit organizations. The movement of power "down and out" with respect to government has changed not just the finances of nonprofit organizations, but also their identity.[9]

Today, most scholars interested in the study of public policy implementation are aware of the important role that nonprofit organizations play in the delivery of publicly funded health and human services. This awareness is in no small part due to a first major wave of empirical research on nonprofit organizations that charted the changing scope of the sector. Beyond documenting an important trend, this early research yielded two important and surprising empirical findings. The first was that by the late 1970s the nonprofit sector had become the principal vehicle for the delivery of government-financed human services. The second was that government had also quietly become the main source of nonprofit human service agency finance.[10] This growing interdependence was the starting point for a new theory of the nonprofit and voluntary sector's service provision role.

According to Lester Salamon, early theories of nonprofit service delivery were problematic because they provided little reason to expect extensive cooperation between sectors. Under Weisbrod's theory of government market failure, nonprofits existed to meet the public's unsatisfied demand for some collective-consumption goods. Nonprofit activity was taken to be a substitute for government provision, and thus there was little theoretical rationale for the cooperation between the two sectors. Hansmann's theory of contract failure was equally problematic because it did not explain government's reliance on nonprofits, or government's regulation of nonprofits. Moreover, the theory appeared to suggest that government, which has even less incentive to betray trust than nonprofits, would be the delivery vehicle used in preference to nonprofits in the case of most public goods.

As an alternative to prevailing approaches to the welfare state, Salamon advanced the concept of "third-party government."[11] Although the American welfare state has grown over the years, an important amount of this growth has been in the form of funds delivered to others for the implementation of programs. Government has turned increasingly to third-party implementers and given them considerable latitude in the way they carry out programs. The idea of third-party government reflects several American political and economic realities, including, perhaps most significantly, the federal structure, through which power and responsibilities are shared with the states, and, in a similar manner, with private institutions. In practice, third-party government has come to be a way in which Americans can reconcile their desire for services with their suspicion of a powerful state apparatus providing them. Third-party government also reflects a commitment to pluralism and enables the service delivery system to remain flexible during changing economic conditions. Independent institutions that contract with the government are usually already in operation, which frees these institutions from shouldering start-up costs, allows them to change direction quickly if needed, and makes it likely that they will operate with better knowledge of local circumstances than a large governmental bureaucracy.

Taking the reality of third-party government as his starting point, Salamon also argued for a "voluntary failure theory" which would serve as an alternative to Weisbrod's and Hansmann's approaches. Salamon saw the nonprofit and voluntary sector not as secondary and derivative of the other sectors, but as the primary response mechanism to the public demand arising from market failure. Rather than picking up the slack, the nonprofit and voluntary sector actually takes the lead in many areas. When nonprofits fail to provide services in sufficient quantities because of resource limitations, government responds to this "voluntary failure" by offering supplemental services or funding to allow greater nonprofit production. The central claim in Salamon's formulation is that when it comes to mobilizing resources for action, government has greater obstacles to overcome and higher costs than the nonprofit and voluntary sector. With its close connection to local communities, the nonprofit and voluntary sector is able to act quickly as issues and concerns arise. Sometimes it does so by mobilizing volunteer efforts; sometimes it does so by raising funds to support professional services. No matter how it chooses to react, the nonprofit and voluntary sector can meet the first alarm that communities sound. Government often enters the fray only when the nonprofit and voluntary response is insufficient: "Government involvement is less a substitute for, than a supplement to, private nonprofit action."[12] Thus, it is voluntary failure that gives rise to government action and to the funding patterns that support third-party government.

Although Salamon portrayed the nonprofit and voluntary sector as playing a leadership role, he eventually reached the conclusion that the sector is not—and probably never was—well suited to being the "independent sector" in either financial or programmatic terms. Salamon saw several areas where the sector was a less-than-perfect mechanism for meeting human service needs. "It is limited in its ability to generate an adequate level of resources, is vulnerable to particularism and the favoritism of the wealthy, is prone to self-defeating paternalism, and has at times been associated with amateur, as opposed to professional, forms of care."[13] These problems were serious but not unmanageable. By joining with government to form a partnership in public service, the nonprofit sector could fulfill its mission of delivering needed services. In areas where the nonprofit sector may lack the ability to attract substantial financial resources, to regulate the way care is provided, and to aspire toward universal provision and neutrality, the public sector could readily provide guidance. Salamon suggested that the nonprofit and voluntary sector's shortcomings nicely complement the government's strengths. "Potentially, at least, government is in a position to generate a more reliable stream of resources, to set priorities on the basis of a democratic political process instead of the wishes of the wealthy, to offset part of the paternalism of the charitable system by making access to care a right instead of a privilege, and to improve the quality of care by instituting quality-control standards."[14]

Salamon was not unaware of the potential problems that a cross-sector partnership might generate, and he correctly identified three fundamental threats to nonprofit organizations brought on by government funding of service delivery activities: (1) loss of nonprofit autonomy and independence; (2) "vendorism," or distortion of the agency missions in pursuit of available government funding; and (3) bureaucratization or overprofessionalization, leading to a loss of flexibility and diversity in program design. Even though he noted that at the time of his writing there was little systematic data available about the effect of government funds on nonprofits, Salamon concluded: "Clearly, dangers to agency independence, pursuit of agency purposes, and internal management style may result from involvement with public programs, but these dangers do not appear to be so severe as to argue for dismantling the partnership that has been created."[15] This conclusion was and continues to be shared by many who see public funding of nonprofits as a simple necessity and an established fact. At the same time, the instrumental value of the sector to government appeared substantial enough to support an argument for increased public funding of nonprofits, even if threats to nonprofit autonomy and mission definition might emerge in the long run.[16]

Since the time that early research first drew attention to the important role public funding plays in supporting nonprofit organizations, a second wave of research has raised serious questions about the nonprofit sector's growing dependence on public funds and whether this might not impair its ability to provide services.[17] Taken together, this research challenges quite directly many of the early analyses of the threats to nonprofits posed by increasing government contracting relations. In fact, the emerging research on public-nonprofit relations[18] has repeatedly found substantial tension and loss of autonomy within nonprofit organizations as a result of dependence on government contracts.

After tracking the financial health of community organizations in Chicago over time, Kirsten Grønbjerg found that government contracts can indeed threaten agency autonomy and lead to bureaucratization.

Heightened degrees of external control and the removal of discretion, which characterize some government contracts, limit the scope of internal management choices that nonprofit organizations can make as they seek to deliver needed services.[19] Many of the nonprofits in the Chicago study assigned staff to each government contract specifically for compliance and reporting reasons. As a result, many nonprofit organizations developed "very complex organizational structures, which largely parallel their public funding streams."[20] Moreover, when asked to compare a variety of funding sources—including government, individual donations, corporate and foundation grants, federated gifts, and fees for service—nonprofit organizations found government grants to be the least flexible, the most difficult to administer and account for, the least reliable over time, and the least sensitive to mission and program priorities.[21] Some nonprofit organizations even reported they no longer pursued public funding because of the threat it posed to their long-term independence. In many ways, Grønbjerg's study of Chicago nonprofits presents compelling evidence of the impact public funding can have on nonprofit organizations—evidence that challenges early thinking about a seamless public-nonprofit partnership.

A second blow to early optimism about public funding of nonprofit organizations can be found in the work of Susan Bernstein, which focused on managers of human services agencies in New York.[22] After conducting detailed interviews, Bernstein concluded that nonprofit agencies are forced to play a perverse game of proposal writing, reporting, and financial planning which bears little connection to the reality of their daily professional lives. She itemized the ways nonprofit organizations suffer from excessive auditing, fluctuating public sector budgets, and multiple reporting requirements to federal, state, and city agencies. Her study effectively captured the mutual dependence—codependence, one is tempted to call it—that the public-nonprofit relationship can create. On the one hand, public sector funders put pressure on nonprofits by threatening to withdraw funding when programs are not designed to their liking. On the other hand, nonprofits are sometimes led to form coalitions so that they can pressure government to increase funding for their particular area of interest. Throughout Bernstein's analysis, embattled nonprofit managers give a vivid firsthand account that contradicts earlier hopes for a fundamental compatibility between the public and nonprofit sectors.

Steven Rathgeb Smith and Michael Lipsky provide the most compelling rebuttal to early minimizations of the threats to nonprofits posed by public funding. Their evidence shows that government contracting has indeed led to the bureaucratization of many nonprofits.[23] In order to receive public funds, nonprofit organizations are obliged to introduce professional staff into their organizations to both administer the new public programs and comply with the terms of the contract. Even when a nonprofit considers that professional staffing is desirable, this requirement frequently demands a change in the way an organization carries out its work. Sometimes this has implications for who gets served: "When nonprofit organizations accept government funds, they often agree to serve clients that are needier than those the organization had previously served. To provide for these clients adequately, nonprofit organizations broaden the qualifications of their staff, adding salary expenses, which may or may not be paid by government."[24] Smith and Lipsky also demonstrate that government contracting has sometimes led nonprofits to compromise their missions in order to hold on to their government contracts. They note that this trend poses a real threat to the long-term diversity of the sector and to its ability to serve as a laboratory for innovation and experimentation. The result has been at times quite unexpected: Smith and Lipsky show that many radical community-based organizations founded in the 1960s have been transformed into docile, homogenized, publicly supported social service bureaucracies—a process driven by years of dependence on government grants.[25]

Beyond the sobering findings of new research on public-nonprofit contracting, two other developments call into question the continuing optimism about frictionless public-nonprofit production partnerships. First, in order for government and nonprofits to work together in true partnership, there must be a balance in power between the sectors. Yet as the data on the sector's birthrate abundantly illustrate, the number of nonprofit organizations has been increasing substantially over the past decade.[26] With more nonprofits competing for what have become, in some areas, increasingly scarce public funds, it is now clear that burgeoning competition among nonprofits has made it harder for nonprofit organizations to achieve an equal partnership with government. Government agencies disbursing funds have been able to be more selective and demanding in their awarding of contracts to nonprofits. Underfinanced and duplicative nonprofit organizations have had to contend with the inability of government (and private funders) to finance the explosive growth of the sector. One consequence of this development has been the rise in nonprofit bankruptcies.[27] Even when nonprofits do secure public funding, a growing literature has raised questions about whether these public funds do not actually end up crowding out private charitable support.[28]

A second problem with the idea of intersector partnership for social provision is more significant: little attention has been paid to the different missions and operating principles of nonprofits and government agencies. Far from heading toward a seamless partnership, the two sectors have experienced severe tensions that have only risen over the past decade, particularly as many faith-based nonprofit organizations have developed contractual relationships with government for the provision of human services. There is a fast-growing disjunction between public sector emphasis on accountability and universalism and the sometimes well-defined missions and commitments of many nonprofit organizations.[29] Thus, in addition to the problems of independence, vendorism, and excess professionalization that have been confirmed in recent research, a fourth type of conflict appears to be emerging—one related to the distinctive moral and religious commitments that guide and animate so many nonprofit organizations.

The idea that the nonprofit and voluntary sector should operate in partnership with government in the efficient delivery of services ultimately commits one to a narrowly instrumental vision of nonprofit and voluntary action. The rationale for the sector's existence and its privileged tax status is to be found in the tasks that it accomplishes, in the work it carries out, and in the outcomes it generates. This instrumental perspective has the benefit of laying out a fairly concrete set of expectations and standards by which the performance of the nonprofit and voluntary sector can be judged. Yet, at the same time, an emphasis on instrumentalism risks turning the nonprofit and voluntary sector into a tool of government action and may shortchange the sector's role as an initiator, innovator, and communicator of values.

The problems created when nonprofits attempt to expand their programs by entering into contracts with government are symptomatic of broader problems that are beginning to confront the sector. As nonprofits struggle to find a place for themselves in the economy and a role in social provision, they must make difficult decisions about how to manage growth and sustain operations. At the same time, they must guard against becoming passive vessels for the accomplishment of neutral public purposes. They must find ways to attract funds while at the same time jealously guarding their charitable missions. There are limits to how far nonprofits can bend before their identities and missions break. When nonprofits become purely instrumental in their orientation, they open themselves up to competition from for-profit firms interested in building new revenue streams. Without a value or expressive dimension, nonprofits are vulnerable to the competitive threat posed by a growing number of for-profit human service firms now working in fields traditionally dominated by nonprofits—a trend that has accelerated as of late.

## Competition with For-Profit Businesses

Increased interest within state and local government in contracting out for service delivery of all kinds has lured large, publicly traded corporations into many fields, particularly the human services, which have long been seen as the purview of nonprofit organizations.[30] Over the past two decades, for-profit firms' share of all government social service contracts has grown from negligible to almost a quarter of all service contracts. Over the same time span, the number of for-profit enterprises in the fields of daycare, home health care, and job training has soared. As business firms have begun entering these new—and traditionally charitable—fields of activity and as nonprofit organizations have become more aggressive in their search for revenues (see Table 3.1), the two sectors have at times come into conflict. The challenges raised by cross-sector competition in service delivery have forced nonprofits to confront their limitations and to respond strategically.

For the nonprofit and voluntary sector, the rise of corporate social services poses major challenges and raises difficult questions of strategy, not least of which is how to hold on to the sector's market share and client base. Some nonprofit organizations will surely be tempted to respond to the new competition by adopting business management tools such as total quality management, benchmarking, reengineering, and other techniques that promise to improve efficiency.[31] While this might help some nonprofits to manage their service delivery operations better in the short run, it is unlikely to be a sustainable long-range strategy. When competition between sectors comes down to the cost, speed, and

Table 3.1. Nonprofit and for-profit social service provision, 1977 and 1997 (includes individual and family services, job training and vocational rehabilitation, child daycare, and residential care).

| Year | Type of social service provider | |
|---|---|---|
| | Nonprofit | For-profit |
| *Number of establishments* | | |
| 1977 | 40,983 | 23,104 |
| 1997 | 92,156 | 69,713 |
| Change | (+125%) | (+202%) |
| *Number of employees* | | |
| 1977 | 676,473 | 177,449 |
| 1997 | 1,586,186 | 662,201 |
| Change | (+134.5%) | (+273.2%) |
| *Receipts (in millions of dollars)* | | |
| 1977 | 9,415 | 2,038 |
| 1997 | 75,683 | 18,894 |
| Change | (+704%) | (+827%) |

*Source:* Census of Service Industries, 1977 and 1997. Data for receipts have not been adjusted for inflation.

quantity of otherwise similar services, nonprofit human services providers will face five serious competitive disadvantages when pitted against profitmaking business firms.[32]

First, the financial and human resources of nonprofits limit their ability to offer complex, large-scale programs as cheaply and efficiently as for-profit firms. Nonprofit organizations are rarely well financed or fully staffed. In fact, they often are run on extremely tight budgets with small staffs. In addition, most smaller nonprofits lack business experience with complex information technology and management systems.

When combined, the resource problems of many nonprofits put business firms in a strong position in the changing field of human services contracting. In some cases, the scale and complexity of the contracts are simply enormous. A small or informal nonprofit organization that has focused its entire history on delivering quality services to a small community seems almost certain to flounder under the substantial management demands placed on organizations seeking large contracts. While some nonprofits may seek to create opportunities for themselves by pursuing contracts that include only direct client services and that leave information-intensive reporting work to for-profit firms, coordinating such a division of labor over the long term would have substantial costs. In terms of sheer scale, however, many nonprofit and voluntary sector organizations do not have the human and financial resources needed to tackle large-scale projects, like those recently funded under welfare reform. Undercapitalization can be a serious problem, given the fact that some government contracts withhold part of the service fee until the client has been served and has achieved some documented outcome. In the job-training field, for example, many contracts pay providers small upfront fees for each processed recipient, with the rest of the fees paid only after the recipient has maintained a job for several months. If a contractor receives all or part of its fees only months after placing a recipient, it must find a way to pay the costs of its services while it waits for those fees to arrive. The relative positions of for-profit firms and nonprofits engaged in raising the capital to meet these expenses could not be more different. For-profit firms are able to raise millions of dollars through initial public stock offerings. By contrast, most nonprofit officials believe their firms are undercapitalized, and few nonprofits have large revenue-generating operations. Moreover, even if nonprofits could raise operating capital through bond issues or other means, watchdog groups might well criticize these charities and accuse them of profiteering or excessive commercialism.[33]

A second problem for nonprofits is that profitmaking firms are able to hire very prominent and well-respected human service officials from both the public and nonprofit sectors for management positions in their growing for-profit human service divisions. High-profile expertise is more likely to gravitate to for-profit human service providers for the obvious reason that an undercapitalized nonprofit cannot offer salaries comparable to the ones large corporations can pay. So long as for-profit businesses can attract the best talent, as they have recently in the job-training and welfare-to-work fields, nonprofit organizations are likely to face tough questions about whether they have the knowledge and experience to manage large and complex operations. Over time, if disparities between the sectors become too great, nonprofit organizations may face a real talent drain that will weaken the sector's productive capacity.

A third potential trouble point for nonprofits is that for-profit firms are able to lobby, while public service nonprofits are somewhat limited in their ability to engage in such activity. Beyond regulatory differences, significant differences in style are obvious between the sectors, in terms of the messages that are conveyed. Lobbyists for businesses often try to "educate" government officials about the advantages of outsourcing and permitting for-profit competition in the human services. There have even been cases where for-profit firms have intervened in the design of the contracting systems under which they would eventually operate. In dealings with the government, for-profit firms are able to present a message of efficiency, while nonprofits often convey a message of equity and caring. The capacity of for-profits to shape the political and funding environment is thus different from that of nonprofits.

The fourth and, in many ways, most important obstacle that nonprofits face when attempting to compete is their lack of a financial bottom line. When for-profit firms sign performance contracts that, for example, require specified reductions in the size of the welfare caseload, or pay a fee whenever a client is successfully rehabilitated, some observers begin to worry about the consequences of these payment systems. One danger is that firms will "cream-skim" or "cherry-pick" clients by focusing their attention on working with the most job-ready or least disabled clients, while writing off those with multiple disadvantages. Additionally, some worry that firms will be tempted to reduce caseloads by cutting off eligible recipients or by taking other steps to achieve performance standards without helping clients become better prepared to function. The whole trend toward outcome funding and performance pay raises all kinds of challenges for nonprofits that want to provide services but that have strong social missions and commitments. Over time, increased competition with for-profit firms for performance-based contracts will likely strain the identity of nonprofit agencies or lead to the slow erosion of funding. Faced with a decision whether to compete or capitulate, many nonprofits may reexamine their service delivery systems and look for ways to increase efficiency and effectiveness. While this work may lead to improved nonprofit operations, it also risks cutting into the "low-return" charity work that nonprofit service organizations have traditionally undertaken. Special-need clients, particularly in the education, health, and social service fields, may find that the quality and availability of their often higher-cost services will change as cross-sector competition and outcome-based funding take root.

The nonprofit sector's competitive limitations have led to a spate of asset sales from nonprofits to for-profits and a number of conversions of nonprofits into for-profits, particularly among hospitals, health maintenance organizations, and health insurance groups. Under federal law, any organization that surrenders its tax-exempt status must contribute an amount equal to the value of its assets to a charity or foundation, which will in turn use these resources for charitable work. Because billions of dollars have been involved in all the sales of nonprofit assets to for-profit firms over the past decade, there is considerable interest in the nature and number of these conversions, especially when a nonprofit hospital sells out to a for-profit entity. Sometimes, hospital conversions are relatively straightforward transactions. In 1985, Wesley Medical Center, the second-largest hospital in Kansas, sold its assets to the Health Corporation of America for $265 million. The proceeds of the sale were then donated to two foundations, one a descendant of the foundation previously associated with the hospital, the other affiliated with the Methodist Church, which had founded the medical center.[34]

At other times, the transactions can be quite complex. One of the more interesting hospital transactions involved a chain of Catholic hospitals operated by the Sisters of Charity of St. Augustine, in Ohio. The purchaser was the Columbia / HCA Health Care Corporation. Under the arrangement that was struck between the parties, the Sisters placed the assets of the hospitals, the health maintenance organization (HMO), and the medical equipment supplier in a joint-venture partnership. Columbia paid the religious order $200 million to acquire half the system, with the understanding that Columbia would then operate the venture. The nuns announced that the funds would be used to create foundations in cities where the hospitals were located and promised that the level of charity care provided would not change. This early conversion, along with dozens of others, were important examples of the interdependence and interpenetration of the for-profit and nonprofit sectors. The trend toward conversions in health care—whether these involve the sale of HMOs or the conversion to for-profit status of large insurers like Blue Cross of California—demonstrates also that when nonprofits are challenged by for-profit entities, they face substantial obstacles to successful competition with business firms. When they surrender through conversions, nonprofit health providers ultimately must relinquish at least part of their ability to achieve their charitable missions in exchange for sustained financial strength. The Sisters of Charity of St. Augustine noted that the sale protected the order's ability to pursue its mission. Without the partnership of the HCA Corporation, the Catholic hospitals would have faced withering competition and a limited ability to cut costs fast enough to stay competitive.[35]

The move to convert nonprofit hospitals to for-profit status was relatively slow in the 1970s, but accelerated in the 1980s and peaked in the mid-1990s (see Figure 3.1). The trend toward conversion also reveals a pronounced preference in recent years for the conversion of large hospitals, rather than small ones. One explanation for the rise of hospital conversions is that changes in Medicare in 1984 led many nonprofit hospitals to worry that their revenues would decline precipitously. When coupled with predictions that for-profit care would compete with nonprofit provision, many charities embraced the idea of conversion as a critical strategic move. The subsequent decline and resurgence in conversion activity can also be understood in terms of the perceived position of nonprofit hospitals in a changing and demanding health care marketplace. Beyond changes in the policy and funding environment, nonprofit hospitals have been converted to for-profit status to gain ac-

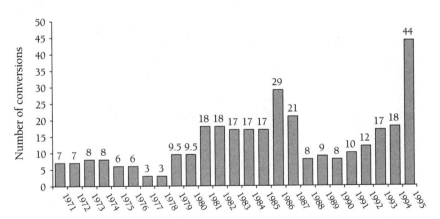

3.1  Hospital conversions, nonprofit to for-profit, 1971–1995. *Source:* David M. Cutler and Jill R. Horowitz, "Converting Hospitals from Not-for-Profit to For-Profit Status: Why and What Effects?" in David M. Cutler, ed., *The Changing Hospital Industry* (Chicago: University of Chicago Press, 2000), copyright © 2000 by the University of Chicago.

cess to new capital, which is easier to do in the for-profit world, where stock offerings can generate quick infusions of cash. In addition, some mergers and sales of nonprofit hospitals have been pursued as a way to relieve substantial debts.[36]

Competition between nonprofit and for-profit health care providers is indicative of a broader trend. The calm and peaceful world that may once have existed for charitable organizations is now long gone. Market pressures have penetrated the nonprofit sector in important ways that cannot but change the sector. As these changes take hold, it is useful to ask whether the scope and quality of services will decline if nonprofits continue to be pressured by the ongoing trend toward greater for-profit activity in traditionally nonprofit fields. To date, comparative data on the relative performance of for-profit and nonprofit organizations remains minimal,[37] in part because there is little consensus on how to obtain accurate measures of program effectiveness. Still, almost everyone is likely to agree that in fields such as early childhood education, community health care, and job training, where knowledge about what works remains highly contested, investment in a plurality of approaches is desirable. With their unique commitments and missions, nonprofit service providers have something important to bring to the table. By continuing to leave public contracting open to a broad range of organizations from across both sectors, government at the federal, state, and local levels can take a critical step toward preserving and affirming the place of nonprofit organizations in the changing landscape of human service provision.

The move by many nonprofits to become more competitive and to meet the challenge posed by profitmaking businesses has led to a major shift in the composition of nonprofit revenues over the past two decades. While many nonprofits continue to rely on charitable contributions to fund their operations, the fastest-growing source of nonprofit revenue is earned income, in the form of fees for service, dues, and charges. Nonprofits have become more commercialized not just because the nonprofit sector has become more crowded and grants thus more difficult to obtain, but also because for-profits are encroaching on domains long thought to be the province of charitable work. One consequence of this move has been the rising importance of the idea of "sustainability"—a word that refers to the ability of a nonprofit to outlast the inevitably close-ended nature of many charitable contributions.

One of the most common ways for a nonprofit to sustain itself over time is to shift away from contributed income and toward earned income. In some measure, the goal of nonprofit sustainability is closely linked to the commercial goal of profitability. In each case, the move to commercialize and commodify services has important consequences for the social mission that a nonprofit or for-profit is able to fulfill.

Growing competition between nonprofits and for-profits is also significant because it risks narrowing the scope and vision of nonprofit organizations. As the nonprofit and voluntary sector becomes locked in increasingly fierce competitive relations with for-profit business, particularly in the areas of job-training, schooling, and day care, it risks becoming ever more instrumental in its approach. When nonprofit organizations are simply efficient intermediaries through which services are produced—efficient enough that differences in costs and methods between the nonprofit sector and for-profit business become obscured—questions about why these organizations should be granted tax-exempt status naturally arise. In short, the competitive drive in some parts of the nonprofit and voluntary sector to produce services at low cost is an important challenge to the sector's traditional charitable mission. How nonprofit organizations balance the competing claims that now pull at them in many areas of services provision will in large measure determine the character and future orientation of the nonprofit and voluntary sector.

## Performance Measurement

As nonprofits have been drawn into competition with for-profit firms and with other nonprofits, a different set of issues concerning performance has surfaced. Although nonprofits often pursue missions whose achievement is difficult to measure, financial and competitive pressures within the sector have led to an increased emphasis on performance measurement. Although the sector has taken significant steps toward professionalizing itself, there is little consensus on what constitutes good evaluation within the nonprofit sector, what should be measured, and how performance indicators should be used by funders and clients in assessing the effectiveness of services. Some outputs of nonprofit activity are difficult to track, while others are more transparent. Measurement in the nonprofit sector is complicated by the range of parties that have a stake in what happens in these organizations. This in turn makes it difficult to ensure that evaluations, once conducted, are actually used to change and improve practices.

The struggle to find tools appropriate for this multidimensional task is taking place even as nonprofits are being asked in many government contracts to produce clearly specified outcomes, not just documented units of service delivery. While for-profit firms are used to focusing on performance measurement, the rise of outcome and performance contracting poses both an opportunity and a challenge to nonprofits. On the one hand, a growing interest in outcomes will focus energies on achieving concrete results and will help nonprofits to confront some of the difficulties in actually carrying out meaningful performance measurement. At the same time, as government seeks to focus on the programmatic outcomes achieved by the organizations it funds, a new kind of freedom may be possible for nonprofits. Performance contracting has the potential to release nonprofits from many of the process regulations, much of the heavy oversight, and the extensive reporting demands that have long characterized government contracts. Since payment is given only upon the achievement of a specified outcome, be it job placement or physical rehabilitation, agencies are able to innovate fairly broadly in their quest for success. There is, however, a dark side to this development: performance contracting is viewed as a threat to some aspects of the nonprofit tradition. Because it makes payment contingent upon success, nonprofits may be tempted to cherry-pick clients and serve those who are most likely to succeed. If this occurs, financial pressures to produce "successful" outcomes may compromise the ability of nonprofits to reach the most needy and pursue social justice. The problem of cherry-picking is exacerbated in fields where for-profit firms are active alongside nonprofits, since profitmaking firms have strong incentives to look for shortcuts to meeting performance goals.

The drive to locate adequate tools for measuring the performance of nonprofits is not an academic matter. Foundations, large individual donors, and government funders are now asking tough questions that probe beneath espoused missions to ask where money can best be invested. Nonprofit organizations of all kinds have had to respond with data to support their requests for continued support. The real challenge lies in the fact that the current demand for solid evaluation data far outstrips the sector's current capacity to deliver meaningful and reliable information on what works and what does not. Thus, the temptation to cut corners or to engage in strategic gaming around performance issues is only getting stronger. With this temptation comes considerable peril to the sector's legitimacy.

Although nonprofits are ownerless organizations, they do have a number of important stakeholders—parties that are interested in and committed to these organizations. Each group has a different stake in the future of nonprofit organizations and each is affected differently by charities that fail to achieve their goals or fulfill their mission. Clients are affected if nonprofits perform poorly or inefficiently, since the quality and affordability of services will decline and make the use of nonprofits less attractive. Contributors, too, are affected: when an organization fails to achieve its goals, their charitable intent is thwarted. And taxpayers and community members are affected because the tax revenue used to support nonprofit organizations is not producing outcomes that are most beneficial to the community. Given these interests, government regulators would appear justified in helping to keep nonprofits from squandering charitable resources. Yet one significant case has made it clear that poorly performing nonprofits have little to fear from the Internal Revenue Service, the principal agency charged with overseeing nonprofit organizations.

The case involved a now-defunct charity named the United Cancer Council (UCC), which benefited from the fact that its name could easily be confused with one of the more established and reputable organizations working to find a cure for cancer. From 1984 to 1989, UCC engaged the fundraising services of the firm Watson and Hughey, which sent out 80 million letters on behalf of the organization and raised a total of $28.8 million in donations from the public. Of this bounty, UCC received only $2.3 million after the costs associated with the fundraising were deducted. The IRS attempted to revoke UCC's tax-exempt status because it had entered into an agreement with a fundraiser that allowed the solicitor to keep the majority of the money sent in by contributors. The United States Court of Appeals for the Seventh Circuit reversed the decision of the Tax Court, ruling that the IRS could not strip a charity of its tax exemption for entering into a foolish business deal. The Appeals Court found that it was unreasonable to penalize a nonprofit simply because it exercised poor judgment in its handling of its finances. While the expense-to-program ratio at UCC was so poor as to call into question the effectiveness of the entire organization, the court found that so long as deals are negotiated at arm's length and the fundraisers are not insiders, charities should have the freedom to pursue their missions as they see fit. This important ruling has effectively put a damper on the government's ability to rein in nonprofits that perform inefficiently and ineffectively.[38]

Although government does not have unlimited oversight of nonprofit performance, some stakeholders have taken an active role in improving the quality of services delivered by nonprofits. In one case, action by stakeholders turned out to be a far more potent tool for regulating nonprofit behavior than the penalties that government might have imposed. The recent history of the United Way provides perhaps the best example of the way in which donors can reshape an organization by exerting pressure and withholding funds. Following a major financial scandal in 1992–1993, the United Way experienced a significant fall-off in the funds it collected within many of its critical chapters. Many faithful donors to the organization demanded change and greater accountability for the use of their charitable dollars. Over the past few years, the United Way has responded to this pressure by giving contributors more of a role in selecting beneficiaries and by developing a new assessment program for the grants that are disbursed. Of course, these reforms occurred only after a national scandal brought enormous publicity to the organization. Yet it is clear that nonprofits can and do respond to pressures brought to bear on them by their stakeholders.

Today, much of the responsibility for watching over the quality and cost-effectiveness of services delivered by nonprofit organizations has been conveyed to government and to private institutional funders that work closely with nonprofits. As a result, some segments of the nonprofit and voluntary sector have seen their ability to deliver services weakened by the general absence of a broad, informed, and committed group of stakeholders. In a few fields, such as services for the disabled, the presence of mobilized and outspoken stakeholders has dramatically improved the accessibility and variety of services. A wider diffusion of responsibility for securing quality services—evidenced in active and engaged clients, contributors, and communities—would go a long way toward ensuring that all nonprofits continue to deliver services that benefit the public.

## Scale and Substance of Nonprofit Provision

Demand-side approaches focusing on the instrumental use of nonprofit organizations for social provision have raised our awareness of the important work performed by these organizations. As nonprofits have assumed a significant role in delivering services, conflicts and tensions with both government and for-profit business have arisen. At the same time, the image of an active and competitive nonprofit and voluntary sector seeking its place within the broader economy raises the difficult question of scale. There are at least two competing perspectives that bear on how much responsibility and how big a role the nonprofit and voluntary sector can play in service delivery and social provision.

The first holds that nonprofit and voluntary action has historically achieved significant scale and can in fact constitute a major contributor to the fulfillment of public needs. Charles Murray has examined the changing levels of private giving since the 1960s and has argued that government spending does appear to crowd out private charity. During the 1960s, when commitment to major social programs was strong and when spending on antipoverty efforts was high, private giving as a percentage of income sank dramatically. As further evidence of a link between government funding and private giving, Murray pointed out that during the early 1980s, when the public perception was that the rate of growth of federal social spending was slowing, there was a boom in private giving. Beyond arguing for a connection between government and charitable activity, Murray asserted that we may never really know the answer to how much responsibility private giving can assume in relation to government provision unless charity is put in a position where it is perceived to be urgently needed.[39]

Taking a different approach to the issue, Alan Reynolds has suggested that in the 1990s private philanthropy supported levels of nonprofit activity that rivaled those of the government's efforts. In making this comparison, Reynolds used data on private giving and nondefense discretionary programs, excluding entitlement programs like Medicare and Social Security. His analysis suggested that private giving is not merely the poor stepchild of government but a large and indispensable part of the social landscape. Reynolds' argument took a more conservative turn when he suggested that, if one brackets public programs which benefit broad parts of the American middle class, the scale of public provision which actually benefits the poor is not that sizable. After making adjustments, Reynolds argued that private philanthropy has more than enough capacity to tackle a range of pressing social problems. Moreover, if tax policy were structured so as to truly promote more charitable giving, the bounds of what the nonprofit and voluntary sector could accomplish might be significantly expanded and its independent role in social provision enhanced.[40]

Not everyone is convinced that a privately supported nonprofit and voluntary sector can ever be or should ever be seen as a central player in social provision. Many critics of devolution and privatization have argued that it is unrealistic to think large-scale human problems will ever be successfully addressed without a strong commitment by the federal government, and that pinning too much responsibility on the nonprofit and voluntary sector will only lead to chaos and inefficiency. After all, the majority of nonprofit organizations operate on a local scale, have modest resources, and rely on the good will of donors and volunteers. Moreover, those nonprofits that do serve large numbers of needy clients almost invariably do so only because government grants and contracts are made available.[41] In the opinion of progressives, overreliance on the nonprofit and voluntary sector might also lead to government's being released from responsibility for important social problems.[42] Thus, even though the idea of an active and independent nonprofit and voluntary sector is appealing, it should not lead anyone to the conclusion that the state's powers are no longer needed to accomplish public purposes. The idea of shifting responsibility for social provision from government to nonprofits is ultimately fraught with many problems. Chief among these is ensuring that the neediest members of society receive the care and assistance they need. While nonprofits have long offered programs and services to the disadvantaged, some people firmly believe that the responsibility for controlling the distribution of these services is too important to be left in private hands, and may need to reside in government if full access and equity are to be preserved.[43]

Part of the reluctance to confer too much responsibility on nonprofits stems from the inability of many nonprofit organizations to achieve real scale. The word "scale" means at least two things. First, it can refer to the variety and scope of the services, the number of clients served, and the geographic coverage of an organization. Organizations that have achieved scale in this sense are those that have set up operation in multiple cities or have had their work replicated by others. The second meaning of "scale" is related more to organizational strength and permanence. Large institutions like the Museum of Fine Arts in Boston, Stanford University, or the Adler Planetarium in Chicago have achieved scale in that they have large institutional presences, offer multiple programs, and have demonstrated that they have the financial wherewithal to persist indefinitely. Scale according to this definition is equivalent to financial strength, often secured by endowment. Although many funders have long sought to assist nonprofits in "going to scale," only a few start-up nonprofit organizations have succeeded. For example, Dress for Success, a provider of free business attire to poor women seeking to reenter the workforce, now operates in fifty-nine cities in four countries. The youth-volunteering organization City Year, which places young people in year-long community service positions and supports them with small stipends and a social network, has become a presence across the United States. While other organizations have had their programs replicated or built their financial base and grown within their local markets, the number of such cases is still small compared to the vast universe of non-profits that work with modest resources on a local basis. Because the achievement of scale is still seen as an elusive goal, there remains considerable doubt about the ability of the nonprofit sector as a whole to take on large areas of social responsibility, particularly when these areas involve critical public needs over which government has long presided.

Beyond arguing whether nonprofits could or should try to play a major role in the provision of services, a different debate has emerged over whether tax policy ought to encourage greater charitable support of certain kinds of nonprofit service providers. One idea that has gained widespread attention is that of a tax credit for contributions to organizations assisting the poor. Under such a system, individuals would be allowed to direct a portion of their tax bill to specific poverty alleviation organizations. Such a policy would change the status quo significantly. Currently, tax filers are allowed to deduct their charitable contributions to public-serving nonprofits from their gross or before-tax income.[44] A tax credit would make this deduction far more potent and would create a much greater incentive to donate. It would divert funds from the government's coffers by means of a more direct transfer between donors and recipient organizations. Moreover, a change in this direction would also signal the government's willingness to prioritize and reward certain kinds of charitable activity, something that the state has been reluctant to do in the past. Other ideas for changing the tax treatment of charitable giving have surfaced over the years, including one that would allow taxpayers who do not itemize deductions to get credit for their giving. Debates over how to treat gifts to charity are often contentious because they raise the question of who should have a say in social provision.

Issues related to the division of labor between sectors are important, yet questions about what *kinds* of services the nonprofit and voluntary sector should provide also loom large. Beyond separating member-serving from public-serving organizations for tax-treatment purposes, government has avoided channeling nonprofit activity into any particular substantive field. At present, tax treatment varies little according to the specific activity of each nonprofit and voluntary entity. All organizations operating under section 501(c)3 of the IRS code are granted tax-exempt status, and contributors to these organizations are rewarded with tax deductions for their gifts. In terms of public policy, it makes no difference whether an individual contribution goes to support an opera company or a soup kitchen. Both are treated the same, in large part because government is reluctant to choose winners and losers in the sector. Given the changing needs of society, it would also be very hard to give preferential treatment to any particular subfield on the basis of the urgency of the problem being addressed. In a short period of time, conditions might well change and new priorities might emerge. Thus, rather than engage in an elaborate game of incentives designed to maximize the social utility of nonprofit and voluntary sector provision, government has decided to remain neutral and to let the market for charitable contributions sort itself out.

One argument against this agnostic stance is that all needs are not equal and that some people find it galling to see a contribution to a puppet theater treated the same as a donation to an AIDS hospice. In part, this reaction is fueled by the fact that we demand more of the nonprofit and voluntary sector than from the for-profit sector. Every year, for-profit firms turn out thousands of products of dubious value for which there is no real social need. But most people devote little thought to the fact that sales of these products are generated by aggressive advertising campaigns. Instead, trusting in the idea of consumer sovereignty, they collectively shrug their shoulders and accept that reasonable people can and do disagree about what constitutes worthwhile commercial activity. When it comes to the services produced by the nonprofit and voluntary sector, people tend to change their standards and reasoning. They may bristle at some of the more frivolous charitable work that is undertaken under the umbrella of tax exemption. Yet when it comes down to making a decision about which causes are worthy and which are not, government has decided to move very slowly. Policymakers may prefer to see private contributions go to an AIDS hospice, but few have attempted to come up with compelling arguments as to why contributors to a puppet theater should be treated differently, particularly when any such action would evoke a flood of arguments, accusations, and charges about which parts of the nonprofit and voluntary sector are truly deserving.[45]

Those who criticize the potential inefficiencies of the tax deduction mainly advocate reliance on other forms of subsidies, ranging from direct grants to service contracts to vouchers to tax-exempt bonding—all designed to ensure that public support flows to organizations working to solve important social problems. These alternative subsidies represent the public sector's desire to discriminate between nonprofits operating in critical fields and those pursuing more esoteric agendas. In this connection, we should note that there are two fundamental rationales for the tax exemption given to nonprofits. The first—that the exemption provides a *subsidy*—rests on the social value of the services delivered by nonprofits. The second argument—that the exemption promotes *sovereignty*—is grounded on the idea of autonomy and independence.[46] Because the subsidy of the tax exemption is distributed evenly across charitable nonprofits, government has had to rely on additional types of support to achieve specific public purposes.

The equity and efficiency questions raised by nonprofit service provision have opened the door for a radical critique of the sector, one that is anchored in concerns over power and "social reproduction."[47] Because parts of the nonprofit and voluntary sector are driven by charitable contributions from wealthy persons, there is a lingering concern that a class bias may well be an inevitable part of nonprofit activity.[48] Research by Teresa Odendahl has suggested that charity really does begin—and end—at home.[49] Large donors tend overall to contribute much more often to organizations and causes that they benefit from or enjoy (such as the arts or education) than to programs that work on unpopular causes or that serve disenfranchised populations. Whether philanthropy is self-interested or not, there can be little doubt that large parts of the productive capacity of the nonprofit and voluntary sector meet private and small-group interests, not the public interest. From the work of membership organizations such as country clubs to the activities of symphonies, whose patrons remain largely drawn from high-income groups, the nonprofit and voluntary sector has not been and probably never will be able to fully answer the charge that it sometimes produces services consumed by a small group of elites who can and will pay.

A more interesting issue is why the question of who benefits from nonprofit activity continues to arise. One obvious explanation is that we have come to hold certain beliefs about the role nonprofit and voluntary organizations *should* play in democracies. At a time when doubts are growing about the ability of government to fund entitlement and assistance programs for those in need, many still view the nonprofit and voluntary sector as a critical buffer or safety net which is ready to provide critical services to those left behind. This may take many forms: churches offering day care at affordable prices, the Salvation Army offering shelter to those with no place to go, Oxfam delivering relief to victims of famine. The benefits these services provide to those in need set a high standard for the rest of the nonprofit and voluntary sector, one that many organizations—particularly those focusing on the more narrow but often less urgent interests of members—cannot meet. The fact that the nonprofit and voluntary sector encompasses both public- and member-serving organizations is, however, a critical source of its strength and a principal reason for its continued popular support. In fact, it is precisely because nonprofits are not all focused exclusively on helping the truly disadvantaged that the productive output of the nonprofit and voluntary sector is able to respond to a wide range of demands expressed by citizens. The service delivery function of the nonprofit and voluntary sector may well be aimed at meeting demand that is not satisfied by government or the market, but this demand is not limited to areas where social injustice may persist. In fact, the productive capacity of the nonprofit and voluntary sector is focused on a very broad range of needs or wants.

Defining the central function of the nonprofit and voluntary sector as service provision has proven to be a powerful starting point for understanding the motivating force behind these special institutions. The earliest theorizing about this service delivery function gave us a basic understanding of how nonprofits operate in the space between the state and the market, at times capitalizing on the failure of government to provide certain collective consumption goods, or on the failure of the market to reassure consumers that the profit motive will not impair the quality of the service delivered. But neither the "government market failure" theory nor the "contract failure" theory fully succeeds in giving us a comprehensive explanation of when and why nonprofit organizations enter into a service provision role. Moreover, neither theory systematically explains the current rising levels of competition and collaboration among the government, business, and nonprofit sectors.

The ability of nonprofit and voluntary organizations to maintain public support depends in great part on their ability to balance competing claims on their time and resources. They must play a role in meeting important social problems through the delivery of services, particularly to the most disadvantaged and least powerful members of society. Yet they must also find their rationale in an ability to produce goods and services that are of interest to a far broader range of clients and consumers. At times using revenues collected from the well-off in order to internally subsidize activities that otherwise would be impossible to finance, nonprofit organizations continue to work to achieve a mix of activities that is sustainable and that produces social value. The service delivery function lies at the core of the sector's rationale. Yet restricting the sector to the task of social provision would be to deny its other roles. These include serving as a channel for the expression of faith and values—a critical function that is taken up in the following chapter.

# 4

# *Values and Faith*

An important part of nonprofit and voluntary activity is expressive in character and speaks to the need people feel to enact their values, faith, and commitments through work, prayer, philanthropy, and volunteerism. The expressive dimension of nonprofit activity need not be conceived as opposed or hostile to the sector's more instrumental dimension. In fact, capturing and taking full advantage of the expressive component of nonprofit activity is critical to the success of the sector and to its more instrumental and productive roles. The expressive, value, and faith-driven aspect of nonprofit and voluntary action has often been overlooked because it is difficult to measure and document. Yet it constitutes a critical component of why these organizations come into existence and how they operate.

From faith-based social service providers that seek to help clients achieve personal change to community activists that work tirelessly for social justice, the nonprofit and voluntary sector is full of people seeking to do something that will not just help others but also be consistent with their own values and beliefs. For many, nonprofit and voluntary work is attractive because it represents a way to connect work activity to core beliefs. At a time when some people must hold down a job that is either entirely divorced from what is important to them or actually in conflict with their espoused values, nonprofit employment and even part-time volunteer work represent a chance to mend this rift. For donors who support nonprofit organizations, charitable contributions can often be about more than just a cash transfer. They are often affirmations of be-

96

liefs that accomplish public purposes while providing donors with the satisfaction of seeing their values put into action.

Taking seriously the idea that values and faith are critical elements of nonprofit and voluntary activity commits one, in some measure, to a supply-side perspective. This means accepting the proposition that the values and beliefs of staff, trustees, volunteers, and donors can be and often are the engines of nonprofit activity. Beyond this descriptive claim, the argument for values and faith can also take on a normative dimension, holding that public policy should actively cultivate and encourage the free expression of beliefs and commitments in nonprofit organizations as a way of ensuring their independence and encouraging innovation. At times, the arguments for the value and expressive content of nonprofit activity are narrower. Because many nonprofits serve a well-defined group of members and not the general public, the private values and beliefs of members sometimes simply enact the right to association, even if the public does not benefit from this activity.

## Theorizing and Harnessing Values

Though not obviously or inherently ideological, the idea that nonprofit organizations can and should be vehicles for the expression of private values and faith has been connected, at least in recent years, with critics of agnostic welfare state policies. Seeing flaws in the broad and neutral design of public programs, some have argued that nonprofits need to do more than just deliver services or encourage political engagement. The idea that there might be a moral dimension to the sector is significant because it allows nonprofits to distinguish themselves from the state and chart for themselves a new direction. The value content of nonprofits is in fact the sector's "value added," which gives nonprofit activity its worth and justifies the effort and expense needed to support it.

One of the most important early explorations of the idea that much of what is important in nonprofit and voluntary action has to do with the expression of values began with the coining of a new term: "mediating structures." Peter Berger and Richard John Neuhaus defined mediating structures as those institutions that stand between the private world of individuals and the large, impersonal institutions of modern society. These structures include neighborhood groups, churches, clubs, and voluntary associations, all of which play a linking or mediating role "by constituting a vehicle by which personal beliefs and values could be transmitted into the mega-institutions."[1] Small, well-connected organizations are critical because they serve two important purposes simultaneously. First, they provide individuals with protection against alienation and anomie by helping to translate public problems into terms that are more recognizable and meaningful. Second, mediating structures are important to the state's ultimate legitimacy because they connect public purposes to the "values that governed the actual lives of ordinary people."[2] Although Berger and Neuhaus coined a popular term, they willingly allowed that the idea of mediating structures can be found in a number of traditions of social and political thought. From Edmund Burke's call for "small platoons" that could operate in opposition to the sweeping changes wrought by the French Revolution, to Ferdinand Tönnies' distinction between *Gesellschaft* (society) and *Gemeinschaft* (community), to the Roman Catholic principle of subsidiarity, the idea of mediating the contact between large public institutions and the individual has long held promise. What made Berger and Neuhaus' formulation important was not just the term they developed, but the timing of their argument.

When it first appeared in 1977, *To Empower People* was seen as an assault on the foundational ideas of the burgeoning welfare state. The argument that mediating structures were essential for bridging private values and public priorities flew in the face of the notion of a national community whose values were defined and enacted by government.[3] Articulating their views before many of the more overtly conservative critiques of the welfare state emerged in the 1980s, Berger and Neuhaus focused attention on the scale and anonymity of "megastructures" that towered above individuals, dictating their behavior and shaping their preferences: "The modern welfare state is arguably the most important case of an enormous exercise of power, by and large motivated benignly, yet having developed into an instrument of oppression as well as corruption."[4]

Berger and Neuhaus argued that government funding and regulation of mediating institutions poses a critical challenge. When small, value-driven, local initiatives are enlarged, professionalized, and replicated by government, the vitality that originally distinguished these initiatives from government risks being undermined. This problem frames two obvious policy options when one is thinking about the relationship of the state to mediating structures. Berger and Neuhaus termed these the "minimalist" and "maximalist" options. The minimalist position holds that public policy should cease and desist from damaging mediating structures. The maximalist position is that the public sector should use mediating structures wherever possible for the realization of public purposes. The preferred solution to this question, according to Berger and Neuhaus, is one that involves rethinking the institutional means through which government carries out its responsibilities. Key to any such reorientation is connecting the massive structures of the state to the little platoons that are meaningful to individuals.

Individual empowerment is a critical ingredient in the resurrection of mediating structures, aimed not at debilitating the state but at making it more meaningful and responsive. Because individuals know their own needs and those of their communities better than anyone else, Berger and Neuhaus offered simple advice: "Mediating structures . . . are the principal expressions of the real values and the real needs of people in our society. They are, for the most part, the people-size institutions. Public policy should recognize, respect, and, where possible, empower these institutions."[5] By affirming that neighborhood groups, churches, voluntary associations, and other mediating structures have an important role to play in public life—as both a channel through which the voices and values of communities can be heard, and as an affirmation of the importance of pluralism—Berger and Neuhaus set out a powerful normative argument. Their vision was grounded in the idea that nonprofit and voluntary action is important in large measure because it represents an affirmation of individual values and beliefs. In the 1970s, when arguments for small-scale intervention and localism were vastly outnumbered by argument for broad national responses to public problems like poverty, this was a bold and counterintuitive set of claims. Of course, during the 1980s these ideas found a receptive audience, when alternatives to large federal spending programs were actively being sought. Today, these ideas are embraced by many conservatives and liberals, who variously argue for the importance of devolution and privatization or for the importance of community empowerment and self-determination.

The idea that nonprofit and voluntary organizations are important because they reflect the values and concerns of little platoons has a number of important implications. It requires that one think systematically about the role values play in the design and management of nonprofit programs. This means asking, as Berger and Neuhaus do, whether the trend toward professionalization within nonprofit organizations has been entirely salutary or whether it has not begun to rob nonprofit activity of some of the individual values and commitments that are so critical. It also leads to the question of whether there is a way to operate nonprofit and voluntary organizations that maximizes the expressive value-driven side of these organizations.

In recent decades, one of the most pronounced trends in the nonprofit and voluntary sector has in fact been the push to professionalize large parts of the workforce.[6] Professionalization has turned out to be a mixed blessing across the many fields of nonprofit and voluntary activity. On the one hand, the rise of a cadre of professional nonprofit managers has ushered in training and certification, ethical standards of conduct, new research efforts, and associations aimed at creating networks of collaboration. Moreover, professionalization in the human services has long promised to replace the amateurism of volunteers with the trained expertise of social workers and health professionals. In areas where the problems of clients can often involve life and death decisions on the part of service providers, professionalization has created a sense of confidence that those delivering services are prepared to do so effectively. For those concerned about a quality gap between nonprofit and business or government services, the rise of nonprofit professionals has been a great reassurance, one that has increased client trust by offering a promise of consistent performance.

On the other hand, professionalization has contributed to at least three problems. First, it has brought with it a general diminution in the eclecticism that lies at the heart of the expressive dimension of the sector. Diffusion of practices through networks of professionals may replicate models of service delivery that are not optimal and that may preempt the continued search and development of alternative, more effective models. To the extent that professionals are bound together through professional associations, electronic communities, and many other forms of communication, the channels through which ideas and practices can be diffused have clearly multiplied. One concern that these networks raise is the ability of service providers to understand and respond to local needs and concerns with programs that are appropriately tailored. If the workforce of the nonprofit and voluntary sector continues to become professionalized and normalized, it is fair to ask whether the capacity to customize and localize may be threatened in the process. Whether the field be alternative medicine or early childhood education, methodological pluralism is less likely to flourish in an environment where standard operating procedures are well defined and universally accepted.

A second problem associated with professionalization is the rise of an increasingly specialized and disconnected array of services. Specialization in the sector is a response to increased competition for clients and contributors. Many nonprofits stake out very narrow market niches as a way to focus on a client base that donors are committed to serving, or as a way to reach groups of clients that can readily afford to purchase the services offered. To the extent that the market niches occupied by nonprofits become narrower, it may be harder for nonprofits to build integrated service delivery systems that are easy for clients to navigate. The issue of specialization is particularly significant from a coordination perspective. The narrower the menu of activities carried out by nonprofits, the harder it will be to move toward a one-stop or integrated model of service delivery. There is more than a little irony in this trend, given the historical roots of many social service agencies. In the early years of the twentieth century, the settlement house movement led to the establishment in many major American cities of multiservice agencies dedicated to meeting the complex problems confronted by the poor and by new immigrants. Today, more than a century later, the initial insight of institutions like Jane Addams' Hull House seems to have been overlooked. Instead, the sector has evolved a professionally oriented language that includes terms like "service coordination," "collaborative governance," and "program synergies."

Beyond premature convergence and hyperspecialization, a third danger of professionalization is that it may pose a threat to the private values, commitments, and beliefs that often are key drivers of local innovation. Important insights into how to address critical human problems, ranging from family breakdown to drug addiction to persistent poverty, have come from people who have suffered through these problems and then shared their experiences with others. Often these leaders and innovators have little formal training or technical expertise. Instead they have what is most crucial in the nonprofit and voluntary sector: commitment and vision. When service delivery is in the hands of a cadre of well-organized professionals, it can become more difficult for these alternative voices to be heard and given a chance to prove themselves, particularly if the new approach entails deviating from accepted modes of treatment or program design. In short, professionalization can bring with it a whole set of preconceived ideas about how work should be done.

The rise of professional careers within fields of nonprofit activity has also changed incentives and motives. The idea of advancement within a professional field has clearly had an impact on the outlook and approach of frontline workers in nonprofits. Instead of hiring people whose primary desire is to give and to help, nonprofits are increasingly being staffed by persons who seek personal advancement both within their organizations and across similar organizations in their chosen fields. The move away from volunteer labor toward career salaried employees has raised a new set of questions about who is delivering services and why they are doing their work. While volunteers remain an important engine driving nonprofits, most nonprofits use professionals to manage volunteers, rather than using volunteers to manage their organizations. As the nonprofit sector has been buffeted by major demographic shifts over the past century, including the movement of women into the workplace and growing racial diversity throughout the population, the composition and aspirations of its workforce have changed. The question that must now be answered is how professionalization, which can be a valuable tool for achieving important instrumental goals within the nonprofit sector, can be used to promote the value-driven, expressive dimension of work in this sector.

In overcoming the instrumentalism that has dominated much of our thinking about the nonprofit and voluntary sector, we should look to new leadership and management models that are aimed at recognizing and encouraging the special expressive and value-laden character of nonprofit and voluntary activities. Seeking to displace the dominant antiseptic approach to leadership that focuses on gaining authority and influence, Ronald Heifetz has articulated an approach to leadership that embraces and cultivates its adaptive character. He starts by defining leaders as citizens from all walks of life mobilizing people to do something socially useful.[7] This is a definition of leadership that "places emphasis on the act of giving clarity and articulation to a community's guiding values."[8] On this account, when seeking to work with the values and commitments of other people, leaders in the nonprofit and voluntary sector must be prepared to consider competing value perspectives. In fact, one of the core tasks of nonprofit leaders is aligning and interpreting a broad and complex set of values within the context of social and community problems that require action. Heifetz's approach to the adaptive capacity needed by leaders applies to both the challenges of leading staff within a nonprofit organization and to the broader task of mobilizing community support for nonprofit action.

In the area of nonprofit management, David Mason has explicitly emphasized the expressive dimension of nonprofit and voluntary action by pointing to the fact that not all work is a means to an end, and that some work is an end in itself: "Expressive behavior presses out into action certain cognitive, emotional, and/or normative motivational states, including deep-seated beliefs and personality attributes. . . . Expressive activity is directly gratifying action for the sake of the action itself."[9] In searching for a way to capture and promote the expressive dimension, Mason argues that nonprofit organizations can actually succeed more fully in their instrumental purposes if they harness and cultivate expressive behavior. Given the fact that only the largest nonprofits are able to pay high salaries, finding a way of motivating staff and volunteers turns out to be a critical challenge. Rather than focusing simply on the narrow parameters of the task at hand and on ways of completing this task more efficiently, managers need to find ways to allow workers to connect personally with their work and express themselves through their organizations. Allowing and actually encouraging nonprofit workers to see their work as a form of expression and as a manifestation of their values and beliefs can be a powerful way of motivating them to accomplish concrete tasks: "Expressive activity in organizations is important not only because people need it as an end in itself, but because the opportunity for expressive activity attracts and motivates participants to work for instrumental purposes."[10] Harnessing and managing the expressive dimension thus becomes more than a topic of academic interest. It becomes a strategic necessity. Without an expressive component, nonprofit organizations can slowly turn into close analogs of bureaucratic public sector agencies or of unimaginative businesses.

In the end, professionalization can be a useful tool for maximizing the instrumental dimension of the work that goes on within nonprofits, but it can inhibit motivating on the basis of values, which may actually be a more powerful tool for ultimately achieving instrumental purposes. Of course, professionals have commitments to their chosen fields and to the traditions that these fields embody. Often, however, these commitments are to ethical conduct and standards of care or service that the profession expects. This is different from commitments that spring from the pure expression of personal values and beliefs through work or volunteering. Why worry about the expressive content of nonprofits? Nonprofit organizations that do not emphasize, promote, and position themselves around values may have a hard time succeeding in an increasingly competitive and turbulent sector—especially if other organizations are willing and able to use the expressive character of nonprofit work to attract donors, and to motivate and retain staff.

## Value-Driven Donors

The question of values within the nonprofit sector becomes more controversial when one changes the discussion from the values of professional staff and volunteers to those of donors. One of the deepest and most complex questions in nonprofit circles concerns the appropriate role and status of the donor within nonprofit organizations. Two radically different schools of thought have emerged. The first holds that philanthropy is really about public purposes and that donors should focus on the needs of the community, putting their own private interests and values aside. Donors should thus work to elicit the opinions of grantees, involve them in all aspects of the grantmaking process, and fund grassroots organizations that are most in touch with community needs. This is sometimes termed funding "from the bottom up." The goal of this approach is to ensure that philanthropic funds are used wisely and efficiently, that they match the needs of the community, and that the public interest is served. This is the more instrumental and demand-oriented approach that is favored by progressives.

The other perspective is more closely aligned with the expressive and value-centered understanding of nonprofit activity. It holds that only when philanthropy is centered on the values and personal interests of donors will the nonprofit sector become sustainable and successful. For donations to continue to flow into nonprofit organizations, donors must be taken seriously and their expressive needs acknowledged. This means that philanthropy is not just about meeting social needs and the demands of certain communities—no matter how real and documented those needs may be. Philanthropy is also about donors' using their funds to explore their own private visions of the public good. As a consequence of this view, any measurement of grantmaking effectiveness must consider not just the programmatic outcomes generated, but also the experience and sense of satisfaction that donors desire. This expressive output is often difficult to justify in light of the pressing nature of some social problems. Yet if the sector neglects it, it ignores a core part of the system of incentives and motives that sustains giving.

What does donor-driven philanthropy look like? Consider two quite different cases, both of which aimed at translating private commitments into public good. In Indianapolis, the late Pierre F. Goodrich used his philanthropy to build support for his values and beliefs. In 1960 he created the Liberty Fund—an operating, not grantmaking, foundation to "promote the study of a society of free and responsible individuals."[11] A businessman and lawyer who read widely, Goodrich was deeply concerned about the concentration of political and economic power in large institutions and saw the preservation of individual liberty as a critical challenge for society. The fund he endowed was established in perpetuity to reflect these values and to carry out a set of activities that would remain uncompromisingly committed to liberty. Rather than making grants to other organizations, the fund uses its own staff to pursue its mission through three principal programs, all of which it operates with income from its $200 million endowment: an extensive agenda of short seminars (up to 150 a year) convened around the world for scholars interested in reading and discussing libertarian classics, a visiting scholars program, and a vast book publishing program that keeps in print at low, subsidized prices many classic texts in the libertarian canon. The fund has considerable control over the content of its programs, since it supervises both the publishing and the seminars, and is able to focus on the fulfillment of the private vision and values of the donor.

Many donors view their philanthropy as an opportunity to demonstrate in a lasting and public way the things in life that have meant the most to them. Donald and Mildred Othmer were a quiet academic couple. He was a chemical engineering professor at the Polytechnic University in Brooklyn, and she was a former teacher who had become a volunteer at the Brooklyn Botanic Gardens and Planned Parenthood. What set them apart from other couples, however, was a decision they made in the early 1960s to invest with a family friend in Omaha named Warren Buffett. The Othmers' investment was converted into shares in Berkshire Hathaway in 1970 at $42 a share. By the time their estate was settled in 1998, Berkshire Hathaway was trading at $77,000 a share and their estate was valued at nearly $800 million. The Othmers had no children and they chose to leave their estate to charity. The organizations they selected included those that had played central roles in their lives: Brooklyn Polytechnic, which had given Donald Othmer the research support he needed to pursue his work and to secure scores of patents; the Chemical Heritage Foundation, a group dedicated to the history of chemistry and chemical technology; and the University of Nebraska, where Othmer had received his Bachelor of Science degree. While the Othmers went from modestly well off to extremely wealthy, their lifestyle did not change much. They occupied the same townhouse in Brooklyn for decades and kept up their work. The philanthropic choices that they made reflected very clearly an affirmation of their life interests and their deep commitment to science. The organizations the Othmers selected to receive the bulk of their estate were organizations to which they had important personal connections and through which their core commitments had been realized.[12]

Not all of the values affirmed by donors are as lofty as the desire to promote individual liberty or to advance science and research. Several recent mega-gifts, including $100 million to build a world-class arts district in downtown Madison, Wisconsin, and $200 million to bolster the animal shelter system across the country, have more to do with the interests and commitments of the donors than anything else. These gifts reflect one donor's love of his Midwestern hometown and another's boundless affection for his miniature schnauzers.[13] Rather than castigate giving that does not proceed from an analysis of the most urgent human needs, the public may need to be more open to the fact that philanthropy must have a certain autonomy and protection within which donors can operate. Only when donors have the ability to use their philanthropy to do something that is meaningful to them will giving likely flow at high levels. After all, if the choices of donors are subject to second-guessing or public oversight, many donors would no longer see a clear line between giving and paying personal taxes, and then having private funds used for collective purposes defined by others. Even though it may entail a certain amount of deference, it is the ability to direct charitable dollars to causes and organizations important to the donor that animates an important part of philanthropy.

The central role of the donor's beliefs in driving philanthropy is underscored perhaps most clearly in the fact that by far the largest percentage of private charitable giving by individuals has been directed at religion. In recent years, the share of private philanthropy received by religious institutions has consistently been over 50 percent, far outstripping gifts to health, education, arts, or social services. Over time, the hundreds of billions of dollars of private charitable contributions made by individuals to their local congregations and to religious institutions of all varieties demonstrate the close connection between faith and charity. While the larger secular grants made by foundations, corporations, and very wealthy donors tend to attract the most attention, it is the vast flow of individual faith-driven giving—often disbursed in small contributions—that still constitutes the core of American philanthropy. Over the years, the level of individual giving as a percent of personal income has fluctuated moderately, indicating that economic conditions have only a modest effect on charitable giving (see Figure 4.1). Much of the research on giving suggests that income is a good predictor of the

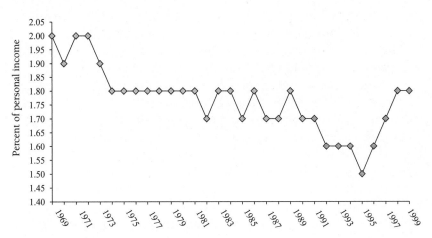

4.1  Giving by individuals as a percentage of personal income, 1969–1999. *Source:* U.S. Department of Commerce data on personal income, in *Giving USA* (New York: American Association of Fund-Raising Counsel, 2000), p. 144.

amount of money donated to charity, but that it is a poor indicator of the decision to give or not to give. Other factors, including beliefs and faith, are needed to explain and predict the philanthropic impulse itself.

Of course, saying that the private values and faith of the donor matter and must be respected is not an entirely respectable position in some political quarters within the nonprofit and voluntary sector. Any donors funding "from the top down," even if their goal is to stimulate new approaches or to challenge conventional practices, open themselves up to the criticism that their philanthropy is a tool of oppression aimed at merely perpetuating the interest of the wealthy. A classic Marxist critique of philanthropy[14]—that it is a tool for the advancement of elite self-interest—has even led some groups to establish foundations that explicitly reject the donor-centered model in favor of an approach that emphasizes the need of communities and their right to determine the use of philanthropic resources. Within these small "alternative funds," usually supported by a small group of wealthy individuals with progressive political views, community members and representatives from recipient organizations play a key role in determining how money will be disbursed. The goal of this transfer of power is to remove the donor's values and interests from philanthropy so that the genuine needs and desires of the community can surface. These experiments in transferring decision-making from the donor to the community represent a very small fraction of philanthropy, but do point to a fairly widespread concern that donor-driven philanthropy can be unacceptable and illegitimate.[15]

The debate over whether the private values of donors should guide the long-term use of charitable funds, particularly many years after the donor's death, raises the thorny question of philanthropic intent and perpetuity. Conservatives such as Robert Bork have argued that the problem of interpreting the charitable intent of the donor is remarkably similar to that of establishing the original intent of the Founders in writing the Constitution.[16] The effort to respect and protect the intent of the donor is important because it preserves the trust that individuals put in foundations and provides a solid basis for defining charitable missions. Moreover, some critics look at the development of some of the largest foundations, including the Ford and MacArthur foundations, and see institutions that pursue agendas which their founders would not approve of and which are at odds with the donors' core values.[17] Of course, progressives counter that the notion of donor intent can interfere with the pursuit of the public interest, particularly in cases when the intent becomes obsolete or when public needs change substantially.

Examples of philanthropic intent that have required updating are not hard to find. In Washington, D.C., the Hurt family endowed a home for the care of the blind in 1923. Located in a large mansion in Georgetown, the residential home saw its occupancy rate slowly decline as blind persons increasingly sought full integration and participation in the broader community. By the mid-1980s, there was clearly a need to adapt the terms of the philanthropic trust, to sell the nearly vacant home, and to fund educational programs that would more effectively meet the evolving needs of the blind. In doing just that in 1987, the trustees modified the mission but stayed true to the underlying values of the donor. Of course, the question of donor intent becomes more complex, and the politics of modifying a philanthropic mission more conflicted, when the shift requires a substantial overriding of the donor's values and intent.[18] This is precisely what happened when San Francisco hosted what has since become known as the Super Bowl of probate.

When the wealthy oil heiress Beryl Buck died in 1975, few could have foreseen that her charitable intentions would trigger one of philanthropy's most important disputes. The dispute centered precisely on the question of how sacrosanct the values and interests of donors really should be and how they should be weighed against the needs of the community. Upon her death, Mrs. Buck, a longtime resident of Marin County, California, left behind what she believed was a modest estate of approximately $10 million. Her will stipulated that the money was to be held in trust by the local community foundation, with the income spent solely on "care for the needy *in Marin County,* and for other nonprofit charitable, religious, or educational purposes *in the County.*"[19] In the years following Mrs. Buck's death, those last three words would take on great importance. Soon, a corporate takeover substantially increased the value of her stock holdings in Belridge Oil Company, which made up the bulk of her estate. In a short period of time, her modest bequest grew into a $350 million fortune. The San Francisco Foundation, which had been given the responsibility of distributing the Buck Trust income, soon faced a dilemma: because of its wealth, Marin County did not appear to some in the Bay Area as the best place to invest philanthropic resources. It was not long before the size and number of grants going to Marin-based groups came under fire. Because Marin County has long been one of the more affluent areas in the nation, some local nonprofit observers at the time believed that the county was rapidly reaching a state of "charitable saturation."

In 1984, the trustees of the San Francisco Foundation asked a state court for permission to distribute part of the Buck fortune, which by then had grown to over $400 million, to other Bay Area charities. The ensuing trial turned into a national forum on the purposes and principles of modern philanthropy. The two conceptions of the responsibilities of foundation administration that were argued out in the Buck Trust case clearly reflected the tension between the private values of donors and the broad interests of the public. In testimony before the court, a series of experts came to opposing conclusions about where the allegiances of foundation managers lie. The positions sketched out by the witnesses were, of course, dependent on whether they believed foundations were private expressions of a donor's philanthropic vision or public trusts to be used for the benefit of all. As the case progressed, a series of rulings by the judge indicated that the San Francisco Foundation would not prevail in their request. First, the judge ruled that evidence of the relative need of other counties was inadmissible. Second, the judge concluded that "there will never be enough dollars to meet even the basic needs of Marin residents. . . . The charitable, educational, and religious needs are effectively limitless." As the tide began running increasingly in favor of Marin, a settlement was arranged by the judge that transferred control of the Buck Trust's income to a newly created Marin Community Foundation. It also stipulated that a small part of the Buck largesse had to be spent on "programs of special significance" that would be located in Marin but that would address major human problems.[20]

The court's decision—while ultimately favoring the residents of Marin and the intent of Buck—nevertheless sent a powerful message to the entire nonprofit and philanthropic world. This message reinforced the view that the donor's intent should not be taken as sacrosanct and that permission to change the mission of foundations could indeed be sought in America's courts. The mission of the Buck Trust was not "impossible" and probably not even "inefficient," in that Marin County did have a core of residents who were living in poverty. Still, the vision and values of the donor had been challenged in the name of the broader community interest. The question of how much sway the values, interests, and commitments of donors should have over the use of charitable money continues to evoke controversy.[21] Other challenges to donors have surfaced, and the notion of donor intent is still the subject of much contention. This is hardly surprising, since philanthropy is an important engine of nonprofit activity and the control of philanthropic resources ultimately dictates a small but critical amount of the content of nonprofit activity.

Today, the struggle to define the role of donors has taken on a new urgency. Two forces are in the process of propelling private philanthropy toward a major transformation—one that will depend in great measure on the values of donors. Over the coming decades, a massive intergenerational transfer of wealth, estimated at well over $40 trillion, is expected to redefine the landscape of giving. The sheer size of this wealth transfer will inevitably place tremendous power in the hands of a broad and diffuse group of individuals with widely divergent values and priorities. In addition to the wealth that will be applied to philanthropic purposes as demographic shifts slowly work themselves out, a second, more immediate development is already under way. A rising number of business entrepreneurs, some with already substantial personal resources, have begun to challenge philanthropy's traditional conventions and practices. With a strong do-it-yourself inclination, many of these wealthy entrepreneurs have expressed a commitment to bringing to philanthropy the personal energy and drive that they have brought to their businesses. As philanthropy braces itself for an infusion of new funds and new practices, the line dividing public and private spheres will all but surely be redrawn in ways that will have consequences for the shape of our democracy.

What are the distinguishing features of the new philanthropy? Although it is still emerging and evolving, two critical philanthropic precepts are apparent. First, many donors have begun to eschew philanthropic consultants and advisors, preferring instead to take full responsibility for their philanthropic decisionmaking. Second, many of the new donors are seeking out deeper, more lasting, and more engaged relationships with recipient organizations. All of which is producing diffuse, pluralistic, and more personal giving patterns.

Beginning in the early 1900s, when major donors like Andrew Carnegie[22] and John D. Rockefeller inaugurated the "scientific philanthropy" which sought to attack social problems at their root, many donors have felt as though philanthropy, to be effective, required professional expertise and oversight.[23] The process of grantmaking seemed complex and fraught with difficult decisions about effectiveness and fairness. Many donors were drawn to the idea of setting up private foundations that would administer their wealth in perpetuity. The creation of large foundations has accelerated over the past three decades (see Figure 4.2). In recent years, however, the basic premise behind foundation giving has been challenged. Just as the trend away from intermediaries has swept through the investment world and empowered individuals to take control of their own finances, donors are now seeking ways to cut out the middleman and make philanthropic decisions themselves, so that their philanthropy will affirm their personal commitments and values.[24] While many donors will continue to rely on foundations, others have begun to experiment in growing numbers with alternative philanthropic vehicles, including community foundations that allow residents to pool their gifts and estates into one large foundation, operating foundations that use investment income to carry out programs run by the foundation's own staff, and other new instruments for giving.

The new donors have responded strongly to the introduction of a range of innovative vehicles for carrying out philanthropic purposes. Large mutual fund companies, which have become eager to meet not just the investment needs of clients but their philanthropic needs as

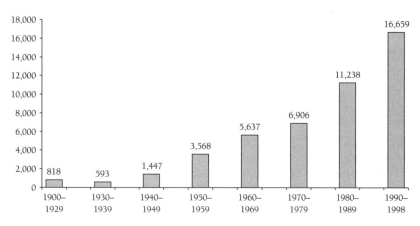

4.2  Number of larger foundations created by decade. *Source: The Foundation Directory* (New York: Foundation Center, 2000). Based on a Foundation Center survey of grantmaking foundations that had at least $1 million in assets or that awarded grants of $100,000 or more in 1997–1998.

well, have been responsible for an important breakthrough. Several families of funds have established their own public charities which act in many ways like community foundations, though they offer great flexibility, practically no regulations, and little paperwork.[25] Donors can deposit funds in their accounts, receive a deduction for the full amount of their gift, and then recommend grants as they see fit. One reason for the surging popularity of these kinds of funds is that they speak directly to the desire of new donors to make their own charitable decisions. Gift funds are not in the business of telling donors what they should be supporting. In fact, the growing market segment that these funds have cleverly claimed is that of new, independent-thinking donors who want control and convenience, not hand-holding and second-guessing. Because these funds typically operate with much lower expenses than traditional foundations and are growing very quickly, they have challenged the mainstream philanthropic establishment to change.[26]

New technology and new ways to give are also changing the approach of smaller donors who are just learning about philanthropy. Today, there are several Internet-based giving sites, where donors can find information about charities and direct contributions to the organizations of their choice.[27] These sites make information easy to access and remove barriers to giving. Like the gift funds, on-line giving sites tend to start with a commitment to empowering donors to make their own decisions. The on-line giving movement is explicitly pluralistic and expressive in its philosophy, and resists attempts to channel and concentrate giving to preselected organizations. At the same time, the push to empower small donors has been endorsed by banks, which now make opening a gift account almost as easy as opening a checking account. Instead of attempting to channel small contributions to a single institutional source, like the United Way, from which grants can then be made, the new vehicles remove this step from the giving process, empowering donors to make decisions themselves which fit their outlook, beliefs, and interests.

Having awakened to the fact that giving need not start and end with the donor's writing of a check or the approval of a grant by foundation trustees, the new philanthropy has begun to change the character of the engagement between donor and donee. Many donors are now seeking closer and more collaborative relationships with their donees and opportunities to reap psychological rewards from giving.[28] Some donors now seek to become more involved in their gifts, by advising on the de-

sign and implementation of the program, by helping the recipient organization connect to other funders, or by providing technical assistance
when the donor has expertise in fields such as law, accounting, or management.[29] Several groups of new donors are now actively teaching
young people about this high-engagement giving and seeking to expand
its currency, in the name of greater donor satisfaction and better results.[30]

The most significant consequences of the rise of donor-driven giving
may well turn out to be the decline of the concept of perpetuity. The
drive for engagement will likely lead to a greater amount of philanthropy being conducted while donors are alive. Many donors now believe that the idea of waiting until old age to begin giving is no longer
personally or socially acceptable. Pressure to start giving is already being
placed on some of the high-tech entrepreneurs who have amassed large
fortunes, and several large gifts have already resulted.[31] As donor-driven
philanthropy picks up pace, one casualty could be perpetuity, an idea
that attracted many people to foundation giving over the past century.
After years of watching many large foundations drift away from their donors' intent, many wealthy individuals are drawn to the idea of taking
charge of their giving.

Overall, the trends toward higher levels of engagement and structural
disintermediation will likely continue to push giving toward a more personal and expressive agenda. The values, commitments, and interests of
donors will play an increasingly important role in the nonprofit sector,
especially as the amount of money dedicated to private philanthropy increases in relation to the amount of public funds available for new,
nonentitlement public spending. The infusion of donor desires and interests into nonprofit activity will not be the only way in which the expressive dimension of the sector expands, however. An important part of
the expressive dimension will be connected to the oldest feature of the
sector: religion.

## Emerging Tensions

Values enter the picture through the decisions about the kinds of people
who will staff nonprofit organizations, and through the beliefs and commitments of individual donors about what are important public purposes. There is, as well, a more concrete and visible way in which ex-

pression manifests itself in nonprofits—namely, through the formation of explicitly religious and faith-based organizations. Faith is a central part of both the financial and the organizational landscape of the sector.[32] After all, America's many congregations are all part of the nonprofit and voluntary sector. And compared to health, social services, education, and the arts, religion receives by far the largest share of individual charitable giving.[33] Religious institutions are also the locus of a significant amount of the volunteer labor that works to address a broad array of concerns. While congregations and faith-based organizations may pursue social justice and seek to meet important social needs, a substantial part of the religious impulse arises from the desire to enact and express one's faith. As Thomas Jeavons has noted, many organizations "come into being primarily to give expression to social, philosophical, moral, or religious values of their founders and supporters. . . . The values-expressive character of many private, nonprofit organizations is what distinguishes them from business and government organizations."[34]

Faith-based organizations range in size and character from the smallest informal groups working to help one family at a time solve its problems to some of the largest and most solidly established religiously affiliated organizations, including Catholic Charities and the Salvation Army.[35] Religiously affiliated schools, universities, and hospitals control a significant part of the total revenue in the nonprofit sector. The degree to which religious conviction shapes the programs and activities of these large organizations varies tremendously.[36] In some organizations, the faith component is at the center of every activity. Storefront churches working in disadvantaged communities see faith not just as part of their services, but as the critical organizing principle that drives the small contributions which make service to the congregation and work in the community possible.[37] At some of the large church-affiliated agencies and hospitals, the role of faith in the design and delivery of services is less transparent. Usually, large hospitals, social service agencies, and universities with religious affiliations open their doors to anyone seeking their services and do not bring faith explicitly into their programs.[38] Through both commercialization and professionalization, some of these religiously based organizations often end up operating much like their secular counterparts, even if faith ultimately animates the organization's worldly mission. Still, because hospitals and universities dominate the

overall revenue structure of the sector and because many of these institutions are religiously affiliated, the role of religion cannot be overlooked or underestimated.

Difficulties in defining exactly what makes an organization "religious"
led Jeavons to develop a functional analysis that focuses on seven key
organizational dimensions: the organization's name and self-description,
the character and beliefs of its participants, the sources of its material
resources, the kinds of products and services it delivers, the way it
processes information and makes decisions, the way it allocates power
within its ranks, and the relationships it has with its environment. By
building a framework around these dimensions, Jeavons reminds us that
religious organizations can be found in all sizes and shapes, and that
they defy simple, unambiguous classifications. The inability to formu-
late a concise and broadly applicable definition has led to considerable
confusion in policy circles about what a religious organization really is.
Although congregations are clearly religious in nature, the definitional
issues for other religious and quasi-religious organizations are anything
but clear-cut.[39]

When one considers only religious congregations, the numbers are
significant (see Table 4.1). While the distribution of religious institutions across faiths has remained relatively constant over the past decades, two trends are noteworthy. First, over the past four decades the
percent of nonprofit entities that are religious in orientation has declined, since the number of congregations has increased at a slower rate
than the number of all other nonprofit organizations. Second, the relative consistency in the numbers of Protestant, Catholic, and Jewish congregations obscures the fact that since 1960 church membership has increased overall by 38 percent. Several groups have experienced rates of
growth of more than 100 percent over the past four decades, including Pentecostals, Jehovah's Witnesses, Latter-Day Saints, and Adventists.
Other groups, such as Episcopalians and Friends, have experienced
membership declines. One of the most difficult problems in tracking
American religious activity is that neither the number of congregations
nor membership size truly captures the underlying phenomenon of
church attendance.[40] Still, congregations and religious activities constitute an important part of the broader nonprofit landscape.

Faith does not find institutional expression in congregations alone.
While values and faith give some organizations distinctive identities

**Table 4.1.**   Number of U.S. religious congregations in the major denominations, 1960–1990.

| Denomination | 1960 | 1965 | 1975 | 1980 | 1985 | 1990 |
|---|---|---|---|---|---|---|
| Protestant | 282,008 | 292,233 | 298,244 | 300,676 | 307,147 | 320,624 |
| Roman Catholic | 21,617 | 23,541 | 23,998 | 25,542 | 24,260 | 23,091 |
| Jewish | 4,079 | 4,079 | 5,000 | 3,500 | 3,500 | 3,416 |
| Eastern churches | 1,363 | 1,531 | 1,469 | 1,583 | 1,656 | 1,689 |
| Old Catholic, Polish National Catholic, Armenian churches | 331 | 329 | 426 | 421 | 436 | 431 |
| Buddhist | 51 | 55 | 60 | 60 | 100 | 100 |
| Miscellaneous | n.a. | n.a. | 1,263 | 1,188 | 1,145 | 1,130 |
| Total | 309,449 | 321,768 | 330,460 | 332,970 | 338,244 | 350,481 |

*Source:* Yearbook of American and Canadian Churches. Data for 1970 not available.

within the sector, they also raise a number of challenges. Dedication to important spiritual and secular missions makes it hard for some groups—particularly smaller, community-based, nonprofit organizations—to function as lean, high-performing organizations. This is especially important because many value- and faith-based nonprofits have missions in the area of human services for the poor. Faith-based organizations are becoming ever more active in the welfare-to-work arena, especially after the passage of federal legislation encouraging faith-based organizations to provide services under government contract. Although many contracts seek to maximize measured results, faith-based organizations march to a somewhat different beat. The espoused beliefs of many religiously affiliated nonprofit service providers are clearly in tension with standards based on pure efficiency and simple measurable outcomes. As a consequence, many faith-driven nonprofit service providers regularly seek out the clients who are the most needy and the most difficult to assist. Often these service providers couch their missions in terms of moral entitlements—an approach that is at odds with giving attention only to the most able clients. Faith-based nonprofits serving only clients who are likely to succeed would entail a tremendous act of betrayal. Hence, these mission-expressive organizations have carved out for themselves a special place in diverse fields of service.

In the social services, faith-based nonprofits and volunteer groups take a more holistic approach to working with the most needy, emphasizing a set of values that providers believe will lead to a better life but that are not necessarily closely linked to increased income or short-term independence. For example, some communities link job preparation to personal development, and personal development to Bible study. These programs attempt to foster the spiritual growth of clients, many of whom need not just technical skills but also support and caring. Faith-based service providers have argued that job-related needs must at times take a back seat to spiritual needs and to the broader goal of building a network of emotional supports. This focus on the whole person distinguishes faith-based programs from secular efforts, which often set up boundaries between professional training and personal development. The personal attention that some church-based programs are now providing is also different from what large agencies—both secular and religiously affiliated—typically offer, in that the small size of these local efforts fosters connections between providers and clients.

Although their small size and aversion to cherry-picking may appear to weaken their competitive position, the ability of faith-based providers to vie for contracts has been substantially reshaped by recent legislation. The "charitable-choice" provision of the welfare reform bill has opened the door to greater funding of faith-based services by government. Inserted by Missouri Senator John Ashcroft, the provision empowers states to use faith-based social service agencies on the same basis as secular agencies in all antipoverty initiatives. Moreover, the provision clearly states that religious providers need not secularize their programs in order to qualify for and obtain contracts. The "charitable-choice" provision has three critical provisions: (1) States may provide welfare services via contracts with religious groups, and/or give beneficiaries vouchers redeemable with such groups; (2) religious groups may participate "on the same basis as any other nongovernmental provider without impairing the religious character of such organizations, and without diminishing the religious freedom of beneficiaries of assistance"; and (3) states may not discriminate against a religious provider "on the basis that the organization has a religious character."[41]

From the perspective of faith-based organizations, the charitable-choice provision has strengthened their ability to provide human services in two ways. First, it offers some written reassurance to religious organizations that they can accept government funds without losing their ability to provide overtly religious support to their members. Many religious organizations have expressed reluctance to accept government funding, or have in the past actively diluted the religious component of their services to secure funds. While charitable choice does not necessarily override state and local laws, and while constitutional concerns will likely still place some limits on the activities churches perform under contract, there is already some evidence that religious organizations are slowly becoming more willing to consider accepting government funds. One major study recently revealed that fewer than 5 percent of religious organizations surveyed now receive government funds for their social services, though about 40 percent say they would be interested in applying for government funds in the near future.[42]

A second important implication of charitable choice for faith-based nonprofits is that it offers states the option of funding nonprofits indirectly by providing vouchers to clients that can be used for the services of their choice. Vouchers will likely increase the opportunities to provide faith-based services, because courts are less likely to interpret the Constitution as limiting a program's religious aspects if those programs are funded indirectly through vouchers. In addition, vouchers reduce the scale of services. Because government frequently offers outsourcing contracts that involve large caseloads (which may run into the thousands), small, church-based programs are not likely to be able to expand to anywhere near the size necessary to compete for these contracts. However, through vouchers, the same program could potentially gain enough additional financial support to increase its program size by a manageable number that the program itself could control.

As faith-based nonprofits compete for clients, staff, and government contracts, faith and values may actually turn out to be a powerful tool of differentiation. While faith-based organizations cannot claim to have the discipline of business's bottom line or the public sector's neutrality, these organizations can make the case that the services they offer may well be better positioned to help clients who face multiple barriers to success. Business will not be attracted to clients needing special attention and services, and government's focus on equity and access limits its ability to customize programs. Yet nonprofits—particularly those with strong value or faith dimensions—can argue that they have philosophies and services designed to take care of the broad range of human problems that keep clients from achieving success. As the competition between all these sectors picks up pace, the value and faith dimension may well end up being a potent tool for defining nonprofit identity and advantage.[43]

Competition for clients is not the only challenge confronting expressive nonprofits. Beyond the independence issue raised by government contracting, faith and values have pitted nonprofits against the state on issues of mission and vision. Three recent conflicts are emblematic of the diverse tensions that can occur between sectors when nonprofits affirm their expressive dimension. In 1997, the city of San Francisco had a highly charged confrontation with Catholic Charities, the area's largest nonprofit provider of children's services. The city's new domestic-partnership law required all contractors to provide benefits to domestic partners. Not surprisingly, Catholic Charities, which annually receives more than $5 million in local social service contracts, strenuously objected. An important exchange ensued, pitting the city's "public policy" against the charity's "private values." At one point, Archbishop William Levada threatened to sue the city, arguing that recognizing domestic partnerships would violate the church's ethical and religious beliefs: "I am against government forcing church agencies to comply with laws that run counter to their religious principles," Levada said.[44] The conflict highlighted the extent and significance of the church-state relationship and the fact that some nonprofit organizations delivering social services hold private beliefs which may conflict with public policies. Contracting with the state may also limit religious freedoms, the archbishop noted. "I believe the ordinance imposes an unconstitutional condition on the recognized right of a religiously affiliated organization such as Catholic Charities to contract with the government for the secular services it offers to clients, while managing its internal operations in a manner consistent with its religious principles."[45]

Complicating matters further was the fact that Catholic Charities was about to open Leland House, a forty-five-unit residential community which had been established for people with disabling HIV infection and which was funded by $4.5 million in local, state, and federal funds. Critics of the archbishop soon attacked him for not immediately complying with the city's ordinance, since Catholic Charities had the status of a nonprofit charity, not a religious charity. The archbishop responded that "religious agencies are entitled to contract with the government to serve the poor. This is our city, too. Catholics are not outside the city. We are part of the city."[46] The conflict was ultimately resolved after Mayor Willie Brown, the archbishop, and four members of the Board of Supervisors agreed to a solution of sorts. Without using the words "domestic partners," the group settled on the following language: "An employee may designate a legally domiciled member of the employee's household as being eligible for spousal equivalent benefits."[47] This meant that the church would extend benefits, but do so in a way that could include an employee's brother, sister, mother, father, or gay lover. The church was thus led to adopt an awkward compromise policy in order to retain its city contracts, which accounted for 40 percent of its local budget.

In New York, a conflict of a somewhat different sort recently erupted between the city's government and a coalition of sixty-eight churches and social service agencies. This time the issue was the implementation of the city's new welfare-to-work policies. The clergy members and non-profit leaders announced that they would not take part in the implementation of the new program, because the program was akin to slavery. They objected to the city's work requirement in exchange for welfare benefits because it would force many recipients to abandon school, would lower the wages of city workers, would provide no possibility of advancement, and would require work in difficult conditions. Unlike the San Francisco case, which turned on the narrow provisions of an ordinance, the New York case illustrates a broader conflict between public and nonprofit agencies. For New York's Mayor Rudolph Giuliani, the new welfare rules were a huge success: they reduced the rolls by more than 285,000 and placed thousands of individuals in community service positions with nonprofit and city agencies. Yet for the coalition the program was a dismal failure, since it did not meet the criteria of justice and fairness. The resulting "implementation boycott"[48] simply highlighted the growing disjunction between public and nonprofit values.

An important fight over the expressive dimension of nonprofit activity has been waged by the Boy Scouts of America (BSA) over the ability of the organization to exclude avowedly gay scout leaders from its ranks. In California, the BSA successfully won a ruling that the organization was a private membership group and that it was not covered by the state antidiscrimination laws. The court held that "the Boy Scouts are not a business establishment and so are free, like any private club, to set membership policies as they see fit. . . . The Boy Scouts is an expressive social organization whose primary function is the inculcation of values in its youth members." In New Jersey, however, the BSA lost a similar lawsuit which had been brought by a gay troop leader. The leader had been dismissed on the grounds that homosexuality was contrary to the organization's values and beliefs, and that it violated the oath which all scouts must take to be "morally straight." After a nine-year legal battle, the New Jersey Supreme Court ruled unanimously that the Boy Scouts did not have the right to exclude the troop leader from the organization, because the large nonprofit was closer to a public accommodation like a restaurant than to a small club where members all share common beliefs. The Court held:

> The Boy Scouts organization constitutes a place of public accommodation because it has a broad membership and forms partnerships with public entities and public service organizations. . . . To recognize the Boy Scouts' First Amendment claim would be tantamount to tolerating the expulsion of an individual solely because of his status as a homosexual, an act of discrimination unprotected by First Amendment freedom of speech. . . . Moreover it is clear that the Boy Scouts does not limit its membership to a particular religion or subscribe to a specific set of moral beliefs.

Because the BSA did not impose a screen on who could enter the organization, the dismissal of the gay troop leader was deemed to be discriminatory. In so ruling, the court rejected the Boy Scouts' First Amendment claim that their organization had a right to "expressive association."

These state court cases are particularly important, not just because they highlight how the expressive dimension of nonprofit activity can and does cause conflict with public policy, but because they represent an important struggle on the part of nonprofit organizations to define a set of beliefs and then to exclude members on the basis of these beliefs. While the Boy Scouts were certainly a private organization not dependent on government funds, the courts in New Jersey and California came to radically different conclusions about whether the freedom to associate includes the ability to exclude some potential members.

The issue eventually reached the Supreme Court, where the scope of the First Amendment protection of the right to assemble—and associate—was reexamined. The court found in favor of the BSA and determined that there was indeed a right to "expressive association" that allowed the Boy Scouts to decide who could act as leaders in its organization. In rejecting the claim that the Scouts were akin to a public accommodation such as a restaurant or hotel, the court found that New Jersey's interests in preventing discrimination did not justify such a severe infringement of the Boy Scouts' right to freedom of expressive association. The court found that the forced inclusion of an unwanted person in a group infringes on this right if the person in question has a significant effect on the group's ability to advocate public or private viewpoints. The court looked at the Boy Scouts' mission ("to serve others by helping to instill values in young people and, in other ways, to prepare them to make ethical choices over their lifetime in achieving their full potential") and at the Scout Oath, according to which each member promises, among other things, "to help others at all times, and to keep myself physically strong, mentally awake, and morally straight." In these words, the court found evidence that the Scouts engaged in expressive activity protected by the First Amendment. The U.S. Supreme Court thus rejected the New Jersey Supreme Court's conclusion that protection should be provided only to organizations that have been established for the purpose of disseminating a certain message. Instead, the court's five-to-four majority saw expressive activity in itself as grounds for protection.

The decision provoked outrage in many parts of the country and resulted in the withdrawal of support by several local chapters of the United Way, the return of Eagle Scout badges by some of the group's members, and talk in Congress about revoking the group's congressional charter. Beyond the legal issue of how to interpret the scope of the right to associate, this case also raised the question of how much discrimination will be allowed in nonprofits, how far the reach of public policy and law will extend into nonprofit organizations, and how central the expressive function of nonprofits is in relation to their more instrumental function. In defining a right to "expressive association," the court left open the difficult issue of when a group's message is central enough to justify allowing the group to exclude persons that hold differing points of view, or when a group message is held broadly enough to constitute a core operating principle. No clear lines were drawn to demarcate when activity becomes expressive and when it remains simply purposive. This issue will surely continue to be argued and litigated as the boundary between the public purposes and private values of nonprofits undergoes further changes.

The question of exclusion and discrimination in nonprofits is not the only one that has brought the sector into conflict with the state. Many other conflicts over the division of labor between the sectors have arisen in recent years, in fields ranging from education (vouchers for religious schools) to the arts (public funding of controversial artists) to health care (public policy allowing for-profit conversions of charity hospitals run by religious orders). Much of the early research on nonprofit organizations never adequately confronted just how easily private values and public purposes can come to be at odds with one another. As conflicts between sectors have arisen around faith and values, the need for resolution of these issues has grown more pressing. Nonprofits are unlikely to shy away from expressing values and faith in their work. In fact, all evidence points in the other direction. As nonprofits face greater pressure to differentiate their services from those of for-profit firms, as well as pressure from the growing number of nonprofits, the role of values and faith in the sector will likely only become more prominent in the years ahead.

## Values, Faith, and Identity

As the nonprofit and voluntary sector's public profile has increased, a major question has emerged about the sector's core rationale. One school of thought about nonprofits has emphasized the sector's instrumental outputs and its partnership with government in the implementation of public programs. As service delivery vehicles, nonprofit organizations are encouraged to focus on operational details as part of the process of becoming an ever more efficient purveyor of programs. This focus on nonprofit capacity was fueled by a concern over the reliability of existing funding sources and a realization that new revenue streams from fees for service and commercial activities might well eventually be necessary to sustain efforts in the future. With an emphasis on instrumental outputs, this perspective led some to believe that nonprofits can learn a lot from business by adopting a management style focusing on efficiency and performance.

A rival vision of the nonprofit sector, however, emerged to counter this emphasis on performance. Rather than seeing nonprofits as instrumentally valuable program implementers, we can view nonprofits as producing important expressive outputs that provide satisfaction to the individuals donating funds, managing programs, and volunteering their time. This alternative perspective holds that only by centering its activity on the expression of important private values and commitments can the nonprofit sector remain vibrant and innovative. The normative rationale for a nonprofit sector—far from residing in the ability of some nonprofit organizations to deliver services efficiently—actually lies in the powerful expressive character of work within the sector. By underscoring the fact that nonprofits embody and allow for the expression of important values and commitments, this alternative rationale for the sector has significantly highlighted the gulf between the nonprofit sector and the more instrumental dimension of profit-seeking work.

These two fundamental but at times conflicting arguments have important consequences for the positioning of nonprofits in a changing environment. The tradeoff between expressive values and instrumental performance in the nonprofit sector is as fundamental as what Arthur Okun termed the "big tradeoff" in politics between equality and efficiency.[49] Of course, depicting the intersection of values and performance in the nonprofit sector as a zero-sum game would do real violence to the complexity of the issues at hand. On the one hand, few nonprofits are either entirely instrumental or wholly divorced from efficiency concerns. On the other hand, few nonprofits are either entirely value-driven or completely devoid of commitment. Instead, each is situated on a continuum, with many organizations falling in the middle. A central—*the* central—challenge for nonprofit managers is to become good at fostering both expressive and instrumental activity.

To respond to this challenge, strategy in the sector must take on a new, more complex identity, one that simultaneously emphasizes the value-laden nature of nonprofit work and the need for effectiveness in pursuit of mission. Unlike business firms, which must produce profits and answer to the expectations of shareholders, and unlike government, which must operate within the bounds of the Constitution and respond to the desires of voters, nonprofit organizations occupy a strange and ambiguous position. They appear to face neither the test of profitability nor the test of constitutionality, but rather a far more complex test of relevance that is linked to their mission. To be sure, a nonprofit's survival depends on fulfilling a mission which is valued by the community it serves, the staff that deliver the services, the board that provides oversight, and the funders that support the organization. In this sense, a central strategic task for nonprofit managers is to create value within a set of operational and environmental constraints that are at once more complex than those faced by corporations and more opaque than those confronted by government. Nonprofits that are able to put such a strategy together will be well equipped to address the new challenges from business and the pressures from the policy environment that are fast becoming an integral part of the nonprofit experience.

Within this broader context, one of the most difficult questions to ask is whether faith and value-based approaches to ever-present human problems have a distinct advantage over more secular approaches. Looking back to the way social needs were met in the past, Marvin Olasky argued that the growth of the welfare state eviscerated personal responsibility and vested too much power in policymakers.[50] Moreover, it led to a belief that poverty could be ended if only enough funds were transferred to the poor. Because the problems of the inner city have never been purely financial, or solvable by ever greater outlays of funds, Olasky suggested that the question of whether charity could mobilize large enough amounts of money was the wrong question. Charities have always had the ability to uplift the poor morally and to convey the kind of values that are needed for self-sufficiency—something that government has never mastered. As government has attempted to play a bigger role in providing a safety net for the poor, it has designed and implemented programs that have failed because they did not require personal responsibility or emphasize character and work habits. For this reason, Olasky suggested that the scope of nonprofit provision should be enlarged and that of government curtailed. For such a reorientation to be feasible and have a chance of succeeding, Olasky argued, Americans will have to do more than pay taxes. They will need to connect to the poor and disadvantaged, and offer help on a personal level.

Conservatives like Olasky agree on the importance of values and faith in solving important social problems, while also noting government's demonstrated limitations. Yet important issues remain unresolved. The first is how the spiritual and value-driven dimension of charitable activity can ever be relied on to solve major social problems on a large scale. A faith and value dimension to social programs does not fit very well with the public sector's commitment to universalism and the line dividing church and state. More critically, the faith and values perspective starts with the assumption that human advancement begins with character and personal change.

Liberals have traditionally been more comfortable conceiving of social programs as structural in nature and requiring systemic change. From this perspective, nonprofits are significant tools for removing structural impediments, not instruments for the transformation of individuals. The idea that nonprofits serve as vehicles for the expression of the values and beliefs of donors, staff, and volunteers is not intuitively obvious to some. After all, it is tempting to look at the tax exemption granted nonprofits as a requirement that this privilege be justified through good works in the public interest. The logic of such a perspective is simple. Since the benefits that this privileged tax status confers can be significant, especially when the organization is engaged in revenue-producing activity, nonprofits "owe" the public or the community something. And when public funds are involved, nonprofits need to carry out their work in ways that are aligned with the public sector's commitment to full access and equal treatment. For some liberals and many civil libertarians, the value and faith dimension of nonprofits appears to have the potential to be exclusionary, or at least particularistic, from the point of view of the clients who are seeking services. For this reason, the move to embrace the expressive dimension of nonprofits has not been universally supported by all parts of the political spectrum. Political perspective clearly shapes not just how the nonprofit sector's role is defined, but also the way the balance between public needs and private values should be struck.

In practice, however, there are huge parts of the nonprofit universe, cutting across both member-serving and public-serving organizations, that define mission around the private values, needs, and interests of individuals and that are not oriented toward a broad and agnostic public purpose. In many of these organizations, instrumental logic does not hold much sway, as people gravitate toward one another out of shared beliefs and principles. The expressive dimension of nonprofit activity thus does not look exclusively at the improvement of the broader community as the rationale for tax-exempt status, but instead at what participation in nonprofit activity can do for those who are giving their time and money to a cause or purpose. The connection between the mission and the satisfaction of the donors, volunteers, or staff can turn out to have powerful benefits to the community in the form of programmatic innovation, greater quality of care, and higher levels of services, as the recent developments in faith-based social services indicate. For those working on the front lines, however, these consequences are rarely the animating force behind the move to enact values through work.

In the fast-changing policy world within which they operate, non-profits have the greatest chance of maximizing their impact by acting as independent innovators that harness private values and direct them toward significant collective ends. Nonprofits need to seize upon their special status to lead society toward new solutions to social problems. A first step is rejecting the vision of nonprofits as passive vessels through which only neutral public purposes can be pursued. The question of nonprofit expressiveness is not one that requires more advocacy on behalf of the sector's financial needs or the needs of clients not served by government or the market. Rather, it requires broader and more serious thought about the underlying rationale for having a nonprofit sector.

The ultimate argument for protecting the independence of nonprofits as a channel for the expression of many private values and visions is clear enough. It holds that nonprofit organizations are important because they provide a unique way for individuals to pursue innovative, iconoclastic, and value-driven solutions to social problems. Much of the first wave of research concerning nonprofit organizations was based on a fairly narrow and limited conceptualization of nonprofit activity, one that lacked an appreciation of the tensions inherent in the value-expressing nature of many nonprofits. Since economic analyses of nonprofit activity were dominant initially, researchers paid little attention to the fundamental "values" differences between the sectors. Instead of longing for a simple and unconflicted identity for the nonprofit sector, we may need to recognize the fundamental value conflicts that are now beginning to characterize this complex realm and accept the fact that the expressive dimension of nonprofits can simultaneously place them at odds with government and enable them to make a unique contribution to society.

# 5

## Social Entrepreneurship

In Chapters 2 and 3, we looked at the nonprofit and voluntary sector as a response to society's need for certain goods and services and as a way of effecting political change. In both cases, we focused on the pull of demand on nonprofit and voluntary organizations and found expressive and instrumental response to demand. We have seen, however, that it is also possible to take a supply-side approach to explaining the rise of the sector. In Chapter 4, we examined nonprofits from a supply-side perspective that emphasized the expressive dimension of values. By combining the supply-side approach with a focus on the instrumental role of nonprofits, we can define a fourth function of the sector: its role as a channel and vehicle for a new kind of social entrepreneurship. This approach to explaining the rationale and rise of nonprofits starts with the motives and characteristics of the people who lead these organizations and the tools they use to pursue their diverse and at times controversial visions. Like the values-and-faith perspective, it starts with the motivation of committed individuals. Unlike the values perspective, which focuses on expression, the entrepreneurship approach looks at how the impulse and vision of individuals lead to the creation of new, growth-oriented organizations that some now term "social-purpose enterprises."

One of the great attractions of the nonprofit and voluntary sector is that it has become a place where new projects can be designed and implemented by people who are willing to take a chance. Almost anyone with an idea or vision can found a nonprofit or voluntary organization quickly. Often organizations are started informally by people seeking a solution to a simple problem through the coordination of action within a community. Other times, formal organizations are created because someone wishes to pursue an idea systematically and within an institutional setting. In both cases, nonprofit and voluntary action is a powerful and increasingly popular vehicle for entrepreneurship—one that can either exist independently from business or work in cooperation with business.[1]

One of the principal reasons the nonprofit and voluntary sector is becoming an attractive vehicle for entrepreneurship is that the barrier to entry is low. Completing the paperwork necessary to receive a 501(c)3 designation is relatively simple and can be done quickly. Financing, managing, and sustaining a nonprofit organization is another matter altogether and requires a great deal of skill. But for people attracted to the idea of developing a vision of the public good and then implementing it in reality, the nonprofit form beckons invitingly. The rise of social entrepreneurs has had a profound impact on the funding of many nonprofits. Instead of relying on private grants or government assistance, many new organizations are conceived from the start as self-supporting operations that generate fees and commercial revenues to support their charitable missions. In this sense, the rise of nonprofit entrepreneurship has been followed closely by a rising tide of fee-for-service and commercial enterprises of all sorts. Some observers worry that the introduction of commerce has become a threat to the charitable orientation of the sector.[2] Yet there is no clear evidence that the new form of financing fueling the sector's growth has significantly undermined the ability of nonprofit organizations to fulfill their missions.

## Elements of a Theory

In the business world, entrepreneurship is an old and trusted practice which has spawned a voluminous literature. Today, business schools display a growing commitment to the teaching of entrepreneurship in response to students' interest in creating start-up companies. Entrepreneurship is an appealing idea because it speaks to the desire of many individuals to take control of their lives and financial futures. Still, definitions vary as to what exactly an entrepreneur is. The entrepreneur has variously been defined as a person who pursues opportunity with or without regard for resources currently controlled;[3] or who brings resources, labor, materials, and other assets into combinations such that their value is greater than before;[4] or who innovates by developing and applying new technology.[5]

The importance of innovation to entrepreneurship was the critical insight of Joseph Schumpeter, who defined an entrepreneur as someone who "revolutionizes the pattern of production by exploiting an invention or, more generally, an untried technological possibility for producing a new commodity or producing an old one in a new way."[6] By linking the idea of entrepreneurship to that of innovation, Schumpeter emphasized the creative aspect of enterprise formation. He also recognized that innovation could take many forms, including product innovation, marketing innovation, process innovation, and organizational innovation. The driving force behind innovation is the entrepreneur and his impulses. "First of all, there is the dream and the will to found a private kingdom, usually, though not necessarily, a dynasty. . . . Then there is the will to conquer, the impulse to fight, to prove oneself superior to others to succeed for the sake not of the fruits of success, but of success itself. . . . Finally, there is the joy of creating, of getting things done, or simply exercising one's energy and ingenuity."[7] By focusing on the social motivations of economic activity, Schumpeter attempted to move beyond the economist's usual affinity for explanations based on rational choice and efficiency maximization.

While traditional thinking about entrepreneurship has focused on start-up activity and new-venture creation, not all entrepreneurial work fits this mold. Many workers are attracted to the idea of building or improving an existing entity—a process that some call "intrapreneurship."[8] It is the powerful impulse to save, to resuscitate, and to grow existing entities. One measure of worker loyalty and commitment within the nonprofit and voluntary sector is the very low rate of organizational closure. While more than one million nonprofit corporations have been formed over the past half-century, the number of closed nonprofits is relatively small. Many organizations often limp along for years waiting for an intrapreneur to breathe life into them and revive them from dormancy. Revitalizing a failing organization can entail as much work as starting from scratch, and in some cases even more. It may involve addressing substantial debt and reputation issues, may demand the redesign of programs, or may require relocation. There is, of course, a point at which intrapreneurship no longer makes sense—when it is better to let the organization simply die a quiet death. Yet if the organization does have real assets or strong name recognition, opportunities to salvage value through intrapreneurship will exist.

As a behavioral phenomenon, entrepreneurship can quickly become a highly creative and personal process. The entrepreneur plays a very important role in shaping the new organization, which often reflects the founder's priorities and visions. How, then, can we understand the process through which entrepreneurs gravitate to different kinds of undertakings and organizations? The answer is that entrepreneurs are attracted to endeavors that fit their personalities, skills, and expertise. Howard Stevenson and his colleagues have argued that there is a spectrum of entrepreneurial types—one that runs from the pure "promoter," who is willing to do anything to achieve the desired result, all the way to the "trustee," who focuses on the effective use of resources currently at hand.[9] Whereas in the past the link between personality and entrepreneurial activity focused on various business fields (manufacturing, retailing, professional services, and so on), we now think of entrepreneurship as occurring across all three societal sectors. Entrepreneurship is viewed as a component not only of the business sector but also of the public sector, where policy entrepreneurs drive ideas from conception through legislation. Social entrepreneurship has been equated with the pursuit of important missions and purposes. It is the force that motivates many young people attracted to the idea of doing good.

Entrepreneurship has emerged as a critical mover and shaper of nonprofit ideas and programs. The impetus for this process has been a generation of nonprofit entrepreneurs who have approached their work with open minds about nonprofit financing and mission definition. Instead of looking at the guidelines of government funders or at the demands of certain constituencies, this new group has started with the questions "What interests me?" and "Where do I best fit?" Because theories of entrepreneurship are essentially behavioral theories, they attempt to develop detailed frameworks and typologies that help us organize the range of possible answers to these kinds of questions. One of the earliest attempts to develop a theory of social entrepreneurship rests on a typology of personalities within the nonprofit world.

Dennis Young has defined a set of models of nonprofit motivation that are a useful starting point.[10] Young's models of entrepreneurs are best thought of as "pure types." In reality, people usually display a combination of the various traits and motivations in Young's pure types. The "artist" is attracted to nonprofits by the promise of finding a place where his own creative energies can be translated into organizational and programmatic reality—where his need to create, nurture, and watch organizations grow can be fulfilled. The "professional" is more discipline-oriented and will seek to implement the latest insights and ideas in the field. The "believer" is an entrepreneur who has a strong commitment to a cause and formulates his plans so as to advance a particular moral, political, or social cause. The "searcher" is out to prove himself, to find a niche, to escape his present employment, and to pursue recognition and a clearer sense of identity. The "independent" enters the sector to find autonomy instead of working under others, to be the boss who calls the shots, and to avoid shared decisionmaking. The "conserver" is a loyalist who is animated by a desire to preserve an organization's character and heritage. Finally, there is the "power seeker," who is drawn to nonprofit work by the urge to wield authority over other people—sometimes because he or she simply enjoys having control over others, and sometimes out of a desire to reap financial rewards.

To build a theory around these pure types, Young goes on to describe a two-part "screening process," the first part of which filters the various types of entrepreneurs into different fields of nonprofit activity. How does this screening or matching process work? Entrepreneurs will gravitate to various parts of the sector depending on four factors: (1) the intrinsic nature of the services delivered, (2) the degree of professional control afforded, (3) the level of industry concentration, and (4) the social priority of the field. To understand how this fourfold screening process might operate, we need only consider two different nonprofit organizations, one a homeless shelter, the other a performing-arts organization. Some individuals will gravitate to shelters because they want to work in a field where services are provided directly to clients, where professional standards for service delivery are far from fixed, where many small organizations populate the field, and where the need for the given services is such that public support for the work is overwhelming. In contrast, other individuals will be attracted to creating an independent theater company because they like the idea of working in a context where the client is a bit removed from the daily work of the organization, where standards of artistic excellence are determined by a small group of opinion makers, where only a few organizations dominate the scene, and where public support is not a major consideration, because work is directed toward pleasing a small, well-defined elite group. Obviously, the motivation behind creating an effective and compassionate shelter is very different from that involved in running a professional theater. Just as obviously, "believers" and "searchers" are more likely to apply their entrepreneurial skills to the delivery of needed social services, whereas "artists" and "independents" are better suited for the cultural world. The goal of behavioral theories of entrepreneurship is to render these broad-brush generalizations more concrete and consistent by elaborating both the motives of the actors and the characteristics of the enterprises in which these actors pursue their work.

Beyond filtering their activities by field, entrepreneurs will also sort out their places through their choice of sector. Entrepreneurial energies may find expression in public agencies, business firms, or nonprofits. According to Young, this second part of the selection process is driven by three factors: (1) the desire to realize income, (2) the level of hierarchy and bureaucracy that is acceptable, and (3) orientation toward service. Thus, for example, "power seekers" striving for financial gain are more likely to gravitate to the business sector while "searchers" are more likely to find their way to nonprofits. Because much variation exists across fields within each sector, and because conditions are constantly changing within fields, we cannot make ironclad predictions. A screening theory based on motives and behavior simply gives us a framework for thinking about how opportunities match up with interests and how skills and motives come into alignment.

If we are to make use of a behavioral theory of social entrepreneurship, involving both a typology of motives and a matching or screening process that connects these motives to specific parts of the organizational landscape, the challenge then becomes one of clearly specifying both these critical elements. While Young's early model moves in the right direction, more work is still needed to define the archetypes of nonprofit motivation and the organizational channels that direct these impulses. In particular, a theory of what draws particular types of people to particular types of entrepreneurial ventures still awaits full elaboration.

One of the more useful attempts to do just this is anchored in the idea of a "social enterprise spectrum," an idea that eschews the traditional sectoral distinctions in favor of a more flexible continuum of organizational types. As defined by J. Gregory Dees, the social enterprise spectrum runs from organizations that are entirely commercial, for-profit, and market-driven to those that are entirely charitable, donative, and voluntary.[11] All social enterprises have certain features in common: they demand that funders sacrifice financial return, they have a workforce that is socially motivated, they offer below-cost pricing to consumers, and they are governed by mission considerations. Entrepreneurs of all kinds will choose activities and organizations that fit somewhere along this spectrum. The idea of a social enterprise spectrum is helpful because it gives us a way of understanding careers that span more than one sector—the sorts of careers that are becoming ever more frequent in today's labor market. Many people may start off in business, in an organization located on the commercial side of the spectrum, only to realize later that they want to work in an organization with a broader, more charitable orientation. Thus, the idea of "nonprofit entrepreneurship" may be impossible to unbundle from the broader notion of social entrepreneurship, which spans sectors and which encompasses a wider variety of organizations.

If we start, however, with Young's theory of nonprofit entrepreneurship and place it in the context of Dees's notion of a spectrum of socially valuable enterprises, a useful perspective on the emergence and growth of the sector emerges. Instead of looking at what pulls donors, staff, and volunteers into nonprofit and voluntary organizations, we begin to get a picture of what pushes these individuals toward doing good. Some may be attracted to socially oriented businesses like Levi Strauss apparel or Ben and Jerry's ice cream. Others will be attracted to commercial nonprofits, such as major nonprofit hospitals. Still others will seek out community groups that are dedicated to a particular social cause. It is clear that social entrepreneurship occurs in all these contexts and many others. Social entrepreneurs will scan the environment and select the causes and organizational forms that best fit their interest and needs. This choice allows the entrepreneur to enact a vision and produce goods or services in a new way.

## Agency and the Entrepreneurial Initiative

The supply-side approach to nonprofits, grounded in the idea of entrepreneurship, has distinct advantages over the demand-side approach.

First, it takes seriously the idea of agency and individualism within non-profit organizations. It explains the rise of nonprofits not by looking at large amorphous phenomena such as government and market failure, but rather by looking into the minds and hearts of individuals. It asks questions about individual values, personalities, and skills, and then strives to explain how these traits come to be mapped onto nonprofits in many different ways. Instead of starting with the question of what public needs exist and then asking how and why nonprofits respond to these needs, the supply-side approach points in the opposite direction. It draws our attention to the behavior of actors, and then explores the confluence of motives and opportunities. Although it represents a useful framework for understanding both the motives and filters that bring entrepreneurs into nonprofits, the supply-side approach leaves open at least one important and nagging question: Who exactly is the entrepreneur? It is tempting to say simply that the entrepreneur is the founder, who raises the funds, defines the mission, and sets up operations. This would be too limiting a definition, however, because entrepreneurial behavior can also characterize program staff, volunteers, trustees, and donors.

In many organizations, the entrepreneur taking the risks and seeking to create value is the executive director, president, or chief executive officer. While titles may vary, almost all formally registered nonprofits have a staff leader who bears the heavy responsibility of sustaining and building the organization. The staff leader is the person internally accountable to the board for fundraising, financial management, and program implementation. In cases where the organization is a start-up, board members will be chosen by this leader. Among the leader's critical tasks will be choosing qualified and motivated directors and hiring staff to carry out the organization's mission. Since funds are often scarce during the early stages of enterprise formation, the staff leader will often need to motivate people to work long hours without overtime pay. Making a strong argument for the importance of the cause or the mission can be the most important tool in this process. For this reason, the staff leader needs to be fully committed to the entrepreneurial goal. One young entrepreneur in Boston engaged in precisely this kind of work when she launched a nonprofit charter school, called City on a Hill, which rapidly expanded and which added teacher training programs as its reputation spread.[12] Starting with very modest initial support, the entrepreneur built the school by securing individual, foundation, and corporate support in addition to the core per-pupil funding provided by the city.[13] A pair of social entrepreneurs founded Jumpstart, an organization designed to give disadvantaged children top-quality preschooling. Jumpstart recruits and places recent college graduates in Head Start and other early-childhood programs. After a modest beginning in 1994, the founders established operations in nineteen communities in less than a decade.

Not all entrepreneurs are staff members. In many cases, volunteers play important entrepreneurial roles, organizing neighborhoods, developing plans of action, and carrying out programs. This is particularly the case with community and grassroots movements, which often start as informal volunteer efforts. The catalyst driving volunteers to take action is often a community problem or social issue that is particularly important or pressing. Instead of waiting for the political process to settle on a policy plan, citizens will often simply band together to address the problem. This kind of behavior is common in a variety of fields, including neighborhood crime control, daycare provision, and environmental restoration. These citizen-led efforts to bring change may look casual and amateurish to some, but often they are very effective because all their energy is focused on the task at hand, not on the administrative burdens that come with operating in a more conventional organizational context. Grassroots entrepreneurs have had considerable success in recent years at operating in areas where more formal nonprofit organizations have been reluctant to go. In Washington, D.C., for example, a group of community volunteers banded together to create a neighborhood crime patrol group called the Orange Hats of Fairlawn.[14] The group was born after several long-time community residents became disgusted with the illegal drug trafficking in their quiet city neighborhood. Drawing exclusively on the time and efforts of local volunteers, the Orange Hats developed methods to take back the streets of the community, while gradually building a strong organization to accomplish this goal. They organized late-night crime patrols, equipped themselves with radio-communication devices and videotape recorders, and coordinated their work with the local police. The leaders of the group built this community organization through personal leadership and example. Countless other informal community efforts have started with little more than commitment, outrage, and faith, and have still accomplished important things.

In some cases, the real entrepreneur may be a trustee who helps found an organization or oversees the daily operations of an existing organization. Often trustees of large organizations provide critical funds for new and existing organizations and play an active role in the management of the organization.[15] The Chicago Symphony Orchestra recently raised hundreds of millions of dollars to fund its expansion into new administrative and performance space. Board members contributed large gifts to this capital campaign and drove the process to a successful conclusion. Because the board was made up of some of the city's most affluent and influential residents, it was able to contribute money as well as to mobilize others in support of the campaign's ambitious goal. Many universities and arts organizations survive and flourish because of fundraising work on the part of their trustees and donations from their alumni and patrons.[16] The idea of trustee entrepreneurs runs counter to the typical vision of board members as quiet, behind-the-scenes overseers, carefully weighing long-term plans and strategies.[17] In many cases, however, trustees will seize the initiative and push organizations to achieve new goals by taking risks. In the case of the Joffrey Ballet, an internationally known dance company located in New York City, trustee intrapreneurship led the company to move to Chicago, where it was able to relieve its debt burden and make a fresh start financially, yet retain its well-known name and strong artistic reputation.[18]

In still other cases, the critical social entrepreneur driving the development of a nonprofit is an independent philanthropist or donor. At times, donors have played critical roles in the creation of new organizations and have stayed involved long after an initial gift helped an organization get off the ground. Major donors do not always serve on nonprofit boards; sometimes, the relationship is purely financial. The decision of Walter Annenberg to devote $500 million to the improvement of major metropolitan public schools was an entrepreneurial effort of the first order, which required the construction of a national network of reform-minded partnerships through which grant money could be disbursed. Other major donors, such as George Soros, have taken a very active role in the creation of institutions that disburse funds and carry out programs aimed at promoting democracy throughout eastern Europe. High levels of donor involvement can create two kinds of conflicts and tensions as an organization matures. First, active and visible donors can make it hard to raise funds from others. If an organization is seen as too closely aligned with the founding donor, new contributors may balk at supplying funds, believing that funds should come from the donor who has shown such a strong commitment to the cause at hand. Second, active and entrepreneurial donors can raise questions about professionalism. Since nonprofits often seek solutions to complex problems and draw heavily on staff expertise, the idea that a wealthy person should play a prominent role in decisionmaking may be resisted.

Many donors are now openly playing the role of venture capitalists—a role that is related to that of the entrepreneur. These donors have sought to move philanthropy away from grants and good will toward social investments and due diligence. Venture philanthropy—as practiced, for example, by the Robin Hood Foundation in New York and Social Venture Partners in Seattle—prefers to talk of "social investments" rather than "grants," the latter implying that little is expected in return for support. By taking a more businesslike approach to social problems, venture philanthropy aims at developing the tools of performance measurement in the nonprofit sector, in order to produce quantifiable social benefits. Another key component of the venture philanthropy model is a lengthening of the relationship between the two parties. Often, funders and their recipients work together over long periods of time and attempt to build a strong relationship which can endure the setbacks and disappointments that new organizations often encounter. The success of such relationships depends largely on two factors: (1) donors must have skills (managerial, legal, accounting) that are useful to the recipient; (2) the financial support must be large enough to justify the demands that this special kind of relationship imposes on nonprofits. Without both expertise and resources, the venture capital model for philanthropy can end up simply burdening and weakening start-up nonprofit organizations. There is a least one other major problem with this model. For all the talk of tracking "social return on investment," there still are few clear measures of return on investment that transform grantmaking into a rigorous process.

The problem of performance measurement comes up more broadly as soon as one conceives of the nonprofit sector in entrepreneurial terms. Despite all the reforms that have swept through the sector aimed at improving performance, nonprofits still operate without a bottom line and without the discipline that the drive for profitability imposes. Still, behavior that looks entrepreneurial is becoming more prevalent among funders, trustees, volunteers, and donors. This has led to a series of problems for the sector, including rapid proliferation of nonprofits and increasing reliance on commercial revenues.

## Critical Perspectives

The entrepreneurship perspective on the creation of nonprofit organizations is primarily a descriptive and analytic one. It grows out of a behavioral theory of enterprise formation that has its roots in economic and management theory. Yet complex normative questions lurk just below the surface. As soon as we describe the emergence of nonprofit and voluntary activity as the matching of behavioral traits of social entrepreneurs, donors, and volunteers with causes, some will raise ethical and political objections to this process. We will see this especially when the part of the sector under consideration is the public-serving and charitable segment that enjoys a special tax-privileged status by virtue of its pledge to fulfill public purposes.

Any supply-side theory of nonprofits must be prepared to address the question of whether the growth of entrepreneurship will lead either to an over-supply of services that benefit those with resources, or to an under-supply of certain other kinds of services that could benefit the most needy. Fueling this concern is a suspicion that the entrepreneurial impulse cannot be trusted to be equitable and fair to all the potential constituencies of nonprofits. If supply is the result of a screening or matching process between, on the one hand, individual interests and personality traits, and, on the other hand, societal sectors and fields of activity, one might reasonably ask whether a responsive nonprofit and voluntary sector will emerge. There is no apparent reason to believe that the mix of programs and activities that ultimately results from the cumulative push of supply will match the most pressing needs of society. In fact, there is even reason to suspect that the mix of activities that ultimately flows from entrepreneurship may differ significantly from the areas of greatest demand, since often many of the most critical community needs involve unglamorous issues and situations. If the social entrepreneur is in the driver's seat throughout the process of enterprise creation and development, some will wonder how many unpopular causes will ever be taken up. In short, the concern is that entrepreneurs will select the most appealing, satisfying, and manageable projects, leaving the most difficult and dangerous work undone.

The simplest response to the equity challenge is to point to the importance of innovation and leadership in nonprofits. In essence, this means countering concerns about distributive justice by arguing that these concerns rest on an inadequate conceptualization of the sector—one that assumes the wrong theory of value creation. Supply-siders hold that the real rationale for nonprofit entities has little to do with the efficiency with which they meet public needs, and has much to do with the way nonprofits challenge our dominant ideas about how society as a whole should respond to its enduring problems. Since the scale of need is enormous and the resources required to satisfy all demands are essentially limitless, a primary focus on equity issues would be misguided. Thus, entrepreneurship claims as its primary goal innovation, not equity. If the final selection and execution of projects do not entirely fit social needs, this is a cost that society must arguably be ready to pay in order to get the innovation that is critical to long-term improvement of social conditions. Residual needs not met by the push of private actors may have to be defined as core problems that the public sector must address, though this approach confers on social entrepreneurship a selfish and shallow character that may not be entirely deserved. After all, the matching or screening process may well channel a group of "believers" or "poets" to the most intractable problems, precisely because these projects can lead to the most challenging and satisfying work.

A second objection to any supply-side approach to nonprofit activity focuses not on equity but on efficiency. It asks whether the continued creation of nonprofits will lead to overproduction and inefficiency. Looking at the phenomenal growth pattern of nonprofit and voluntary organizations over the past century, one might well wonder whether this pattern of growth and organizational creation is in fact efficient.[19] After all, the sector—measured solely by the number of legally registered nonprofit organizations—has gone through a century of exponential growth: from roughly 100,000 organizations in 1950 to 400,000 in 1970 to 800,000 in 1980 to more than 1 million in 1990 to close to 1.5 million today.[20] New industries have emerged and blossomed during this period, while more established fields have experienced substantial growth.

In the area of the arts, there was, for a time, considerable concern that more capacity to deliver performing arts was being built than was actually being demanded. John Kreidler has traced this situation to what he believes was the over-funding of community theaters during the 1970s by large foundations.[21] After reaching the conclusion that theater was not widely enough available, particularly outside the major metro-politan centers, the Ford Foundation began an aggressive grantmaking program to fund the creation of many small theaters. Although this en-terprising vision led to a period of fast growth in the theater community, it ultimately proved unsustainable. Kreidler notes that when the Ford Foundation eventually moved on to other areas of interest, a major financial crisis occurred in the field. Theaters have continued to struggle with financing ever since, even after philanthropic support stabilized at a lower level. To keep their organizations alive, many theaters have tried to raise ticket prices and to create new streams of income. Yet an earn-ings gap has remained, since these new funds have not compensated for the decrease in philanthropic support. The experience with over-capac-ity in the performing arts represents, for some, a textbook case of what happens when nonprofits become supply-driven rather than responsive to demand. The result is hardly an efficient system, because small the-aters now compete intensely with one another for a limited pool of ticket buyers and funders.[22]

In other fields such as social services, the proliferation of agencies has led to considerable concern that these organizations may be duplicating each other's efforts and competing unnecessarily for contributions and clients. Nonprofits often seek to attract private funding on the basis of some new approach or model for addressing problems as diverse as un-employment, literacy, drug abuse, and youth violence through the devel-opment of new models for training, counseling, tutoring, and recre-ational activity. While the need for these services may be great, it is not clear that having large numbers of organizations vying for small grants to carry out this work is an efficient way of operating. As nonprofits compete with one another and search for new and innovative ways to deliver services, a growing number of funders have begun to demand that nonprofits collaborate more actively and eliminate program dupli-cation. Solving the inefficiency of a supply-driven sector is not easy. In many instances, efficiency can be purchased only at the cost of plural-ism, diversity, and innovation.

One provocative answer to the inefficiency argument draws on the work of the eighteenth-century French economist Jean-Baptiste Say, whose famous claim was that "supply creates its own demand." In quot-ing Say, contemporary supply-siders argue that the creation of new en-terprises of any kind, far from occurring in a vacuum, actually creates new markets and demand for new services. By bringing together new combinations of productive capacity, entrepreneurs create projects for which there may be only latent demand. Because their projects often represent new approaches to old problems, initial demand may not be the right test for whether something of value has been created. In fact, the supply-side perspective explicitly argues that it is not. When a new micro-lending program opens in a depressed community, there may not be a group of residents demanding the development of such a program. After years of neglect, the demand may be latent and may require entrepreneurship to unearth and capitalize on it. Of course, the idea of creating demand is not new and has been a centerpiece of the marketing campaigns of many new consumer products. There is a growing sense that marketing is a critical part of any nonprofit initiative and is needed to attract both clients and donors.

The idea that supply creates its own demand is at once liberating and dangerous. On the one hand, it is an open acknowledgment that innovation is a critical part of nonprofit activity. It is also a quiet assertion that clients do not possess all the answers, nor do they necessarily know all the possible questions that are worth answering. This controversial position has the most traction in areas of service where problems are changing quickly or in new areas where programs have not previously been offered. On the other hand, an entirely supply-driven nonprofit and voluntary sector can be a dangerous idea if it commits one to the belief that all innovation should come from the top down. Given the huge disparity in power that often separates giver and receiver, the idea that a nonprofit sector can create its own demand reasonably alarms some and evokes concern about responsiveness and accountability, particularly when organizations are dealing with the most needy and vulnerable members of society.

In thinking about this argument, we should consider a broader implication of the supply-side position—namely, that efficiency may not be a prime rationale for nonprofits. Nonprofit and voluntary organizations will not always match up perfectly with the most pressing needs of communities or represent the single most efficient way to achieve narrow programmatic objectives. But this may be a small price to pay for innovation as individuals bring their interests and ability to bear on issues that are important to them. By focusing on innovation and not efficiency, nonprofit entrepreneurs differentiate themselves from entrepreneurs in the business sector, where achieving cost efficiency is a critical part of the process of building a successful strategy. Because nonprofits are driven by mission and do not seek to generate a profit for shareholders, the drive to be cost-effective is simply not as strong.

One way in which the imperfect match between private resources and public needs has been addressed is through the creation of enterprises aimed at creating new flows of funds. By raising revenues from fees for service and from internally operated commercial enterprises of all sorts, many nonprofit entrepreneurs have advanced their mission while meeting a market test. The turn to earned sources of income has been greeted by some as the great emancipator of nonprofits, a development that frees the organization from the demands of private donors and government funders. Others believe that such income entails a considerable loss in organizational clarity and purpose.

## Commercial Ventures and Fees

If the nonprofit and voluntary sector is a place where entrepreneurs of all kinds begin projects and programs that fit with their interests and commitments, it is also a place where money is often in short supply. Even the most well-meaning social entrepreneur can accomplish only so much when operating on good will and a shoestring. It is not uncommon, therefore, for commerce and commitment to come into contact with each other. Entrepreneurship thus can take a second form: in addition to creating nonprofit and voluntary organizations, social entrepreneurs have relentlessly and aggressively gone about raising earned income to support their organizations. Over the past thirty years, basic changes in the funding patterns of nonprofits have altered the nonprofit landscape. Private contributions have declined as a percentage of nonprofit revenues, from more than 53 percent in 1964 to less than 24 percent by 1993. During this same period, earned income—which includes everything from fees for program services to royalties derived from licensing agreements to revenues from the operation of commercial ventures—has exploded.[23] The substitution of earned income, complemented by rising public sector contracts, for charitable contributions is a clear sign of more than just a change in the balance sheet of nonprofit organizations. It is evidence of a new vision of the function of nonprofits, one that emphasizes the entrepreneurial side of the sector. Few successful nonprofits finance their growth through greater fundraising efforts. Instead, such growth has been fueled in significant measure by ever-greater levels of earned income.

The attraction of earned income is undeniable. Unlike charitable dollars, which often come with narrowly circumscribed purposes, earned income can be used to meet any expense within the nonprofit organization. Some might argue that the commercialization of nonprofits is a direct response not just to the squeeze put on charitable dollars but also to the increasing demands that donors are putting on their gifts. Often, elaborate proposals and reports are needed to secure foundation or corporate support. Once the funds are received, more work follows, since reports and evaluations must be filed regularly. Both fundraising and reporting require substantial amounts of staff time and impose significant accountability.[24] Given these constraints, nonprofit organizations are in greater need of funds that can be used to just sustain and maintain capacity—something that donors tend to ignore in favor of new initiatives and pilot programs. Instead of generating new projects to please funders, many nonprofits simply need money for the unglamorous purpose of meeting the payroll and paying the rent.

Earned income can answer this need and can come in many forms. Program revenues are fees routinely charged by organizations for the services they render to their clients or customers. To ensure that these fees do not discourage needy clients from seeking service, some nonprofits, such as community mental health clinics, adopt sliding scales that allow clients to pay what they can reasonably afford. Even the Metropolitan Museum in New York has a flexible program fee: visitors are asked to pay a certain admission charge, but a sign indicates—in small letters—that this amount is recommended, not required. Many public-serving 501(c)3 organizations seek to remain flexible on their fees because they see a potential threat to their charitable mission if fees discourage entire segments of their client base from taking full advantage of their services. Private colleges and universities have long been especially dependent on tuition revenues to cover annual expenses (see Figure 5.1). Even institutions with substantial endowments charge tuition, while offering financial assistance to those whose family income is insufficient to meet the rising costs of higher education. Nevertheless, such increases pose difficult questions about the accessibility of college education.

Beyond charging fees, nonprofit organizations have turned to a second source of revenue to finance their growth: they create commercial ventures that are closely related to their mission. In their quest for funds unencumbered by restrictions and reporting requirements, some organizations have taken a commercial turn, directing their entrepreneurial energies toward the creation of revenue-producing operations. These ventures include everything from thrift stores operated by the Salvation Army to university-run foreign tours for alumni. These ventures do not always connect directly with the organization's mission, though they do allow a nonprofit to generate tax-exempt funds that can be used for core program activity.

The entrepreneurial impulse can also be manifest in the sale or licensing of the name of the organization. A common form of this kind of arrangement is termed "cause-related marketing."[25] These arrangements generate a small corporate contribution for every sale of a given business

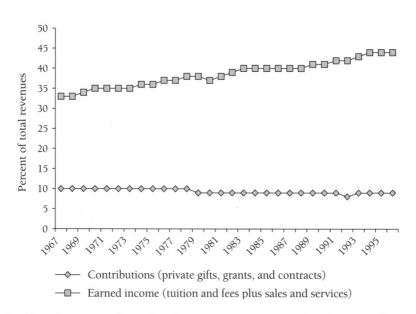

— ◆ — Contributions (private gifts, grants, and contracts)
— ▣ — Earned income (tuition and fees plus sales and services)

5.1 Earned income and contributed income as a percentage of total revenues for private colleges and universities. *Source:* U.S. Department of Education, National Center for Education Statistics, "Integrated Postsecondary Education Data System" and "Higher Education General Information Survey," Finance survey, 1966–1996.

product or service. Thus, for example, consumers are told that for every pair of stockings they purchase a contribution will be made to help fight breast cancer, or that for every dollar they charge to a credit card a small percentage will be donated to the restoration of a national monument. These deals are often attractive to nonprofits because they do not usually demand much in the way of time or resources. All they usually require is the signing of an agreement. For this reason, nonprofits often view cause-related marketing as found money, since the revenue generated is money that the organization would likely not raise on it own. While these deals appear to have little immediate downside no matter how small the contribution is in relation to the sales generated by the charity's name, there are growing concerns about the long-term impact of these arrangements. After all, among the most precious commodities controlled by a nonprofit are its name and reputation, which together create the good will and trust needed to generate clients and contributors. Cause-related marketing deals that depend on corporate sales to generate contributions to charities and simple endorsement arrangements that lend a charity's name to a product could explode into bad publicity for the nonprofit if the corporation is shown to have a poor labor or environmental record or if the deal itself is exposed as exploitive and deceptive.

One of the most controversial examples of such an arrangement was the ill-fated collaboration between Sunbeam, a manufacturer of small appliances, and the American Medical Association (AMA), the membership organization that represents the medical profession. Under the agreement that was struck between these two parties, the manufacturer was given permission to place the AMA logo and endorsement on the packaging of its medical products, such as blood pressure gauges. This particular deal ultimately failed when members of AMA objected to the commercial nature of the transaction and eventually ousted their president for arranging it.[26] Other major health charities have endorsed products more successfully. The American Heart Association (AHA) changed its charter in 1988 so that it could enter into product endorsements. It created a "HeartGuide Seal" program that companies could display on their packaging if their products were low in fat, sodium, and cholesterol and if the companies were willing to pay an annual fee as high as $500,000. Although the Food and Drug Administration was concerned that the AHA's inability to make sound scientific judgments about products might ultimately mislead consumers, the AHA forged ahead with its endorsement program and struck deals with numerous cereal makers. The American Cancer Society also entered the endorsement business and struck deals with food producers, including a very lucrative arrangement with Florida's Department of Citrus to promote the consumption of oranges.[27] One reason that licensing and marketing agreements continue to raise eyebrows is that they appear to move nonprofits uncomfortably close to the market. These arrangements are designed both to raise funds for the nonprofits and to sell more products for the businesses. Because the amount of money that actually reaches smaller and needier nonprofits can be quite small, some observers worry that the power asymmetry in the relationship makes true partnerships difficult to achieve. Nonprofit organizations can rarely negotiate with a corporation because at the slightest sign of resistance the firm can move on to another cause and organization.

Finally, a growing number of nonprofit organizations have taken the most aggressive step of all—namely, the establishment of ventures or enterprises that bear no real connection to their core charitable missions, but that generate a stream of income which can be used for social purposes. The regulation of these "unrelated businesses" has increased in recent years as competitors in the business world have raised complaints about unfair competition. When revenues are derived from an enterprise that is "not substantially related to the mission" of the nonprofit, the IRS applies a tax. This "unrelated business income tax" (UBIT) is intended to limit the expansion of nonprofit enterprise into areas that businesses occupy, or at least to level the playing field. The range of unrelated businesses operated by nonprofits is enormous, and can include everything from a bakery operated by a youth center to a real estate development firm operated by a university.

As unrelated commercial activity by nonprofits has increased in recent years (see Figure 5.2), enforcing the rules that protect fair competition has become difficult. As nonprofits expand their involvement in commercial ventures, their annual reported profits remain small and hence the taxes they pay on their unrelated business income have stayed relatively low (see Figure 5.3). One explanation for this phenomenon lies in the clever accounting techniques employed by nonprofits—techniques that allow them to report minimal gains or even losses related to the generation of the unrelated income. They do this by shifting costs from

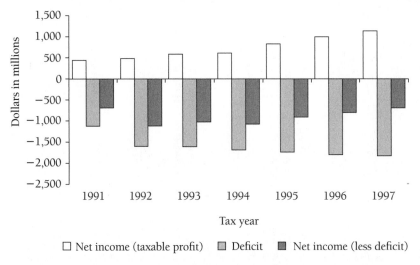

5.2  Unrelated business net income (taxable profit), deficit, and net income (less deficit) in constant dollars, tax years 1991–1997. *Source: Statistics of Income Studies of Exempt-Organization Business Income Tax Returns, 1991–1997* (Washington, D.C.: Internal Revenue Service, 2001).

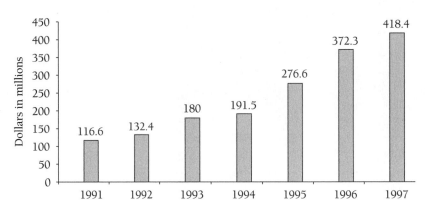

5.3  Unrelated business income tax reported by nonprofit organizations, tax years 1991–1997. *Source: Statistics of Income Studies of Exempt-Organization Business Income Tax Returns, 1991–1997* (Washington, D.C.: Internal Revenue Service, 2001).

**Table 5.1.** Scope of nonprofits' commercial activities on a continuum showing relation to mission.

Very close to mission ← → Very far from mission

| Type of nonprofit | Program revenues | Commercial enterprises closely related to type of organization | Commercial enterprises distantly related to type of organization | Marketing of the organization's name to patrons | Licensing of name and endorsements aimed at the public | Commercial ventures that are totally unrelated to any aspect of the program |
|---|---|---|---|---|---|---|
| Theater | Sells tickets | Offers acting classes | Operates a coffee bar in the lobby | Sells theater posters | Sells broadcast rights to its productions | Runs a resale shop |
| Community health clinic | Charges fees for medical services (sliding scale) | Sells medical supplies and prescriptions | Runs a cafeteria that is open to the public | Sells T-shirts and mugs | Enters into multiparty cause-related marketing agreements with local retail companies | Operates a local van service for community residents |
| College | Charges tuition | Operates a bookstore | Sponsors educational travel for alumni | Sells tote bags and ties | Endorses prep course for Scholastic Aptitude Test | Engages in commercial real estate development |

*Source:* Adapted from James C. Crimmins and Mary Keil, *Enterprise in the Nonprofit Sector* (Washington, D.C.: Partners for Livable Places, 1983).

program-related activities to commercial ventures. In other words, as nonprofits have created flows of income from ventures that sometimes compete directly with for-profit firms, they have learned to move staff, overhead, and capital expenses from the program side of the balance sheet to the commercial side. As this cost shifting occurs, any profits generated by unrelated business activity are quickly turned into losses.[28] Through this cost shifting, the tax liability of nonprofits is often reduced or eliminated. The IRS has grown suspicious of this practice, wondering why nonprofits continually engage in activities that incur losses.[29] Of course, the answer is that often profits are being made but the rules designed to level the playing field between business and nonprofit enterprises are being skirted.[30]

The many faces of nonprofit commercial activity can be depicted across a continuum; the range extends from activities closely related to mission, all the way to those completely unrelated to mission. As an organization's activities shift from the left side to the right side of the spectrum (see Table 5.1), difficult questions clearly arise about the costs and benefits of entrepreneurial activity within the nonprofit and voluntary sector.

The commercial turn in the nonprofit sector raises important issues about the ability of the sector to execute its many and diverse missions. First, the sector's shift from a base of contributed income to one that is earned through the charging of fees may make it more difficult for nonprofits to pursue missions involving social change aimed at assisting disadvantaged populations. Second, commercialization may lead to profound cultural changes in the workforce of the nonprofit and voluntary sector, as a new generation of leaders enters these increasingly businesslike organizations. Third, the changing nonprofit workforce has made some decidedly businesslike demands concerning the compensation levels in large nonprofit organizations, raising difficult questions about the use of tax-exempt funds. It is useful to take up the issues of mission adherence, organizational culture, and employee compensation separately.

*Mission*

For years, arguments have raged about whether the charging of fees by nonprofits adds or detracts from their ability to fulfill their missions.

The battle lines are fairly clear. On the one hand, some argue that the creation of a more entrepreneurial sector brings new and unrestricted resources to bear on social problems. Since funds generated through fees can be directed to any purpose designated by an organization, these revenues may allow organizations to cross-subsidize activities that funders would not support or that cannot generate their own stream of earned income to support them. At the same time, greater reliance on fees has been seen as exposing nonprofits to a real market test. Services for which clients pay have a demonstrated value that free services cannot really match. Moreover, when nonprofits rely on the fees paid by their clients, they are driven to achieve efficiencies that are impossible when the funds supporting their activities are donated. In this way, the commercial transformation of the sector has been seen as a disciplining process which has tightened the operations of many nonprofits, since it forces them to meet the exigencies of a bottom line.

On the other hand, critics increasingly claim that the rise of fee-for-service arrangements in the nonprofit sector, far from being a bellwether of mission achievement through managerial improvement, actually threatens the sector's commitment to serving those in need. Some worry that as nonprofits become more and more businesslike and entrepreneurial, the core social concerns that define them will be replaced by much narrower efficiency concerns. In the case of nonprofit hospitals, there is a heated debate over whether the quality and quantity of charity care is decreasing in the ever more market-driven and competitive health care market.[31] In higher education, as costs have escalated, similar questions about social mission have arisen. The ability of a student to pay may not be a factor in admissions at some of the most selective colleges and universities, but students still shy away from assuming the large debt burdens that are part of the aid packages offered to them. The issue of access is even more critical to many smaller, community-based organizations operating in disadvantaged neighborhoods. For these organizations, maintaining a flow of funds from the charging of fees can be both a necessity and a severe challenge. Even when the fee scale is designed to accommodate the poor, the absence of free services can be an impediment to reaching the clients that are critical to the organization's ability to accomplish its mission.

In practice, the fee-charging side of nonprofit activity is often inextricably linked to the charitable work of nonprofit organizations. Perhaps the clearest example of this link can be found in the work of the American Red Cross, one of the largest nonprofits in the United States. The Red Cross delivers services in two ways. First, it operates a national network of blood banks and an expanding biomedical division that are driven almost entirely by the fees hospitals pay for these products. Second, it works through a national network of more or less autonomous chapters that deliver emergency relief when storms, floods, or fires strike. In addition to this charitable work, which is paid for largely from donations, the chapters offer first-aid training courses that raise revenues for other local programs. For a large organization such as the American Red Cross, the link between commercial and charitable work lies at the heart of the organization's identity. After all, the blood services cannot operate without the contribution of free blood to its centers. Key to securing the good will that makes this enterprise function is the perception that the Red Cross is an agile and responsive organization that assists those in need. In this way, the charitable disaster-relief work of the chapters is a critical guarantor of the Red Cross's position as a leading nonprofit deserving of support, be it in the form of blood donations, cash contributions, or volunteer labor. The commercialized half of the organization could not exist without the halo effect generated by the delivery of charitable services. There is a close link between the charitable work and the entrepreneurial work in nonprofits of all varieties, and it is difficult to imagine that either an organization or the entire sector could ever function effectively without a balance between charitable and commercial activity. For the Red Cross, managing these two forms of activity so that they support each other has proven to be a major challenge over the past decade.

Not all nonprofits have carried off this delicate managerial task with ease. Commercialism's challenge to the nonprofit mission has been felt particularly acutely in higher education. When universities make deals with business corporations, some people see these agreements as running contrary to the goals of teaching and research. At the University of California at Berkeley, a major dispute erupted in 1998 when the school entered into an agreement with Novartis, a large Swiss pharmaceutical firm and producer of genetically engineered crops. Under the deal, Berkeley's Department of Plant and Microbial Biology would receive $25 million for the support of basic research. In return, Berkeley gave Novartis substantial authority to negotiate licenses for the department's discoveries, including the results of research funded by government grants. The most controversial part of the agreement was the control Berkeley authorities granted Novartis over how its money would be spent: the company was allotted two out of the five seats on the department's research committee. Also irksome to many was the company's right to keep the results and methods of research secret for up to four months, so as to prevent industry competitors from stealing the ideas generated by Novartis' investment at Berkeley. Student groups and some faculty members objected to this arrangement, arguing that it gave a corporate interest unprecedented influence within the university. Moreover, the deal also caused some on campus to ask why a public university, whose mission was to teach and conduct research, was allowing a corporation to determine the way faculty members spent their time.[32]

## Organizational Culture

The commercial turn within some nonprofits has led to a concern that the personnel and culture within many nonprofit organizations have changed. In the social services, the image of the dedicated social worker laboring for decades on the front lines to combat urgent social problems has slowly been replaced with a new model. Many people starting nonprofit organizations are young, ambitious, and trained in business and policy schools. Increased levels of nonprofit entrepreneurship are one of the consequences of the rise of nonprofit management as a field of study and practice. Over the past three decades the number of management training programs for individuals pursuing leadership careers in the nonprofit sector has risen enormously. It is now possible in most cities to locate several degree-granting programs that teach the essentials of nonprofit program and financial management. Alongside these new programs, there is now an extensive literature on the effective management of nonprofits which has fostered improved operations and a more sophisticated understanding of nonprofit entrepreneurship.

The proliferation of fellowship programs such as Ashoka and Echoing Green, which promote the formation of new nonprofit endeavors by young people, has created a pool of talented social entrepreneurs eager to test their ideas and skills around the world. Many of these new social entrepreneurs deliberately choose nonprofits over government, where it might take years of service to reach a position of real authority and responsibility. In the nonprofit and voluntary sector, these same young people are often able to create their own organization and greater levels of responsibility at earlier stages in their careers. As the nonprofit workforce has changed at the same time that commercialism has taken root, some observers question whether nonprofits still manifest a distinct culture. The shift in revenue streams has clearly influenced the composition of the sector's labor force. Not only has the sector been affected by the rise of a cadre of young professionals, but nonprofits have also brought in many people from the business world, sometimes with powerful cultural consequences.

Not surprisingly, the emerging centrality of fees as a source of agency finance has engendered proposals to curb nonprofit commercialism by cracking down on nonprofits that stray too far from charitable work. Some critics have argued, for example, that commercialism has pushed nonprofits so close to commercial business that the tax exemption of many organizations is no longer fully justified.[33] After examining a number of nonprofits that served affluent communities and compensated their executives well, James Bennett and Thomas DiLorenzo suggested that unless nonprofits can prove their tax exemption allows them to pursue a charitable mission, there is no good reason to countenance the unfair competition that the current system often promotes.[34] From upscale fitness centers serving young professionals to university-directed foreign tours for alumni to large museum retail shops, nonprofit organizations are constantly pushing into new territory in search of revenues. Because these cash-generating ventures require staff time and commitment to succeed, they have undeniable implications for the culture and character of nonprofits. A theater that devotes substantial resources to building its café or a university that aggressively seeks out corporations to lease its banquet facilities may not diminish in a zero-sum fashion the amount of time and effort it spends improving its productions or strengthening its faculty. Nevertheless, commercialism can be a real distraction that diverts the attention of leaders from critical mission-related work. Controversies over commercialism have also focused attention on the compensation decisions within some nonprofits and the broader issue of financial accountability.

## Employee Compensation

Earned income is helping to fill the coffers of many nonprofits, but rising salaries are causing the funds to disappear at an accelerating pace.

One of the most significant developments in the nonprofit sector is the rise of professionals who command extremely generous salaries, particularly at large institutions such as universities and hospitals. This has re-opened the question of whether compensation levels in nonprofits need to be regulated. This issue was raised in a visible and lasting way by a case involving the largest charity in Hawaii, the Bishop Estate, which was responsible for managing and using a multi-billion-dollar endowment to operate schools for Hawaiian children. It was revealed that, over the course of a decade, the organization had paid its trustees millions of dollars in "fees." The scandal eventually led to a settlement with the IRS, one that included stiff financial penalties and the resignation of all trustees. The settlement was designed to send a message that limits on compensation would be enforced.

Of course, reasonable people can and do disagree about whether there should be any limits at all on nonprofit compensation. Two competing perspectives on this subject have emerged. For some individuals, the idea of paying nonprofit executives salaries that rival those in the business world is anathema. After all, the reasoning goes, those who choose to work in the nonprofit world do so knowing that few charitable organizations can afford generous financial rewards and that personal satisfaction is the coin of the realm. Accordingly, anyone seeking a generous compensation package should look to other parts of the economy for more lucrative opportunities. Focusing on the intersection of mission, stewardship, and accountability, this side of the argument reasonably concludes that nonprofit organizations cannot responsibly direct substantial charitable resources to their employees when the same resources could in many instances be used to serve needy clients or fulfill the organization's programmatic mission.

Not everyone sees nonprofit employment as demanding a vow of poverty. Many argue that the nonprofit sector needs to pay its best workers wages that are competitive with those of business firms if charitable organizations are ever to attract and retain the most capable people. Those embracing the idea of comparable pay across sectors sometimes claim that it is precisely because there is no clear bottom line in the nonprofit sector that good managers are critical. Since reliable metrics of achievement are hard to define in the absence of measures such as earnings per quarter, share price, and debt-to-equity ratio, nonprofit managers must be especially creative and resourceful in deploying an organization's human and financial capital. Leaders of large nonprofit organizations must be able to juggle multiple tasks and be able to motivate both professionals and volunteers. These tasks require people with strong management and leadership skills. For this reason, some people think compensation packages competitive with those in the for-profit sector are needed to ensure that nonprofit organizations do not become the employers of last resort to which managers turn after exhausting all other alternatives.

Rising nonprofit salaries clearly have the potential to undermine the trust that lies at the heart of at least one powerful rationale for the existence of nonprofit organizations. If staff salaries and directors' fees become too high, they can siphon off organizational resources for private advantage, which, for all intents and purposes, is equivalent to a "distribution" of revenue. This kind of distribution through salaries and fees rather than through the payment of dividends is problematic for three reasons. First, it undermines a community's confidence in the motives of nonprofit workers and weakens support for the tax exemption that charitable nonprofits enjoy. Second, it shakes the confidence of clients in the services that are being rendered, because providers' motives are different when constraints on profiteering are lifted. Third, it means that donors cannot assume a link between the size of their gift and the extent and quality of charitable services delivered. The clients of nonprofits, the donors, and the communities in which the organizations operate are thus all affected when the spirit of the nondistribution constraint is violated.

Pressures to pay higher and higher salaries to nonprofit leaders threaten to undermine the fragile identity of public charities as mission-driven organizations where motives and rewards resist quantification in dollars and cents. For some nonprofits, such as the Salvation Army, low wages are part of the identity of the organization and a critical factor in clients' trust and loyalty.[35] Clients and donors are attracted to organizations that spend money on programs devoted to a charitable mission rather than on compensation and perks for those who are doing the work. The ability of the largest and most visible nonprofits to attract the best talent and preserve their own identity as charitable organizations will depend in large measure on how well the compensation issue is resolved in the years ahead.

If nonprofits are to operate like businesses, they need oversight, especially given the bedrock fact that nonprofits do not have owners and lack clear lines of accountability.[36] This raises the question of who is responsible for eradicating inappropriate policies and financial abuses within nonprofits. At times, greed and dubious ethics have led to unlawful behavior. Over the past decade a number of major financial scandals have rocked the nonprofit world: the president of the United Way of America was convicted of embezzlement;[37] the head of the Foundation for New Era Philanthropy was found to be perpetrating an enormous investment fraud;[38] leaders of the Episcopal and Baptist churches were prosecuted for outright theft.[39] Lesser ethical lapses have also hurt the credibility of the sector and some of its largest institutions. The head of the National Association for the Advancement of Colored People was fired for improper transfer of funds (to his former mistress),[40] and the president of Adelphi University was forced to resign when it was revealed that he was enjoying a lavish lifestyle made possible by an extraordinarily generous compensation package.[41] Such incidents further tarnished the image of the sector.

While the best solution to the ethical problems facing the sector is simply better judgment on the part of its leaders, greater levels of oversight and disclosure are also needed. Nonprofit organizations must file an annual disclosure statement with the Internal Revenue Service. This statement, known as Form 990, has gone through a number of changes over the years, though it is still outdated and confusing. Making the annual financial reporting instrument easier to access, interpret, and complete would be a first step in improving the supply of data about nonprofits. To date, this information has been used in only limited ways. Independent nonprofit watchdogs and oversight organizations have been established in many fields to collect and disseminate it, but the results have been mixed. The Better Business Bureau, for example, reviews charities' compliance with various standards—for example, those concerning the use of a high percentage of funds for program activities, evidence of active board governance, and the provision of complete and accurate solicitations and informational materials to donors. It also catalogues government actions against national charities. Other organizations have taken on the task of disseminating information about nonprofits. The National Charities Information Bureau acts as a kind of accreditor for charities by collecting data on nonprofits, and reporting which organizations have complied with requests for information and which have not. Both of these broad voluntary systems rely to some extent on the good will of charities to provide information and to report data accurately. The main problem with these approaches is that they are unable to monitor groups that ignore requests for information—and it is in such organizations, of course, that problems are most likely to occur.

The difficulties inherent in voluntary reporting have led some to argue that the only real solution to the accountability problem in an increasingly commercialized and entrepreneurial nonprofit sector, and to the narrower compensation question that has emerged more recently, may lie in the establishment of a public agency that could ensure openness and disclosure. A nonprofit equivalent of the Securities and Exchange Commission would, among other things, impose uniform accounting techniques on public charities, disseminate information on the financial condition of organizations, and create channels through which donors, volunteers, clients, and community members could access and use this information. Of course, this would be a far more complex proposition in the nonprofit sector, where lines of ownership are overlapping and ill-defined, than in the business sector, where one group of owners (namely, shareholders) have a clear interest in solid information. If information is to work as part of a regulatory system and if the idea of a "nonprofit SEC" is to succeed, a major transformation is needed not just in the kind of information that is made available but in the outlook of the many stakeholders of nonprofit organizations, including donors, clients, and the general public.[42]

There is at least one major development on the horizon that may help expose the nonprofit sector to the bright light of disclosure. Several new nonprofit organizations have been formed to disseminate financial information about nonprofits over the Internet. These projects promise to overcome at least part of the information problem by allowing any person to access essential financial data for a large number of nonprofit organizations.[43] Figures on operating expenses, administrative overhead, and fundraising costs will all be available to potential contributors and volunteers. The goal is to make research on nonprofits simpler for the average donor by putting this information where it is easiest to access.

Ultimately, the real danger of commercialism is not greater regulation of nonprofits or even the curtailment of a new and powerful revenue stream, but rather a loss of identity and purpose within nonprofit organizations. If all nonprofit services had a price attached to them and were negotiated through market arrangements, one might reasonably wonder how the sector could ever fulfill its public-service role. Of course, some services will be sold at below-market prices and the charitable mission will consist in making the difference between market cost and nonprofit cost as great as possible. This is ultimately a very narrow and impoverished vision for the sector, one that aims merely at producing services at a state-subsidized rate.

## The Supply-Side Perspective

While entrepreneurship—along with the commercial activity it has spawned—has emerged as a powerful alternative theory for explaining the rise and growth of nonprofits, it can and does intermingle with other explanations. In many cases, it is not easy to determine whether the key driver of nonprofit activity is really the private impulse of the entrepreneur or some combination of various types of entrepreneurship made possible by government or market failure leading to unsatisfied demand. The interaction of supply- and demand-side explanations of nonprofit activity was most clearly illustrated recently in Hartford, Connecticut, where a very important confrontation occurred between leaders of the city's nonprofit social service agencies and the local government.[44]

Like many American cities, Hartford fell on hard times in the early 1990s, when many businesses relocated or downsized. This downward spiral was alarming enough, but soon city leaders began to worry about something else. Over a period of years, the number of nonprofit service providers in the city had mushroomed from two dozen to well over a hundred. The city government became particularly concerned that the downtown area was becoming a center not for business firms but for social service agencies, including soup kitchens, homeless shelters, and drug-abuse counseling centers. The influx of these service providers was, in the eyes of the city, dangerous for two reasons. First, it was further eroding the city's tax base, since the nonprofits paid no property taxes. Second, it was hurting the image of the city and making redevelopment harder. As a response, the city enacted a zoning ordinance that restricted the entry of social service providers into the downtown area. In taking this step, the city believed it was countering a tide of nonprofit entrepreneurship that was creating—or relocating—demand for services from all parts of the region to Hartford's downtown. Of course, the local nonprofit leaders argued that they were only responding to demand and meeting critical needs.

In the fight over Hartford's zoning ordinance, two very different understandings of the way nonprofits work were pitted against each other. In the opinion of nonprofit professionals, the growth of agencies for the disadvantaged and the disabled was simply a sign that the need for these services was acute. The homeless and the addicted, they believed, have both needs and rights, and these human service professionals felt they were responding compassionately to a growing demand. To the city's leaders, the picture looked radically different. Instead of seeing the growth of social services in Hartford as a response to increased demand, they believed that the supply of services had attracted clients from all over the region to Hartford. Though they did not attribute to the nonprofit workers anything but the best intentions, they nevertheless saw the problem of demand as inexorably linked to the supply of services. For this reason, the city took aggressive steps to curb the availability of new social services through new zoning regulations. While many activists were outraged by the city's actions and the reasoning that appeared to lie behind them, the demand- and supply-side explanations could not be clearly distinguished from each other.

In the end, explaining the rise of nonprofit and voluntary organizations from a supply-side approach is challenging for at least two reasons. First, when one is building a rationale for the sector, this approach commits one to looking not just at the beneficiaries, clients, and recipients of nonprofit activity but also at the social entrepreneur, the donor, and the volunteer. While this turning of the tables is unproblematic when the mission of the organization is to provide services to a well-defined, dues-paying membership, it becomes more controversial when the purpose of the organization is to provide services to the public. After all, we expect membership organizations to be oriented toward the needs and interests of the members, and we have crafted a public policy framework for these organizations that takes this into account: member-serving organizations enjoy tax exemptions but not the privilege of offering a tax deduction to contributors. When we come to the broad universe of charitable nonprofits (the public-serving part of the sector), the supply-side approach becomes more problematic. We want to believe that organizations which receive tax exemptions and have the ability to offer contributors a tax deduction for their gifts exist to serve the needy and provide important services. The idea that the driving rationale for any part of nonprofit activity may be not the clients and their unmet demands but

rather the interest and ideas of social entrepreneurs is unnerving because it forces us to rethink what the sector is all about and the nature of
the populations it serves.

Second, centering nonprofit activity on entrepreneurship means accepting that some services will be delivered to clients through increasingly marketlike conditions. As competition for charitable contributions
becomes ever more intense, many of the new social entrepreneurs are
turning to new, more commercial sources of revenue to support their
agendas. The rise of entrepreneurial managers within the sector has
brought with it a set of revenue-producing tools that may conflict at
times with the mission-orientation of nonprofit organizations and with
their ability to serve neglected people who may not be in a position to
pay even subsidized rates for needed services. Balancing the market's potent incentives with its potential distortions is a critical task for the diverse spectrum of increasingly entrepreneurial nonprofit organizations.
To the extent that this balance is achieved, nonprofits will be able to attract talented people to the sector, give them a measure of personal satisfaction, and produce public benefits that extend broadly across society.

# 6

# Balancing the Functions of Nonprofit and Voluntary Action

The preceding chapters considered the ability of nonprofit and voluntary organizations to intervene in the political realm, their efforts to provide needed services, their capacity to express values and commitments, and their role as vehicles for social entrepreneurship. These functions have taken nonprofits outside the quiet role they played in earlier times, and put them in conflict with both government and business. As the sector has grown and become more complex, both the range of nonprofit organizational forms and the scope of their activities have changed dramatically. Today, the presence and contribution of nonprofit organizations can be felt in almost every part of public life. Because nonprofits still have an unsettled relationship with the state and the market, they must now wrestle with and resolve a broad range of challenges. One factor is essential if this endeavor is to succeed: the sector must achieve a balance among its multiple roles. Only when nonprofit organizations speak to their broad and diverse range of stakeholders will they gain the kind of public support and understanding that has at times proved elusive.

In isolation, each of the four functions of nonprofit organizations brings them into contact and at times conflict with business or government. Community organizing and political advocacy often challenge entrenched interests in public sector bureaucracies. Political mobilization can also speak directly to corporate labor and environmental practices. Nonprofit service delivery work may seem neutral and unassuming, but increasingly nonprofits are struggling to get funding from government and maintain some kind of programmatic independence. At the same time, service organizations are encountering new competition from large business corporations seeking to enter new markets. The value-and-faith dimension of nonprofit activity is equally rife with possible inter-sector frictions, since ethical, religious, and social justice commitments can be wedges that create division and factionalism. Finally, the entre-preneurial character of nonprofits, when taken too far, makes nonprofits look like unfair competitors with business and appear to be more sensi-tive to the bottom line than to meeting the needs of the most disadvan-taged. As intersector tensions rise, understanding and responding to these issues is critical to the long-term advancement of nonprofit and voluntary organizations.

As a starting point for thinking about where the universe of nonprofit organizations is headed and how these organizations might best respond to future challenges, it may be useful to return to the functional dis-tinctions presented earlier in the book. The four functions of nonprofit organizations—civic and political engagement, service delivery, val-ues expression, and social entrepreneurship—are permeable and inter-connected. As nonprofits become one-sided in their work, they expose themselves to difficult questions about why they deserve their special tax-privileged position and identity. Returning to Figure 1.1 and devel-oping it further, we can sketch a new table that highlights the principal challenges confronting the sector. Just like the functions, these chal-lenges blur the borders of the table and interact with one another (see Figure 6.1).

This concluding chapter returns to the main analytic distinctions in-forming the book and summarizes the logic of each of the four functions of nonprofit and voluntary action. In the process, it will become clear how each function, when taken to an extreme or pursued in isolation from the other functions, can lead to significant problems. The complex-ity of the policy issues facing the nonprofit and voluntary organizations is ultimately a product of the divergent roles and responsibilities that the sector has assumed. Dissecting and diagramming these functions, and clarifying the challenges that are raised by one-sided nonprofit activity, are critical first steps toward defining an integrated vision of how non-profit and voluntary organizations might operate most successfully in the years ahead.

|  | Demand-side orientation | Supply-side orientation |
|---|---|---|
| Instrumental rationale | **Service delivery**<br><br>Core problem<br>◆ Vendorism<br><br>Manifestations<br>◆ Weakened autonomy as a result of dependence on government funding<br>◆ Excessive focus on scale of nonprofit provision<br>◆ Isomorphism and decreased diversity of services | **Social entrepreneurship**<br><br>Core problem<br>◆ Commercialism<br><br>Manifestations<br>◆ Neglect of underserved communities<br>◆ Drift in organizational mission<br>◆ Cases of private inurement |
| Expressive rationale | **Civic and political engagement**<br><br>Core problem<br>◆ Polarization<br><br>Manifestations<br>◆ Narrow factionalism between organizations<br>◆ Blurred boundaries around lobbying<br>◆ Disconnect between grassroots and leadership | **Values and faith**<br><br>Core problem<br>◆ Particularism<br><br>Manifestations<br>◆ Rise of private agendas<br>◆ Cases of exclusion and discrimination<br>◆ Problems of accountability |

6.1 Problems and issues in the nonprofit and voluntary sector.

## Civic and Political Engagement and the Problem of Polarization

The first role of nonprofits centers on the civic-and-political-engage-ment model described in Chapter 2 and depicted in Figure 6.2. It starts with the claim that nonprofit and voluntary action is a response to im-portant social and political demands, which are translated through action into engagement and participation. By opening the public sphere to people whose interests have been underrepresented or ignored, non-profit and voluntary civic and political action aims at generating change. An important part of this political work is aimed at channeling more public resources to particular social issues and, often as a consequence, at obtaining more funding for certain nonprofit organizations. The polit-ical work of nonprofits drives toward change, both by bringing pressure to bear on government and by mobilizing grassroots action at the local, state, and national levels. Although much of the local political work of nonprofits is aimed at empowering and engaging populations that have not always had their voices heard, entrenched interest groups, industry trade associations, and business lobbies have devoted substantial re-sources to advocacy efforts.[1] It is important to remember that all of the trade and professional associations in Washington, D.C., are tax-exempt, not just those associations pursuing social justice or empower-ment agendas. Because the resources of nonprofit organizations are lim-ited, acting through politics is seen as a potent form of leverage. The civic and political engagement work of nonprofit and voluntary organi-zations can thus be understood as an attempt to use limited resources in a way that catalyzes action by others.

Although encouraging civic and political engagement is desirable, clearly it is sometimes possible to have too much of a good thing. If civic and political engagement becomes so dominant that it overwhelms the other three functions, nonprofits run the risk of being perceived as ex-cessively partisan and polarizing. Community groups have the ability to bring people together around common concerns, and this process

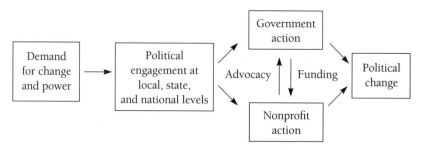

6.2 Model of civic and political engagement in the nonprofit and voluntary sector.

can be exhilarating and empowering. But when the political activity of nonprofits moves from grassroots organizing to advocacy and lobbying, challenges to their tax-exempt status are raised. Recent efforts in Congress to limit the lobbying activities of nonprofits that receive public funds are the most recent example of this suspicion of excess partisanship. Over the past decade, lawmakers have proposed a series of bills aimed at curtailing the political activity of nonprofits, particularly when these organizations receive federal funds.

Legislative action—such as the famous Istook Amendment—targeting the political advocacy work of nonprofits has at times been supported by the argument that it is unclear whom some nonprofits speak for and why the tax code should grant their voices special support.[2] In the case of union political activity, Congress has also considered limiting the ability of unions to use membership dues to fund political advertising without first seeking the approval of members. Outside the Beltway, the growing political power of membership organizations representing the elderly, advocacy groups working on behalf of children, coalitions of religious believers, and unions representing teachers have contributed to the public perception that the national interest has been reduced at times to a mere aggregation of interest group positions.

While it is critical that the political voices of nonprofits be heard, it would be wrong to believe that political work by itself could serve as the basis for a strong nonprofit and voluntary sector. Nonprofit political advocacy and lobbying, especially when these activities are polarizing or based on narrow interest group agendas, all too often do not speak to broad public needs or to the necessity for coalition building and consensus. Only when nonprofits expand the reach of their political work and combine it with other kinds of activities will these organizations garner the support they need both within and beyond their ranks.

## Service Delivery and the Problem of Vendorism

Beyond shaping the political realm through action and ideas, nonprofit and voluntary organizations provide a range of concrete services to the public and to their members. The service delivery role of nonprofits has one important thing in common with their civic-and-political-engagement role: it, too, starts as a response to demand, this time for goods and services (see Figure 6.3). While the government may attempt to respond to this demand—particularly if mobilized constituencies press for action—there will often be areas that are underserved by the market and the state. When such shortfalls occur, nonprofit and voluntary organizations can and do enter the picture, sometimes even before government acts, by providing needed services to those who lack the ability to pay or who seek specialized services.

Nonprofit organizations must strive, however, to be more than mere engines of service production if they are to claim a compelling rationale for the sector. After all, government is more than capable of delivering a great range of critical human services. Thus, nonprofits run some risk when they fail to differentiate themselves and simply vend services on behalf of the public sector. If nonprofits are merely obedient vessels for the execution of narrowly defined public purposes, they will have considerable difficulty developing and sustaining innovative approaches and programs. The threat of vendorism is augmented by the growing role that government funds play in the human services. Combating the loss of autonomy that accompanies narrow service delivery activity on behalf of government requires both the definition of distinctive missions and the pursuit of creative funding strategies. Some nonprofits have sought to avoid vendorism by acquiring greater financial independence from public funders, principally by developing commercial sources of revenue. Yet this move has turned out to be fraught with its own challenges. Nonprofit fee-for-service work will continue to be challenged by for-profit firms, which have greater incentives to be efficient. When non-

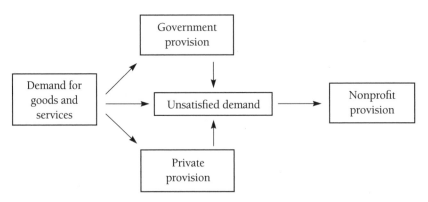

6.3 Model of provision of social services, involving the public, private, and nonprofit sectors.

profits fail to produce goods and services in ways and at prices different from those elsewhere in the market, they invite challenge for being redundant and less efficient than for-profit ventures. Given the proliferation of business firms capable of fulfilling many human service and education needs, nonprofit providers need to be perceived as more than well-meaning vendors of services if they are to make a compelling argument for their privileged tax-exempt status.

While delivering services will always remain central to the sector's identity, nonprofit organizations must be understood and used as more than tools of production. When nonprofit organizations become nothing more than tools of government action or efficient private producers, they lose the middle ground between the public and private that defines the character of nonprofit and voluntary action. Today, nonprofits are increasingly being pressured to produce only goods and services for which there is a demand. Competition has pushed many agencies in this direction. It is a trend, however, that must be resisted if nonprofit and voluntary organizations are to achieve their full potential.

## Values and Faith and the Problem of Particularism

Clearly, it is possible to take an entirely different approach to the explanation of nonprofit and voluntary action—one that starts with the impetus of donors, volunteers, and staff (see Figure 6.4). There are large parts of the nonprofit and voluntary sector that cannot be understood as a strategic response to unmet demand, but rather must be seen as an ex-

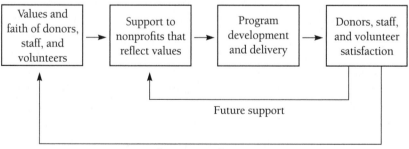

6.4 Model of nonprofit dynamics, based on the values and beliefs of donors, volunteers, and staff.

pression of belief and faith on the part of individuals. Indeed, many voluntary and nonprofit efforts draw attention to issues and opportunities which have long been overlooked, for which no clear constituency exists, or for which no demand is present. Nonprofits can and do give voice to the beliefs and values of individuals. In the vast realm of faith or religiously based activity, it would be useless to interpret action strictly as a result of demand and instrumental concerns. The impulse to help and to serve often has its roots in private convictions, personal values, and religious faith. For this reason, the value-and-faith model of nonprofit activity starts and ends with the commitments of donors, volunteers, and staff. Nonprofit and voluntary action is about their experience, even though, in the long run, social benefits are achieved as well.

The very virtue of expressive action constitutes the basis of its perceived weakness. Critics of value- and faith-based nonprofits see these organizations as exclusionary or excessively particularistic because their missions speak for only a subset of the population—a group that has a common outlook or set of beliefs. This is especially problematic if the nonprofits adhere to exclusionary membership criteria or espouse divisive views. The sectarian tendencies of faith- and value-driven nonprofits also raise concerns about a narrowing or closing of the sector. Particularism can affect the services offered by nonprofits or the flow of charitable funds within the sector.[3] The rise of a new class of mega-donors capable of using private funds to shape the public agenda has made some observers even more suspicious of the increasing ability of private individuals to use their wealth to project their views into the public sphere and bypass public policy. When a privately funded voucher program is started or a donor provides substantial backing to a ballot initiative on altering drug control policy, the private values and beliefs of some individuals are clearly able to carry more sway than others. For this reason, the expressive character of nonprofit and voluntary action contains within it a threat of balkanization and particularism that can appear less than democratic.

The risks of excessive particularism inherent in a values-and-faith-driven sector are worth shouldering, however, given the importance of having a plurality of voices on the full range of major public issues. The private values and commitments that get aired through nonprofit activity may not always please everyone. Nevertheless, when enough voices and perspectives are brought into the public sphere, it is likely the resulting cacophony will embody some wisdom. Just as with the other functions of nonprofit and voluntary action, however, the value-expressing rationale must not and should not overwhelm the other roles of nonprofit organizations. It must be pursued in support of and in balance with the other functions of nonprofit and voluntary action.

## Entrepreneurship and the Problem of Commercialism

The social entrepreneurship model of nonprofit action starts with the drive and creativity that private individuals bring into the public realm (see Figure 6.5). Social entrepreneurs of all kinds start nonprofit organizations—not just because demand and need beckon, but because there are entrepreneurial opportunities to develop programs and supportive streams of revenue. The entrepreneurship model is also clearly oriented toward the supply side, and sees the production of nonprofit goods and services from the perspective of innovation and income-seeking activity by individual social entrepreneurs. This approach is different from both the civic engagement and service delivery models in that it does not point to the state and to public funding as a critical driver for nonprofit and voluntary action. While many nonprofit organizations do at some point secure public funding, many of the new social entrepreneurs are seeking ways to support their work through commercial ventures and fees for service. These revenues, which have few or no strings attached to them in terms of how they may be spent, can be used inside the organization to subsidize programs and activities that lack their own revenue streams.

The entrepreneurial character of the nonprofit and voluntary sector

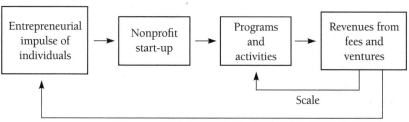

6.5 Model of nonprofit dynamics, based on entrepreneurship.

should not be seen as entirely altruistic, however. Organizations driven by membership dues and fees often deliver services to affluent communities and operate in ways that increasingly resemble the methods of aggressive for-profit businesses, focusing as much on marketing, sales, and margins as would any profitmaking operation. When an enterprise appears to be either narrowly targeted at exclusive membership groups or when its primary function appears to be the expansion of staff salaries and organizational resources, the case for public support of nonprofits becomes harder to make.[4] In this sense, an aggressive entrepreneurial agenda risks exposing nonprofits to charges of crass commercialism.

Nonprofit organizations are turning "profits" at record levels. The revenues generated by commercial activities of all kinds raise difficult questions about the coherence and identity of the sector as a whole. The growing commercialism of nonprofit organizations—seen in the charging of fees, the operation of fundraising businesses, and the generation of revenue through licensing and sponsorship agreements—raises important questions about mission coherence. The issue of mission distortion or drift is one that has been raised repeatedly. After all, when a youth service organization decides to operate a thrift store or when a museum commits to developing and marketing a line of furniture, the staff time and energy expended can be substantial. Nonprofits need to weigh whether the financial benefits of commercial activity outweigh the headaches that these activities can often cause. As the range of commercial activities becomes broader and broader, new kinds of business staff will be needed—ones that may not be attuned to the organization's mission.

Since nonprofits pay no taxes on related business activity and because they have shown themselves to be fairly agile in shifting program costs to cover profits from commercial activity (so that they pay little or no unrelated business income tax), cries of unfair competition have become more pronounced. Nonprofits are particularly vulnerable to such charges when their services are aimed at middle-class clienteles and when there is little apparent cross-subsidization. More importantly, the question of commercialism is relevant because it may well end up shaping public perception and support for nonprofit tax exemption. At a time when public scrutiny is being trained on large commercially oriented nonprofits, the devotion of nonprofits to the sale of goods and services can raise questions about why special tax treatment is extended to nonprofits. After all, one national organization (the American Association of Retired Persons) recently had to set up a for-profit subsidiary to assuage concerns that its commercialism—as evidenced in its sale of life insurance, travel, and other services to its members—had made it too big and politically powerful.[5] Other nonprofits with aggressive commercial orientations, such as fitness clubs that operate in affluent neighborhoods and cater primarily to young professionals, have encountered criticism for not really having a charitable mission that is worthy of favorable tax treatment.

In many ways, the rising commercialism of the nonprofit sector is a product of the increasing focus on the entrepreneurial function within the sector. Many organizations are focused less on their mission than on the marketing and sale of their products and services. To the extent that a nonprofit organization is narrowly focused on instrumental goals and the advancement of the social entrepreneur behind it, commercialism and its rewards will be an attraction—one that may have a steep price attached to it in the long run if pursued in excess and to the exclusion of other ends.

## The Limits of Growth

Over the past half-century, as nonprofits have sought to balance their multiple and competing roles, the nonprofit and voluntary sector has grown at a tremendous rate, both in terms of the number of organizations delivering services and the resources devoted to these organizations. One of the most difficult and painful questions today, however, is whether these two trends have proceeded in alignment with each other or whether the expansion of the sector is beginning to outstrip society's ability to support these endeavors adequately. While private philanthropy has increased steadily over the years, the sheer number of causes and organizations competing for philanthropic resources has exploded. It is thus possible to view the growth of the sector from two quite different perspectives.

On the one hand, the increasing number of nonprofits—each seeking to deliver services and each with its own identity and mission—can be seen as a very positive development for the field. The fact that there are a great many organizations is an affirmation of pluralism and diversity. A large and diverse nonprofit sector, it can also be argued, is likely to provide innovation and overcome the pitfalls of vendorism. To the extent that the nonprofit world continues to grow and attract new people and new ideas, its capacity to challenge received wisdom is likely to be enhanced. There are other benefits to a broad dispersion of power and resources across a large number of organizations. Diversity and diffusion of resources may lead nonprofits to be more attuned and responsive to local communities. As the number of nonprofits continues to rise, there are more opportunities to develop services that are culturally and contextually appropriate. This constitutes a strong argument in favor of pluralism and variety within the sector, even if some efficiency must be traded to achieve it. After all, nonprofits are often a critical link among residents of communities. Having many small, local, and accessible organizations becomes critical if these organizations are to build strong networks of trust that can make service delivery more effective.

While pluralism and local control are powerful attractions, the growth of the sector's service delivery capacity can be interpreted quite differently, particularly if efficiency is a serious concern. As the number of organizations climbs and as the level of resources devoted to nonprofits rises as a percent of GDP, some aspects of the sector's growth do appear less than optimal. In particular, there is much duplication of services, even within relatively tight geographic boundaries. Often an organization is established to address a problem even when existing organizations are already in place. Sometimes the rationale for this expansion starts with an appeal to pluralism. But these arguments wear thin when one considers the underfinancing and instability of many organizations. The fragmentation and duplication that have resulted in an ever-expanding nonprofit sector are at least in part a function of two factors. First, nonprofit activity appeals to individuals who want to be their own bosses or who do not want to work in a bureaucratic or corporate environment. Second, the barriers to entry are extremely low and can be crossed, initially at least, with the filing of few documents.

The fragmentation of effort that uncoordinated growth has brought to many fields of nonprofit activity may have serious implications for nonprofits committed to delivering high-quality services. If there are large numbers of nonprofits working in isolation on common problems, they will find it hard to achieve economies of scale and instead may be drawn into an exhausting struggle for organizational survival. To date, the evidence that fragmentation interferes with sustainability is suggestive but not conclusive. Even as the number of nonprofit organizations has soared, hundreds of thousands of nonprofits are apparently inactive despite remaining on the IRS rolls.

Fragmentation and redundancy have also fueled heightened competition within the sector. As charitable resources have tightened, more nonprofits are pursuing fewer funding streams. Competition has not led to mergers and acquisitions, however.[6] Most organizations believe strongly that their missions, values, and local ties make such strategic consolidation impractical and ill-advised. Thus, while the business sector is able to respond to competitive pressures by merging operations and downsizing, nonprofits tend to resist such moves. Competition among nonprofits is therefore rarely productive. Nonprofits compete for private and public funds in a zero-sum game where the stakes can be very high. This leads many nonprofits to devote substantial time and energy to fundraising and positioning.[7] Moreover, nonprofits are finding that volunteers—who contribute valuable free labor—must be courted and attracted in an environment where the number of choices is multiplying and where information about volunteering opportunities has made people more selective in the kinds of positions they are willing to assume.

Whether one views the exponential growth of the sector in a positive or negative light depends to a certain extent on how one prioritizes the instrumental and expressive dimensions of nonprofit activity. If the expressive quality is accepted as a critical rationale for the sector, then growth offers many exciting opportunities for pluralism to flourish. If, however, the function of the sector is conceived primarily in terms of its ability to deliver certain services in a efficient way, then the growth of the sector takes on a far more problematic character.

## The Challenge of Balance

The four functions of the nonprofit and voluntary sector cut across two dimensions. The first depends on the distinction between demand- and supply-side theories of nonprofit and voluntary action. This distinction is significant because it raises the basic question of who benefits from this sector and where its energies ought to be directed. Demand-side theories see nonprofit and voluntary action as aimed at the provision of goods and services or at mobilizing political support for collective decisionmaking, with public needs as the driving force. Taking this perspective commits one to a positive and normative theory of the sector. Demand is seen as pulling nonprofit activity into the areas of greatest need, often where the market and the state cannot or will not go. This positive perspective can take a normative turn when the resources de-voted to nonprofit activity are said to be justified based on the social benefits that are produced. The demand-side perspective, in its effort to explain and justify the nonprofit sector's privileged position in society, looks at what comes out of the sector.

The supply-side perspective, as we have seen, takes a substantially dif-ferent tack. The push of social entrepreneurs, value-driven donors, and committed volunteers is considered the animating force behind the sec-tor. In constructing a positive theory, supply-siders identify the inclina-tions and innovations of donors, staff, and volunteers as the engine that drives the sector forward and that pushes demand. More critically, tak-ing a supply-side approach commits one to seeing the sector's underly-ing normative rationale in a very different way. Rather than focusing on how the sector meets public needs, the supply-side perspective focuses on what nonprofit and voluntary organizations do for those who propel the sector forward. As a normative principle, this translates into an argu-ment that the experience of the donors, staff, and volunteers should be acknowledged and respected, not shunted off as some irrelevant concern in the organization's effort to achieve greater levels of public utility. While this perspective does not exclude the public benefits that accrue from individual action, it does focus on the private benefits that are real-ized. It also leads to the following two claims. First, increasing the flow of charitable funds and activities requires the full expression of private interests and values. Second, some individual choices, which in them-selves may appear socially suboptimal, lead in the aggregate to collective benefits in the form of innovations and pluralism.

The second distinction we have drawn is between the instrumental and expressive purposes behind nonprofit and voluntary action. This di-mension cuts across the demand-supply dimension, while recognizing that instrumentally valuable activity, such as effective entrepreneurship and the efficient delivery of services, is qualitatively different from ex-pressive activity, such as political speech or the practice of religion. In-strumental activity has as its goal the accomplishment of concrete ends, and the work of nonprofits is valued in terms of how they contribute to the achievement of these ends. Accordingly, when nonprofit organizations deliver services to the homeless or to battered women, what is significant is that public needs are fulfilled and that nonprofits act as useful vehicles for the achievement of public ends. Instrumental logic attaches value to use and application above all else.

The expressive dimension of nonprofits points one's attention in another direction. It reminds us that part of nonprofit and voluntary action is important and valuable independently of what is achieved in the name of the public. The very act of coming together to accomplish a public purpose is important. It can be transformative for the individual and allows for the actualization of deeply held beliefs. Thus, when a community organizes a book collection for the local senior-center library, the satisfaction that residents take in helping their community is just as important as the project's success in locating many interesting books. The act of joining together is important because it enacts values and beliefs and gives them expression, which is a significant end in itself. Nonprofit and voluntary action allows people to speak for themselves, and on behalf of others, through action. This expressive dimension is different from the instrumental dimension because it validates a part of nonprofit activity that is often overlooked or downplayed in the name of more practical deeds. Reaffirming the private expression of values and faith, especially when the call for nonprofit provision is strong, is controversial because it appears intangible and something of a luxury. Proponents of the expressive dimension counter this critique by pointing to the fact that when people act on their beliefs and values through nonprofit work, it is more likely that they will achieve concrete instrumental purposes.

The distinction between demand- and supply-side approaches and the contrast between instrumental and expressive dimensions bring to the surface conflicting ideas about whom nonprofits should benefit, what kinds of activities they should undertake, and how they should operate. To be sure, there are important links that can be drawn across these two divides. Both the demand-side and instrumental perspectives share a view that nonprofits are fundamentally public organizations with important responsibilities to all. Both the supply-side and expressive perspectives see nonprofits as essentially private institutions that spring from the rights individual hold. Rights and responsibilities thus provide a third way to think about the arguments made on behalf of the sector. Of course, rights and responsibilities themselves are not mutually exclusive, and many extremely successful nonprofits have both a demand-side and a supply-side orientation *while* combining expressive and instrumental work. In fact, one of the most important principles of nonprofit management and leadership is that an organization can *simultaneously* deliver services, advocate for policies that are important to the community, express values through a unique and individualistic mission, and generate funding streams through the creative use of commercial ventures. In practice, the number of organizations with diverse portfolios of activities and orientations is too limited. More often, functional diversity in the sector is achieved across organizations rather than within organizations. And herein lies one source of the mounting criticism that has been leveled at the sector. After all, each of the four core challenges described here is closely connected to the others. Improving nonprofits' ability to achieve balance will likely demand a complex set of integrated responses, both at the level of public policy toward the sector as a whole and at the level of the day-to-day management of nonprofit organizations.

All of which brings one back to the four basic functions of nonprofit organizations. The recent evolution of the nonprofit and voluntary sector has demonstrated a simple truth: when nonprofit organizations are seen as delivering only on one function, legitimacy and support may be hard to secure over the long term and nonprofits will have difficulty addressing their many pressing challenges. In this sense, the very strength of the sector can be a source of weakness. Individuals can motivate nonprofit organizations with a broad range of public and private purposes. The freedom that these special organizations provide, however, opens the door for excess. As nonprofits become narrower in the goals they pursue, questions about the balance between the instrumental needs of the public and the expressive desires of individuals become more penetrating and more difficult to dismiss. Nonprofits that are exclusively political in their orientation will have a hard time countering criticism that they are part of the problem which plagues all levels of our political system. Nonprofits that simply deliver services, and offer nothing different from what government agencies and for-profit firms already provide, will have trouble making an argument for their continued privileged tax position. Nonprofits that simply allow a group of people to express their commitments and values will be seen as narrowly focused underachievers. And nonprofits that are too aggressive in their entrepreneurship will be criticized for excess commercialism.

At the sector level, there are two possible ways to achieve the kind of functional balance that is needed. The first is to place hope in an invisible hand, one that directs nonprofits to pursue one-sided agendas at the organizational level with the belief that things will balance out at the sector level. While there is tremendous variation in the sector's activities, it is not clear that the four functions are now being fulfilled evenly. Financial pressures have led to an emphasis on the service delivery and entrepreneurship functions, with government contracts and earned income fueling much of the sector's growth. The laissez-faire solution has been the approach adopted to date, in part because the alternative is even less plausible.

The second way to achieve balance at the sector level is through coordinated action by nonprofits or through changes in the regulatory environment designed to shape the composition of the sector. There is, however, reason to doubt the feasibility of this method. The nonprofit and voluntary sector is a complex and conflicted amalgam of institutions and impulses that are difficult to govern. The sector has rarely, if ever, demonstrated a capacity for taking coordinated action on behalf of any cause and concern, much less a complex task such as ensuring the achievement of balance across the four functions of nonprofit and voluntary action. Government could adjust its tax treatment or its funding of the various kinds of nonprofit organizations so as to promote certain kinds of activities and discourage others. But this approach is fraught with problems. Relying on government to structure the activities of nonprofits more actively than it does now would likely only push the sector closer to the service delivery function at the cost of the other functions.

Fortunately, balance can be achieved at the organizational level because it simply represents good strategy. While the four functions are distinct conceptually, in practice successful organizations embody several or all of these roles. Multiple and overlapping functions can strengthen an organization and help it adapt to changes in the policy and funding environments.[8] Thus, for example, in the case of an organization working to provide after-school programs for disadvantaged youth, there may be times when advocacy for greater levels of volunteerism and local funding of education is needed, and other times when the delivery of effective services is most useful. Some faith-based organizations, such as those striving to move people from welfare to paying jobs, have also worked hard to achieve balance across the expressive and instrumental dimensions. Many of these programs try not just to help members express their religious convictions, but also to channel this powerful impulse into entrepreneurial activity designed to build revenues in support of the organizational mission. By transcending narrow roles and missions, nonprofits can achieve two important ends. First, they can create a mix of public and private value that satisfies the donors, staff, and volunteers while simultaneously providing goods and services that meet important public needs. When nonprofits do stretch themselves and work across traditional programmatic boundaries, new ideas and program models often emerge. Second, when nonprofits become active across diverse functions, they expand the base of support for their work within the local community. After all, when a nonprofit has multiple programs, the range of people interested in using or funding these programs inevitably expands. This can be very important, especially given the fluctuations and swings in nonprofit finance. Having more than one program or product can allow an agency to deal with sudden changes in the funding environment that might otherwise bring hardship.

In the end, when nonprofit organizations become too one-sided, they become vulnerable to charges of politicization, vendorism, particularism, and commercialism. In fact, many of the crises and scandals that have shaken the nonprofit sector can be traced in some degree to lack of balance across the four broad functions defined here. The search for fit among the four functions can be seen as one of the most important challenges to nonprofit managers. One positive response to this challenge would be to accept that virtue in the nonprofit sector ultimately lies in moderation and balance among the four functions.

For the complex and conflict-ridden universe of nonprofits to grow and prosper in the long run, these organizations will need to avoid the excessive pull of any one of the four central functions. Actors within the sector will need to engage in politics in ways that enhance all public life, and not just the interests of small, well-organized constituencies. Managers will need to demonstrate that their organizations can play an effective role in delivering critical services, and that they deserve the confidence of public and private funders and clients. Community leaders acting through nonprofit and voluntary organizations will need to give voice to the private values and distinctive beliefs of groups that separate nonprofit activity from both government and commercial business. Entrepreneurs will likewise need to continue to use nonprofits as vehicles for social innovation. In delivering on all of these functions, nonprofit and voluntary organizations will have to strive for balance among these varied roles.

If those committed to nonprofit and voluntary action work to achieve multiple purposes that defy easy categorization, they may well succeed both in satisfying the donors, staff, and volunteers and in creating broad public benefits for deserving clients and communities. This would be a result that everyone interested in the future of nonprofit organizations could embrace. It would also fulfill the essential mission of the nonprofit and voluntary sector.

# Notes

## 1. The Idea of a Nonprofit and Voluntary Sector

1. The literature on the nonprofit and voluntary sector has burgeoned over the past two decades. One of the early attempts to bring the sector's many competing research agendas together can be found in Walter W. Powell, *The Nonprofit Sector: A Research Handbook* (New Haven, Conn.: Yale University Press, 1987). Other overviews of the sector that have provided basic data on the dimensions of nonprofit and voluntary activity include Lester M. Salamon, *America's Nonprofit Sector: A Primer,* 2nd ed. (New York: Foundation Center, 1999); William G. Bowen et al., *The Charitable Nonprofits: An Analysis of Institutional Dynamics and Characteristics* (San Francisco: Jossey-Bass, 1994); and Jon Van Til, *Growing Civil Society* (Bloomington: Indiana University Press, 2000). For the most detailed statistical profile of nonprofit activity, see the most recent version of the *Nonprofit Almanac: Dimensions of the Independent Sector* (San Francisco: Jossey-Bass, 1996), which is updated periodically.

2. On the growth of nonprofit and voluntary organizations around the world, see John Burbidge, ed., *Beyond Prince and Merchant: Citizen Participation and the Rise of Civil Society* (New York: Pact Publications, 1997); John Keane, *Civil Society: Old Images, New Visions* (Stanford, Calif.: Stanford University Press, 1998); Víctor M. Pérez-Díaz, *The Return of Civil Society: The Emergence of Democratic Spain* (Cambridge, Mass.: Harvard University Press, 1993); Lester M. Salamon and Helmut K. Anheier, *Defining the Nonprofit Sector: A Cross-National Analysis* (New York: Manchester University Press, 1997); and Robert I. Rotberg, ed., *Vigilance and Vengeance: NGOs Preventing Ethnic Conflict in Divided Societies* (Washington, D.C.: Brookings Institution Press, 1996).

3. Joseph S. Nye, Jr., Philip D. Zelikow, and David C. King, *Why People Don't Trust Government* (Cambridge, Mass.: Harvard University Press, 1997).

4. The idea of nondistribution constraint is clearly outlined in Henry B. Hansmann, "The Role of Nonprofit Enterprise," in Susan Rose-Ackerman, ed.,

*The Economics of Nonprofit Institutions: Studies in Structure and Policy* (New York: Oxford University Press, 1986), pp. 57–84.

5. The literature on the management of public sector organizations provides insights into some of the challenges of sustaining and leading a nonprofit organization. Some of the best studies of public management include Michael Barzelay, *Breaking through Bureaucracy: A New Vision for Managing in Government* (Berkeley: University of California Press, 1992); Sanford Borins, *Innovating with Integrity: How Local Heroes Are Transforming American Government* (Washington, D.C.: Georgetown University Press, 1998); Laurence E. Lynn, Jr., *Public Management as Art, Science and Profession* (Chatham, N.J.: Chatham House, 1996); Mark H. Moore, *Creating Public Value: Strategic Management in Government* (Cambridge, Mass.: Harvard University Press, 1996); David Osborne and Ted Gaebler, *Reinventing Government: How the Entrepreneurial Spirit Is Transforming the Public Sector* (New York: Plume, 1992).

6. A good discussion of the legal framework guiding accountability in the nonprofit sector can be found in Laura Chisolm, "Accountability of Nonprofit Organizations and Those Who Control Them: The Legal Framework," *Nonprofit Management and Leadership* 6, no. 2 (Winter 1995): 141–156.

7. Kevin P. Kearns, "The Strategic Management of Accountability in Nonprofit Organizations: An Analytic Framework," *Public Administration Review* 54, no. 2 (1994): 185–192; Kevin P. Kearns, *Managing for Accountability: Preserving the Public Trust in Public and Nonprofit Organizations* (San Francisco: Jossey-Bass, 1996).

8. Henry Hansmann, *The Ownership of Enterprise* (Cambridge, Mass.: Harvard University Press, 1996).

9. Kirsten A. Grønbjerg, *Understanding Nonprofit Funding: Managing Revenues in Social Services and Community Development Organizations* (San Francisco: Jossey-Bass, 1993).

10. Most notably, Wisconsin and New York City transformed their public assistance programs and made community service or part-time employment a requirement.

11. Thomas Haskell, ed., *The Authority of Experts: Studies in History and Theory* (Bloomington: Indiana University Press, 1984).

12. One critique of philanthropy has emphasized that some funders have channeled social protest and deradicalized grassroots social movements by imposing constraints and attempting to shape these efforts. See J. Craig Jenkins, "Channeling Social Protest: Foundation Patronage of Contemporary Social Movements," in Walter W. Powell and Elisabeth S. Clemens, eds., *Private Action and the Public Good* (New Haven, Conn.: Yale University Press, 1998), pp. 206–216; and Rosa Proietto, "The Ford Foundation and

Women's Studies in American Higher Education: Seeds of Change?" in Ellen Condliffe Lagemann, ed., *Philanthropic Foundations: New Scholarship, New Possibilities* (Bloomington: Indiana University Press, 1999), pp. 271–286.

13. The nonprofit and voluntary sector also includes fringe organizations that espouse extreme political and racial views and rely on violence and intimidation. Although these organizations are a small part of the organizational universe, they undercut the image of a sector that does nothing but good. On the dangers of voluntarism, see Morris P. Fiorina, "Extreme Voices: The Dark Side of Civic Engagement," in Theda Skocpol and Morris P. Fiorina, eds., *Civic Engagement in American Democracy* (Washington, D.C.: Brookings Institution Press and Russell Sage Foundation, 1999).

14. The issue of how much nonprofit workers earn, and the need for complete public disclosure that compensation decisions create, is taken up in Peter Frumkin, "Transparent Nonprofits," *The Public Interest* 142 (Winter 2001): 83–94. See also Peter Frumkin and Alice Andre-Clark, "Nonprofit Compensation and the Market," *University of Hawaii Law Review* 21, no. 2 (Winter 1999): 425–485.

15. See Henry Hansmann, "Why Do Universities Have Endowments?" *Journal of Legal Studies* 19, no. 1 (January 1990): 3–42.

16. Steven E. Permut, "Consumer Perceptions of Nonprofit Enterprise: Comment on Hansmann," *Yale Law Journal* 90, no. 7 (June 1981): 1623–1632.

17. The adoption by most states of the American Bar Association's Model Nonstock Corporation Statute had a significant impact on accountability and ownership issues in nonprofit organizations. Among other things, the statute shifted the fiduciary standard toward a business judgment standard and away from that traditionally applied to trusts. In so doing, it enabled nonprofit boards to use proxy voting, change by-laws without membership approval, and delegate powers to executive committees. The main effect of these changes was to empower boards and to weaken the role of members (in membership organizations). For a detailed account of this shift, see Michael C. Hone, "Aristotle and Lyndon Baines Johnson: Thirteen Ways of Looking at Blackbirds and Nonprofit Corporations: The American Bar Association's Revised Model Nonprofit Corporation Act," *Case Western University Law Review* 39, no. 3 (1989): 751–762; and Peter Dobkin Hall, "Law, Politics, and Charities in the Post-Liberal Era," in Paul Pribbenow, ed., *Serving the Public Trust: Insights into Fundraising Research and Practice* (San Francisco: Jossey-Bass, 2000), pp. 5–31.

18. For a good overview of the issues related to the conversion of hospitals from nonprofit to for-profit status, see John H. Goddeeris and Burton Weisbrod, "Conversions from Nonprofit to For-Profit Legal Status: Why Does It Happen and Should Anyone Care?" *Journal of Policy Analysis and Management*

17, no. 2 (1998): 215–233; John H. Goddeeris and Burton Weisbrod, "Why Not For-Profit? Conversions and Public Policy," in Elizabeth T. Boris and C. Eugene Steuerle, eds., *Nonprofits and Government: Collaboration and Conflict* (Washington, D.C.: Urban Institute, 1999), pp. 235–266. See also Gary Claxton, Judith Feder, David Shactman, and Stuart Altman, "Public Policy Issues in Nonprofit Conversion," *Health Affairs* 16, no. 2 (March–April 1997): 9–26; and Jerome P. Kassirer, "Mergers and Acquisitions: Who Benefits? Who Loses?" *New England Journal of Medicine* 334, no. 11 (March 1996): 722–723.

19. Studies of nonprofit organizations have tended to focus on large established nonprofits because they control the bulk of the finances within the sector. Yet one recent estimate suggested that there may well be a substantial number of small, informal organizations that operate under the radar screen of researchers. See, for example, David Horton Smith, "The Rest of the Nonprofit Sector: Grassroots Associations as the Dark Matter Ignored in Prevailing 'Flat Earth' Maps of the Sector," *Nonprofit and Voluntary Sector Quarterly* 26, no. 2 (June 1997): 114–131.

20. On the discontinuity between traditional voluntary associations and more modern voluntary organizations, see Peter Dobkin Hall, "Vital Signs: Associational Populations and Ecologies in New Haven, Connecticut, 1850–1990," in Skocpol and Fiorina, eds., *Civic Engagement in American Democracy,* pp. 211–248. On the broad evolution of voluntary associations, see Gerald Gamm and Robert Putnam, "The Growth of Voluntary Associations in America, 1840–1940," *Journal of Interdisciplinary History* 29, no. 4 (Spring 1999): 511–557.

21. The importance of trust is examined in an increasing number of studies, including Roderick M. Kramer and Tom R. Tyler, *Trust in Organizations: Frontiers of Theory and Research* (Thousand Oaks, Calif.: Sage Publications, 1996); Francis Fukuyama, *Trust: The Social Virtues and the Creation of Prosperity* (New York: Free Press, 1995); and Adam B. Seligman, *The Problem of Trust* (Princeton, N.J.: Princeton University Press, 1997).

22. On the evolution of nonprofit nomenclature, see Van Til, *Growing Civil Society.*

23. Brian O'Connell, *Powered by Coalition: The Story of Independent Sector* (San Francisco: Jossey-Bass, 1997), is a history of the association as told by its first leader.

24. See most notably Michael O'Neill, *The Third America: The Emergence of the Nonprofit Sector in the United States* (San Francisco: Jossey-Bass, 1989).

25. Roger A. Lohmann, *The Commons: New Perspectives on Nonprofit Organizations and Voluntary Action* (San Francisco: Jossey-Bass, 1992).

26. Ibid., p. 58.

27. Barry D. Karl, "Nonprofit Institutions," *Science* 236 (May 1987): 984–985.

28. Peter Dobkin Hall has argued that in fact the nonprofit "sector" is a construct which is becoming harder and harder to justify, given the blurring of boundaries between nonprofit, business, and government organizations. See Hall, "Philanthropy, Public Welfare, and the Politics of Knowledge: Acquiring Knowledge by Taking Risks," in Deborah S. Gardner, ed., *Vision and Values: Rethinking the Nonprofit Sector* (New York: Nathan Cummings Foundation, 2000).

29. On the diverse organizational forms that populate the nonprofit landscape, see Jeremy Kendall and Martin Knapp, "A Loose and Baggy Monster: Boundaries, Definitions and Typologies," in Justin Davis Smith et al., eds., *An Introduction to the Voluntary Sector* (New York: Routledge, 1995), pp. 66–95.

30. For a clear overview of the special rules governing the operation of private foundations, see David F. Freeman and the Council on Foundations, *The Handbook on Private Foundations,* rev. ed. (New York: Foundation Center, 1991).

31. See, for example, Peter Dobkin Hall, *Inventing the Nonprofit Sector* (Baltimore: Johns Hopkins University Press, 1992).

32. The idea that nonprofits sit somewhere between the business sector and the public sector is captured in Robert Wuthnow, "Introduction," in Wuthnow, ed., *Between States and Markets: The Voluntary Sector in Comparative Perspective* (Princeton, N.J.: Princeton University Press, 1991). Some of the tensions that the idea of boundaries between sectors raises are explored in James M. Ferris and Elizabeth Graddy, "Fading Distinctions among the Nonprofit, Government, and For-Profit Sectors," in Virginia A. Hodgkinson et al., eds., *The Future of the Nonprofit Sector: Challenges, Changes, and Policy Considerations* (San Francisco: Jossey-Bass, 1989), pp. 123–139.

33. Lee Staples, *Roots to Power: A Manual for Grassroots Organizing* (New York: Praeger, 1984).

34. The desire to find new ways to argue for social initiatives has been part of a broader trend toward a politics of moderation and centrism. Rather than arguing for additional federal spending measures, much of the liberal agenda has been translated into the simple preservation of existing entitlement programs and the funding of local—often nonprofit—initiatives aimed at solving discrete community problems.

35. One attempt to examine the broad array of nonprofit activities for new insights about "what works" is Lisbeth B. Schorr, *Common Purpose: Strengthening Families and Neighborhoods to Rebuild America* (New York: Anchor Books, 1997).

36. Critiques of Great Society social programs proliferated in the early 1980s,

but few were as influential as Charles Murray, *Losing Ground: American Social Policy, 1950–1980* (New York: Basic Books, 1984).

37. Many of the core conservative themes were articulated in Charles Heatherly, ed., *Mandate for Leadership* (Washington, D.C.: Heritage Foundation, 1981); and again in Newt Gingrich, *To Renew America* (New York: Harper Collins, 1995).

38. Marvin Olasky, *The Tragedy of American Compassion* (Washington, D.C.: Regency Publishing, 1992). Of course, long before the conservative revolution embraced faith-based approaches, the government had in various ways assisted religiously affiliated organizations. See Amos Warner, *American Charities* (New York: Thomas Cromwell, 1908).

39. Great Society programs provided extensive financial support to community empowerment programs, many of which were affiliated with inner-city congregations. Catholic Charities, the Salvation Army, and Lutheran Social Services have long been the recipients of some of the largest social service grants from the government. What made the conservative approach distinctive was the active involvement of theologically conservative religious bodies that had traditionally avoided commitment to social service delivery.

40. Richard C. Cornuelle, *Reclaiming the American Dream: The Role of Private Individuals and Voluntary Associations* (New Brunswick, N.J.: Transaction Publishers, 1993).

41. Avner Ben-Ner and Theresa Van Hoomissen, "Nonprofit Organizations in the Mixed Economy: A Demand and Supply Analysis," in Avner Ben-Ner and Benedetto Gui, eds., *The Nonprofit Sector in the Mixed Economy* (Ann Arbor, Mich.: University of Michigan Press, 1993), pp. 27–58.

42. A good summary of early theorizing about nonprofit activity can be found in Avner Ben-Ner, "Nonprofit Organizations: Why Do They Exist in Market Economics?" in Susan Rose-Ackerman, ed., *The Economics of Nonprofit Institutions: Studies in Structure and Policy* (New York: Oxford University Press, 1986), pp. 94–113.

43. Dennis Young, *If Not For Profit, For What? A Behavioral Theory of the Nonprofit Sector, Based on Entrepreneurship* (Lexington, Mass.: Lexington Books, 1983).

44. The literature on nonprofit strategic management is expanding quickly. Important work to date has often straddled the line between the public and nonprofit sectors. See, for example, John M. Bryson, *Strategic Planning for Public and Nonprofit Organizations: A Guide to Strengthening and Sustaining Organizational Achievement* (San Francisco: Jossey-Bass, 1995); Kevin P. Kearns, *Managing for Accountability: Preserving the Public Trust in Public and Nonprofit Organizations* (San Francisco: Jossey-Bass, 1996); and Paul C. Light, *Sustaining Innovation: Creating Nonprofit and Government Organi-*

*zations That Innovate Naturally* (San Francisco: Jossey-Bass, 1998). Other work has extended and adapted concepts from business management to nonprofit organizations. See, for example, Peter F. Drucker, *Managing the · Nonprofit Organization: Principles and Practices* (New York: Harper, 1992); Sharon Oster, *Strategic Management for Nonprofit Organizations* (New York: Oxford University Press, 1995); Alceste Pappas, *Reengineering Your Nonprofit Organization* (New York: Wiley, 1995); Christine W. Letts, William P. Ryan, and Allen Grossman, *High Performance Nonprofit Organizations: Managing Upstream for Greater Impact* (New York: Wiley, 1999).

45. For a good discussion of the challenges of managing a nonprofit in a way that allows workers to express their values and commitments, see David E. Mason, *Leading and Managing the Expressive Dimension: Harnessing the Hidden Power Source of the Nonprofit Sector* (San Francisco: Jossey-Bass, 1996).

46. See Douglas Henton, John Melville, and Kimberly Walesh, *Grassroots Leaders for a New Economy: How Civic Entrepreneurs Are Building Prosperous Communities* (San Francisco: Jossey-Bass, 1997).


## 2. Civic and Political Engagement

1. Paul Hirst, *Associative Democracy: New Forms of Economic and Social Governance* (Amherst, Mass.: University of Massachusetts Press, 1994).

2. On the women's movement, see Mary Fainsod Katzenstein and Carol McClurg Mueller, *The Women's Movement in the United States and in Europe* (Philadelphia: Temple University Press, 1987); and Jane Mansbridge, *Why We Lost the ERA* (Chicago: University of Chicago Press, 1986). On the labor movement, see Thomas Geoghegan, *Which Side Are You On? Trying to Be for Labor When It's Flat on Its Back* (New York: Farrar, Straus and Giroux, 1992). On the environmental movement, see Mark Dowie, *Losing Ground: American Environmentalism at the Close of the Twentieth Century* (Cambridge, Mass.: MIT Press, 1995).

3. Antony Black, *Guilds and Civil Society in European Political Thought from the Twelfth Century to the Present* (Ithaca, N.Y.: Cornell University Press, 1984).

4. See Thomas Hobbes, *The Leviathan,* ed. C. B. Macpherson (New York: Penguin, 1977).

5. D. B. Robertson, "Hobbes' Theory of Associations in the Seventeenth-Century Milieu," in D. B. Robertson, ed., *Voluntary Associations: A Study of Groups in Free Societies* (Richmond, Va.: John Knox Press, 1966).

6. See C. B. Macpherson, *The Political Theory of Possessive Individualism: Hobbes to Locke* (Oxford: Clarendon Press, 1964); and Isaiah Berlin, *Four Essays on Liberty* (New York: Oxford University Press, 1969).

7. John Locke, *The Second Treatise on Government and A Letter Concerning Toleration* (Oxford: Basil Blackwood, 1948).

8. George Washington, *Writings of George Washington* (New York: Library of America, 1997), p. 968.

9. John Stuart Mill, *Utilitarianism, Liberty and Representative Government* (London: Dent, 1960), p. 164.

10. A. D. Lindsay, *The Modern Democratic State* (Oxford: Oxford University Press, 1943), p. 258.

11. Ibid., p. 258.

12. One of the best accounts of Tocqueville's visit to America can be found in Andre Jardin, *Tocqueville: A Biography* (New York: Farrar, Straus and Giroux, 1988).

13. Alexis de Tocqueville, *Democracy in America,* trans. Lawrence G. Mayer (New York: Harper and Row, 1969).

14. Ibid., p. 513.

15. Ibid., p. 107.

16. Ibid., p. 521.

17. See William Ellery Channing, "Remarks on Associations," in *Collected Works of William Ellery Channing* (Boston: American Unitarian Associations, 1929). Quoted in Peter Dobkin Hall, "Philanthropy, Public Welfare, and the Politics of Knowledge: Acquiring Knowledge by Taking Risks," in Deborah S. Gardner, ed., *Vision and Values: Rethinking the Nonprofit Sector* (New York: Nathan Cummings Foundation, 2000).

18. See, for example, Don E. Eberle, *America's Promise: Civil Society and the Renewal of American Culture* (Lanham, Mass.: Rowman and Littlefield, 1998): pp. 19–38; Theda Skocpol, "Don't Blame Government: America's Voluntary Groups Thrive in National Network," in E. J. Dionne, Jr., ed., *Community Works: The Revival of Civil Society in America* (Washington, D.C.: Brookings Institution Press, 1998), pp. 37–4; and Theda Skocpol, "The Tocqueville Problem: Civic Engagement in American Democracy," *Social Science History* 4, no. 4 (Winter 1997): 455–477.

19. See, most recently, Sidney Verba, Kay Lehman Schlozman, and Henry E. Brady, *Voice and Equality: Civic Voluntarism in American Politics* (Cambridge, Mass.: Harvard University Press, 1995).

20. Robert Nisbet, *Community Power* (Oxford: Oxford University Press, 1962).

21. Ibid., p. 279.

22. C. Wright Mills, *The Power Elite* (Oxford: Oxford University Press, 1956).

23. The literature on civic participation and democracy is vast. Two of the better recent treatments can be found in Michael J. Sandel, *Democracy's Discontent: America in Search of a Public Philosophy* (Cambridge, Mass.: Harvard Uni-

versity Press, 1996); and Michael Schudson, *The Good Citizen: A History of American Civic Life* (New York: Free Press, 1998).

24. Robert D. Putnam, *Bowling Alone: The Collapse and Revival of American Community* (New York: Simon and Schuster, 2000); idem, "Bowling Alone: America's Declining Social Capital," *Journal of Democracy* 6, no. 1 (1995): 65–78; idem, "The Prosperous Community," *The American Prospect* 13 (Spring 1993): 35–42.

25. The capacity of small-town civic associations and voluntarism to build strong communities is described in Robert N. Bellah et al., *Habits of the Heart: Individualism and Commitment in American Life* (Berkeley, Calif.: University of California Press, 1985).

26. Robert D. Putnam, with Robert Leonardi and Raffaella Y. Nanetti, *Making Democracy Work: Civic Traditions in Modern Italy* (Princeton, N.J.: Princeton University Press, 1993).

27. Robert Putnam, "Bowling Alone, Revisited," *The Responsive Community* 5, no. 2 (Spring 1995): 18–33.

28. Robert D. Putnam, "The Strange Disappearance of Civic America," *The American Prospect*, no. 24 (Winter 1996): 34–48.

29. Robert Wuthnow, *Loose Connections: Joining Together in America's Fragmented Communities* (Cambridge, Mass.: Harvard University Press, 1998). See also idem, *Acts of Compassion: Caring for Others and Helping Ourselves* (Princeton, N.J.: Princeton University Press, 1991); and idem, *Sharing the Journey: Support Groups and America's New Quest for Community* (New York: Free Press, 1994). Other criticism of Putnam's thesis has come in the form of data showing a rise, not a collapse, of volunteerism. See Everett Carll Ladd, *The Ladd Report* (New York: Free Press, 1999).

30. Wuthnow, *Loose Connections*, p. 8.

31. Jane Jacobs, *The Death and Life of Great American Cities* (New York: Vintage, 1961).

32. A discussion of the history and evolution of the concept of social capital can be found in Putnam, *Bowling Alone*, pp. 15–28.

33. James Coleman, "Social Capital in the Creation of Human Capital," *American Journal of Sociology* 94, supplement (1988): S95–120.

34. Ibid., p. S98.

35. Mark S. Granovetter, "The Strength of Weak Ties," *American Journal of Sociology* 78, no. 6 (May 1973): 1360–78.

36. Ibid., p. 1378.

37. On the challenge of bridging the gap between individuals and the political sphere, see Margaret Weir and Marshall Ganz, "Reconnecting People and Politics," in Stanley B. Greenberg and Theda Skocpol, eds., *The New Major-*

*ity: Toward a Progressive Politics* (New Haven, Conn.: Yale University Press, 1999). For a more sobering perspective, see Jean Bethke Elshtain, "Not a Cure-All: Civil Society Creates Citizens; It Does Not Solve Problems," in Dionne, ed., *Community Works,* pp. 24–29.

38. An important discussion of the promise and problems of pluralism can be found in Robert A. Dahl, *Dilemmas of Pluralist Democracy: Autonomy and Control* (New Haven, Conn.: Yale University Press, 1982). See also idem, "On Removing Certain Impediments to Democracy in the United States," *American Political Science Review* 60 (1966): 296–305.

39. Joseph S. Nye, Jr., Phillip D. Zelikow, and David C. King, eds., *Why People Don't Trust Government* (Cambridge, Mass.: Harvard University Press, 1997).

40. For an overview of the challenges of mobilizing citizens for action, see Kim Bobo, J. Kendall, and S. Max, *Organizing for Social Change* (New York: Seven Locks Press, 1996).

41. Sidney Verba, Kay Lehman Schlozman, and Henry E. Brady, *Voice and Equality: Civic Voluntarism in American Politics* (Cambridge, Mass.: Harvard University Press, 1995).

42. Ibid., p. 9.

43. Ibid., p. 8.

44. See, for example, Laura Woliver, "Mobilizing and Sustaining Grassroots Dissent," *Journal of Social Issues* 52, no. 1 (1996): 139–152.

45. Saul Alinsky, *Reveille for Radicals* (New York: Vintage, 1960; orig. pub. 1946); idem, *Rules for Radicals* (New York: Random House, 1971); Scott M. Wilson, *Organizing for Power and Empowerment* (New York: Columbia University Press, 1994).

46. Various examples of urban grassroots mobilization can be found in Robert Matthews Johnson, *The First Charity: How Philanthropy Can Contribute to Democracy in America* (Washington, D.C.: Seven Locks Press, 1988). See also Marshall Ganz, "Resources and Resourcefulness: Strategic Capacity in the Unionization of California Agriculture, 1959–1966," *American Journal of Sociology* 105, no. 4 (January 2000): 1003–62.

47. Charles C. Moskos, *A Call to Civic Service: National Service for Country and Community* (New York: Free Press, 1988); Morris Janowitz, *The Reconstruction of Patriotism: Education for Civic Consciousness* (Chicago, Ill.: University of Chicago Press, 1983); Robert Coles, *The Call of Service: A Witness to Idealism* (Boston: Houghton Mifflin, 1993).

48. Elizabeth Reid, "Nonprofit Advocacy and Political Participation," in Elizabeth T. Boris and C. Eugene Steuerle, eds., *Nonprofits and Government: Collaboration and Conflict* (Washington, D.C.: Urban Institute Press, 1999).

49. See John B. Judis, "The Pressure Elite: Inside the Narrow World of Advo-

cacy Politics," *The American Prospect* 9 (Spring 1992): 15–29; and Nicholas Lemann, "Citizen 501(c)3," *Atlantic Monthly* (February 1997).

50. For a summary of the strategy of conservative funders, see Sally Covington, *Moving a Public Policy Agenda: The Strategic Philanthropy of Conservative Foundations* (Washington, D.C.: National Committee for Responsive Philanthropy, 1997). On the other side of the political spectrum, see Michael Schuman, "Why Liberal Foundations Give So Little to So Many," *The Nation* (January 1998): 11–16, which suggests that grassroots funding by the left has been less than effective at creating broad movements for public policy change.

51. Nonprofit advocacy efforts have been pursued through independent policy think tanks and through business-funded efforts to shape regulatory policy. See James A. Smith, *The Idea Brokers: Think Tanks and the Rise of the New Policy Elite* (New York: Free Press, 1991); and David Vogel, *Fluctuating Fortunes: The Political Power of Business* (New York: Basic Books, 1989).

52. The idea of leverage is an old one. It simply denotes an activity that achieves a maximum amount of social impact for a minimum amount of financial expense. On the various ways that funders have sought to increase the effectiveness of their giving, see Peter Frumkin, "Philanthropic Leverage," *Society* 37, no. 6 (Fall 2000): 40–46.

53. A practical guide to nonprofit lobbying can be found in Bob Smucker, *The Nonprofit Lobbying Guide* (Washington, D.C.: Independent Sector, 1999). A broader treatment of the politics of lobbying is Bruce C. Wolpe and Bertram J. Levine, *Lobbying Congress: How the System Works* (Washington, D.C.: Congressional Quarterly, 1996).

54. For a good history of the rise of interest groups, see Elisabeth Clemens, *The People's Lobby: Organizational Innovation and the Rise of Interest Group Politics in the United States, 1890–1925* (Chicago: University of Chicago Press, 1997).

55. A classic account of lobbying in the United States can be found in Lester W. Milbrath, *The Washington Lobbyists* (Chicago: Rand McNally, 1963).

56. See David E. Rosenbaum, "Tax-Exempt Status Rejected, Christian Coalition Regroups," *New York Times,* June 11, 1999, p. A18; and Richard L. Berke, "Ruling Bolsters Christian Group: Judge Rejects Most Charges of Illegal Role in Elections," *New York Times,* August 3, 1999, pp. A1, A10. For an account of the Christian Coalition's political strategy, see Ralph E. Reed, *Politically Incorrect: The Emerging Faith Factor in American Politics* (Dallas: World Publications, 1994).

57. The effect of globalization on nongovernmental organizations is explored in a special issue of *Nonprofit and Voluntary Sector Quarterly* 28, no. 4, supplement (1999). See also Thomas Risse-Kappen, ed., *Bringing Transnational Re-*

*lations Back In* (Cambridge: Cambridge University Press, 1995); and Jackie Smith, Charles Chatfield, and Ron Pagnucco, *Transnational Social Movements and Global Politics: Solidarity beyond the State* (Syracuse, N.Y.: Syracuse University Press, 1997).

58. L. David Brown, Sanjeev Khagram, Mark H. Moore, and Peter Frumkin, "Globalization, NGOs and Multi-Sectoral Relations," in Joseph S. Nye, ed., *Governance and Globalization* (Washington, D.C.: Brookings Institution Press, 2000).

59. Edward Shils explored the broad sociological problem of centrality and remoteness in *Center and Periphery: Essays in Macrosociology* (Chicago, Ill.: University of Chicago Press, 1975).

60. The problem of creating change through political action is one that often raises questions about leadership. For the best discussion of what leadership in any sector of society entails, see Ronald Heifetz, *Leadership without Easy Answers* (Cambridge, Mass.: Harvard University Press, 1994).

## 3. Service Delivery

1. Burton Weisbrod, "Toward a Theory of the Voluntary Nonprofit Sector in a Three Sector Economy," in Susan Rose-Ackerman, ed., *The Economics of Nonprofit Institutions: Studies in Structure and Policy* (New York: Oxford University Press, 1986), pp. 21–44.

2. Ibid., p. 22.

3. For a fuller exposition of the idea of government failure, see Burton Weisbrod, *The Nonprofit Economy* (Cambridge, Mass.: Harvard University Press, 1988).

4. Weisbrod, "Toward a Theory of the Voluntary Nonprofit Sector in a Three Sector Economy," p. 30.

5. Ibid., p. 31.

6. Ibid., p. 39.

7. Ibid., p. 31.

8. Henry B. Hansmann, "The Role of Nonprofit Enterprise," in Rose-Ackerman, ed., *The Economics of Nonprofit Institutions,* pp. 57–84.

9. See John D. Donahue, *Disunited States* (New York: Basic Books, 1997); idem, *The Privatization Decision: Public Ends, Private Means* (New York: Basic Books, 1989).

10. Lester M. Salamon, "The Changing Partnership between the Voluntary Sector and the Welfare State," in Virginia A. Hodgkinson et al., eds., *The Future of the Nonprofit Sector: Challenges, Changes, and Policy Considerations* (San Francisco: Jossey-Bass, 1989), pp. 41–60.

11. Lester M. Salamon, "Of Market Failure, Voluntary Failure, and Third Party Government: Toward a Theory of Government-Nonprofit Relations in the Modern Welfare State," in Salamon, *Partners in Public Service: Government-Nonprofit Relations in the Modern Welfare State* (Baltimore, Md.: Johns Hopkins University Press, 1995), pp. 33–52.

12. Ibid., p. 44.

13. Ibid., p. 48

14. Ibid., p. 49.

15. Lester Salamon, "The Government-Nonprofit Partnership in Practice," in Salamon, *Partners in Public Service,* p. 109.

16. See Marilyn Taylor and Jane Lewis, "Contracting: What Does It Do to Voluntary and Non-Profit Organizations?" in Perri 6 and Jeremy Kendall, eds., *The Contract Culture in Public Service: Studies from Britain, Europe and the USA* (Brookfield, Vt.: Ashgate Publishing, 1997), pp. 27–46.

17. See Nicholas Deakin, "The Perils of Partnership: The Voluntary Sector and the State, 1945–1992," in Justin Davis Smith, Colin Rochester, and Rodney Hedley, eds., *An Introduction to the Voluntary Sector* (New York: Routledge, 1995), pp. 40–65.

18. For an overview of the issues and tensions created by contracting, see H. Brinton Milward and Keith G. Provan, "The Hollow State: Private Provision of Public Services," in Helen Ingram and Steven Rathgeb Smith, eds., *Public Policy for Democracy* (Washington, D.C.: Brookings Institution, 1993), pp. 222–240. See also Margaret Harris, "Contracting and the Changing Politics of Need in the USA," in Perri 6 and Jeremy Kendall, eds., *The Contract Culture in Public Service,* pp. 69–78.

19. Kirsten A. Grønbjerg, *Understanding Nonprofit Funding: Managing Revenues in Social Services and Community Development Organizations* (San Francisco: Jossey-Bass, 1993).

20. Ibid., p. 193.

21. Ibid., p. 183.

22. Susan Bernstein, *Managing Contracted Services in the Nonprofit Agency* (Philadelphia: Temple University Press, 1991).

23. Steven Rathgeb Smith and Michael Lipsky, *Nonprofits for Hire: The Welfare State in the Age of Contracting* (Cambridge, Mass.: Harvard University Press, 1993). See also Steven Rathgeb Smith, "The New Politics of Contracting: Citizenship and the Nonprofit Role," in Helen Ingram and Steven Rathgeb Smith, eds., *Public Policy for Democracy* (Washington, D.C.: Brookings Institution, 1993), pp. 198–221.

24. Ibid., p. 105.

25. Ibid., pp. 134–144.

26. Elizabeth T. Boris, "Nonprofit Organizations in a Democracy," in Elizabeth T. Boris and C. Eugene Steuerle, eds., *Nonprofits and Government: Collaboration and Conflict* (Washington, D.C.: Urban Institute Press, 1999), pp. 3–29.

27. See Mark Hager et al., "Tales from the Grave: Organizations' Accounts of Their Own Demise," *American Behavioral Scientist* 39, no. 8 (August 1996): 975–994; Joseph Galaskiewicz and Wolfgang Bielefeld, *Nonprofit Organizations in an Age of Uncertainty: A Study of Organizational Change* (New York: Aldine de Gruyter, 1998); Mark Hager, "Explaining Demise among Nonprofit Organizations" (Diss., University of Minnesota, Department of Sociology, 2000).

28. There is a lively debate over whether and to what extent public funding crowds out private contributions. See Bruce R. Kingma, "An Accurate Measure of the Crowd-Out Effect, Income Effect, and Price Effect for Private Contributions," *Journal of Political Economy* 97, no. 5 (1989): 1197–1207; Richard Steinberg, "Does Government Spending Crowd Out Donations? Interpreting the Evidence," in Avner Ben-Ner and Benedetto Gui, eds., *The Nonprofit Sector in the Mixed Economy* (Ann Arbor, Mich.: University of Michigan Press, 1993), pp. 99–125; Arthur C. Brooks, "Is There a Dark Side to Government Support for Nonprofits?" *Public Administration Review* 60, no. 3 (May–June 2000): 219–229.

29. Joe Laconte, *Seducing the Samaritan: How Government Contracts Are Reshaping Social Services* (Boston: Pioneer Institute, 1997).

30. See Peter Frumkin and Alice Andre-Clark, "The Rise of the Corporate Social Worker," *Society* 36, no. 6 (September–October 1999): 46–52; and William Ryan, "The New Landscape for Nonprofits," *Harvard Business Review* (January–February 1999): 127–136.

31. See Alceste Pappas, *Reengineering Your Nonprofit Organization* (New York: Wiley, 1995); and Thomas Wolf, *Managing a Nonprofit Organization* (New York: Prentice Hall, 1990).

32. The discussion here draws on work conducted collaboratively with Alice Andre-Clark on nonprofit/for-profit competition in the field of welfare-to-work services. See Peter Frumkin and Alice Andre-Clark, "When Missions, Markets, and Politics Collide: Values and Strategy in the Nonprofit Human Services," *Nonprofit and Voluntary Sector Quarterly* 29, no. 1 (2000): 141–164.

33. See Reid Lifset, "Cash Cows or Sacred Cows: The Politics of the Commercialization Movement," in Hodgkinson et al., eds., *The Future of the Nonprofit Sector* (San Francisco: Jossey-Bass, 1989), pp. 140–167. Hospitals have been the subject of considerable scrutiny and criticism, particularly with regard to the amount of charity care they offer. See Monica Longley,

"Nonprofit Hospitals Sometimes Are That in Little but Name," *Wall Street Journal,* July 14, 1997, p. 1.

34. For a comprehensive discussion of the trends in hospital conversions, and of the effects of these transactions, see David M. Cutler and Jill R. Horowitz, "Converting Hospitals from Not-for-Profit to For-Profit Status: Why and What Effects?" in David M. Cutler, ed., *The Changing Hospital Industry* (Chicago: University of Chicago Press, 2000).

35. Anne Lowery Bailey, "Health Care's Merger Mania," *Chronicle of Philanthropy* 7, no. 3 (November 16, 1995): 1.

36. The issue of when and why nonprofit hospitals should consider converting is taken up in James R. Schwartz and H. Chester Horn, *Health Care Alliances and Conversions: A Handbook for Nonprofit Directors and Trustees* (San Francisco: Jossey-Bass, 1998).

37. The major exception is in the field of health care, where numerous studies of hospitals have sought to document differences in patient satisfaction and levels of uncompensated care.

38. David Cay Johnston, "Court Rules against IRS in Charity Case," *New York Times,* February 12, 1999.

39. Charles Murray, "The Tendrils of Community," in David Boaz, ed., *The Libertarian Reader* (New York: Free Press, 1997), pp. 108–111.

40. Alan Reynolds, *Death Taxes and the Independent Sector: Reflections on the Past and Future Growth of Private Charities and Foundations* (Washington, D.C.: Hudson Institute, 1997).

41. For an overview of the evolving role of government in provision, see Carolyn Webber and Aaron Wildavsky, *History of Taxation and Expenditure in the Western World* (New York: Simon and Schuster, 1986); and Salamon, *Partners in Public Service.*

42. For a critique of conservatives' attempts to emphasize the moral content of private charitable efforts on behalf of the poor and to give such efforts priority over more neutral public programs, see Mark Rosenman, "A Return to Alms," in Deborah S. Gardner, ed., *Vision and Values: Rethinking the Nonprofit Sector* (New York: Nathan Cummings Foundation, 2000).

43. For a critical rebuttal of Reynolds' arguments, see Julian Wolpert, *What Charities Can and Cannot Do* (New York: Century Foundation, 1996).

44. For an overview of the determinants of individual contributions, see Charles T. Clotfelter, *Federal Tax Policy and Charitable Giving* (Chicago: University of Chicago Press, 1985).

45. One proposal which was seriously debated would have given taxpayers a $500 tax deduction for gifts to nonprofits working to help the poor. The Coats-Kasich Bill, as it was called, was ultimately defeated, in part due to

the difficulty of deciding which nonprofits were in fact engaging in poverty alleviation. See John Buntin, "Tax Incentives for Charitable Giving," Kennedy School of Government, Teaching Case no. 1357.0, Harvard University, 1994.

46. Evelyn Brody, "Of Sovereignty and Subsidy: Conceptualizing the Charity Tax Exemption," *Journal of Corporation Law* 23, no. 4 (Summer 1998): 585–629.

47. For a discussion of the Marxian perspective on philanthropy, see Robert F. Arnove, "Introduction," in Arnove, ed., *Philanthropy and Cultural Imperialism: The Foundations at Home and Abroad* (Bloomington: Indiana University Press, 1992). The *Great Soviet Encyclopedia* (1950) defined philanthropy as "a means the bourgeoisie uses to deceive workers and disguise parasitism and its exploiter's face, by rendering hypocritical, humiliating aid to the poor in order to distract the latter from class struggle." Suspicion of the wealthy and their motives lives on.

48. See Eduard C. Lindeman, *Wealth and Culture* (New Brunswick, N.J.: Transaction Books, 1988); Nelson W. Aldrich, Jr., *Old Money: The Mythology of America's Upper Class* (New York: Vintage Books, 1989); Francie Ostrower, *Why the Wealthy Give: The Culture of Elite Philanthropy* (Princeton, N.J.: Princeton University Press, 1995); Waldemar Nielsen, *Inside American Philanthropy* (Norman: Oklahoma University Press, 1996).

49. Teresa Odendahl, *Charity Begins at Home: Generosity and Self-Interest among the Philanthropic Elite* (New York: Basic Books, 1990). See also idem, ed., *America's Wealthy and the Future of Foundations* (New York: Foundation Center, 1987).

## 4. Values and Faith

1. Peter L. Berger and Richard John Neuhaus, *To Empower People: From State to Civil Society*, ed. Michael Novak (Washington, D.C.: AEI Press, 1996; orig. pub. 1977), p. 148.

2. Ibid., p. 149.

3. For a set of excellent historical accounts of private efforts to help the poor, see Donald T. Critchlow and Charles H. Parker, eds., *With Us Always: A History of Private Charity and Public Welfare* (New York: Rowman and Littlefield, 1998).

4. Berger and Neuhaus, *To Empower People*, p. 146.

5. Ibid., p. 164.

6. For an overview of the complex interplay of professions in society, see Andrew Abbott, *The System of Professions* (Chicago: University of Chicago

Press, 1988). In the field of private foundations, professionalization has increased the size of the workforce and changed the way foundations relate to the public. See Peter Frumkin, "Private Foundations as Public Institutions: Regulation, Professionalization, and the Redefinition of Organized Philanthropy," in Ellen Condliffe Lagemann, ed., *Philanthropic Foundations: New Scholarship, New Possibilities* (Bloomington, Ind.: Indiana University Press, 1999), pp. 69–100; and Peter Frumkin, "The Long Recoil from Regulation: Private Philanthropic Foundations and the Tax Reform Act of 1969," *American Review of Public Administration* 28, no. 3 (September 1998): 266–286.

7. Ronald Heifetz, *Leadership without Easy Answers* (Cambridge, Mass.: Harvard University Press, 1994).

8. Ibid., p. 23.

9. David E. Mason, *Leading and Managing the Expressive Dimension: Harnessing the Hidden Power Source of the Nonprofit Sector* (San Francisco: Jossey-Bass, 1996), p. 46.

10. Ibid., p. 14.

11. Quoted from "Liberty Fund," a pamphlet which is published by the Liberty Fund and which describes Goodrich's life and ideas.

12. See Karen W. Arenson, "Staggering Bequests by Unassuming Couple," *New York Times,* July 13, 1998, A1.

13. See Evelyn Nieves, "A Campaign for a No-Kill Policy for the Nation's Animal Shelters," *New York Times,* January 18, 1999, pp. A1, A12.

14. This critique is often grounded in the work of the Italian Marxist theorist Antonio Gramsci, whose writings focused on the use of culture by elites.

15. Susan A. Ostrander, *Money for Change: Social Movement Philanthropy at Haymarket People's Fund* (Philadelphia: Temple University Press, 1995); J. Craig Jenkins and Abigail L. Halcli, "Grassrooting the System? The Development and Impact of Social Movement Philanthropy, 1953–1990," in Ellen Condliffe Lagemann, ed., *Philanthropic Foundations: New Scholarship, New Possibilities* (Bloomington: Indiana University Press, 1999); J. Craig Jenkins, "Channeling Social Protest," in W. W. Powell and Elisabeth Clemens, eds., *Private Action and the Public Good* (New Haven, Conn.: Yale University Press, 1998), pp. 206–216; Susan A. Ostrander, "The Problem of Poverty and Why Philanthropy Neglects It," in Virginia A. Hodgkinson et al., eds., *The Future of the Nonprofit Sector: Challenges, Changes, and Policy Considerations* (San Francisco: Jossey-Bass, 1989), pp. 219–236.

16. See Robert H. Bork, "Interpreting the Founder's Vision," in *Donor Intent* (Washington, D.C.: Philanthropy Roundtable, 1993).

17. See Martin Morse Wooster, *The Great Philanthropists and the Problem of Donor Intent* (Washington, D.C.: Capital Research Center, 1998).

18. See Peter Frumkin, "Fidelity in Philanthropy: Two Challenges to Community Foundations," *Nonprofit Management and Leadership* 8, no. 1 (Fall 1997): 65–76.

19. Last Will and Testament of Beryl Buck, Marin County Counsel Office archives.

20. See John G. Simon, "American Philanthropy and the Buck Trust," *University of San Francisco Law Review* 21 (1987): 641–679.

21. Since the seventeenth century, jurists and legislatures have claimed the right to define appropriate kinds of charitable activity and to reform charities that did not serve the public interest as they defined it. The issue of the permanence of donor intent has been the subject of extensive legal study, particularly as it relates to the ability of future generations to alter the mission of a foundation or trust when the original mission has become impractical or impossible to fulfill. See C. Ronald Chester, "Cy Pres: A Promise Unfulfilled," *Indiana Law Journal* 54 (1979): 407–425; Vanessa Laird, "Phantom Selves: The Search for a General Charitable Intent in the Application of the Cy Pres Doctrine," *Stanford Law Review* 40 (1988): 973–987; and Rob Atkinson, "Reforming Cy Pres Reform," *Hastings Law Journal* 44 (1993): 1111–1156.

22. Andrew Carnegie, "The Gospel of Wealth," in Dwight F. Burlingame, ed., *The Responsibilities of Wealth* (Bloomington: Indiana University Press, 1992). See also the discussion by Barry Karl, "Andrew Carnegie and His Gospel of Philanthropy: A Study in Ethics of Responsibility," in Burlingame, ed., *The Responsibilities of Wealth*; and Ellen Condliffe Lagemann, *The Politics of Knowledge: The Carnegie Corporation, Philanthropy, and Public Policy* (Chicago: University of Chicago Press, 1989).

23. The best overview of the history of philanthropy can be found in Robert H. Bremner, *American Philanthropy* (Chicago: University of Chicago Press, 1988). See also Judith Sealander, *Private Wealth and Public Life: Foundation Philanthropy and the Reshaping of American Social Policy, from the Progressive Era to the New Deal* (Baltimore, Md.: Johns Hopkins University Press, 1997). Earlier important treatments of foundation philanthropy are F. Emerson Andrews, *Philanthropic Giving* (New York: Russell Sage Foundation, 1950); and Warren Weaver, *U.S. Philanthropic Foundations: Their History, Structure, Management, and Record* (New York: Harper and Row, 1967). For an overview of the more recent evolution and activity of large private foundations, see Waldemar A. Nielsen, *The Golden Donors: A New Anatomy of the Great Foundations* (New York: Truman Talley Books, 1985); Dennis P. McIlnay, *How Foundations Work: What Grantseekers Need to Know about the Many Faces of Foundations* (San Francisco: Jossey-Bass, 1998); Gerald Freund, *Narcissism and Philanthropy: Ideas and Talent Denied* (New York: Vi-

king, 1996); and James Allen Smith, "The Evolving Role of American Foundations," in Charles T. Clotfelter and Thomas Erlich, eds., *Philanthropy and the Nonprofit Sector in a Changing America* (Bloomington: Indiana University Press, 1999), pp. 34–51.

24. There are now several handbooks designed to guide wealthy donors in determining how much they can afford to give and how to give away their funds creatively. See Claude Rosenberg, Jr., *Wealthy and Wise: How You and America Can Get the Most Out of Your Giving* (Boston: Little, Brown, 1994); Renata J. Rafferty, *Don't Just Give It Away: How to Make the Most of Your Charitable Giving* (Worcester, Mass.: Chandler House Press, 1999).

25. The special features of the new gift funds are described in George Pieler, "Foundations Meet the Market: Charitable Checkbooks and Donor Choice," *Philanthropy* (July–August 1998): 25–28.

26. Several of the larger community foundations have in fact responded to the changing market for philanthropic service. No longer focused on raising unrestricted funds that foundation staff can allocate to causes they select, community foundations have been aggressively marketing their donor-advised funds, which give donors, not staff, the chance to make philanthropic decisions.

27. Internet giving does have its drawbacks; chief among these is the lack of oversight and evaluation of the quality of the organizations seeking funds. See Reed Abelson, "As E-Giving Sites Spring Up, Some Say It's Donor Beware," *New York Times,* November 17, 1999, p. H21; Reed Abelson, "Pitfalls for Internet Shoppers with Charitable Bent," *New York Times,* March 31, 1999, pp. A1, C10.

28. The tendency of donors to identify with the organizations and causes they support through philanthropy is discussed in Paul G. Schervish, "Wealth and the Spiritual Secret of Money," in Robert Wuthnow et al., eds., *Faith and Philanthropy in America* (San Francisco: Jossey-Bass, 1989), pp. 63–90. See also Susan A. Ostrander and Paul G. Schervish, "Giving and Getting: Philanthropy as a Social Relation," in Jon Van Til et al., eds., *Critical Issues in American Philanthropy: Strengthening Theory and Practice* (San Francisco: Jossey-Bass, 1990).

29. The idea of turning philanthropy into an engaged and consultative form of venture capital investing is explored in Christine W. Letts, William P. Ryan, and Allen Grossman, "Virtuous Capital: What Foundations Can Learn from Venture Capitalists," in *Harvard Business Review on Nonprofits* (Boston: Harvard Business School Publishing, 1999), pp. 91–110. This approach focuses attention and resources on building strong organizations, not just on writing checks that support isolated initiatives. For a broad description of the move to adapt the venture capital model for use in philanthropy, see *Ven-*

*ture Philanthropy: Landscape and Expectations* (Reston, Va.: Morino Institute, 2000).

30. See Judith Miller, "A Hands-On Generation Transforms the Landscape of American Philanthropy," *New York Times,* December 9, 1997, p. 8.

31. Sam Howe Verhovek, "Internet's Fortune Makers Giving It Away, Their Way," *New York Times,* February 11, 2000, pp. A1, A21. Patricia Leigh Brown, "Turning Baby Internet Moguls into Big Givers," *New York Times,* November 17, 1999, p. H4.

32. For an account of the intersection of religion and charitable activity, see Peter Dobkin Hall, "The History of Religious Philanthropy in America," in Wuthnow et al., eds., *Faith and Philanthropy in America,* pp. 38–62.

33. See *Giving USA* (New York: American Association of Fund-Raising Counsel, 1999); Jeff E. Biddle, "Religious Organizations," in Charles T. Clotfelter, ed., *Who Benefits from the Nonprofit Sector?* (Chicago: University of Chicago Press, 1992), pp. 92–133.

34. Thomas H. Jeavons, "When Management Is the Message: Relating Values to Management Practice in Nonprofit Organizations," *Nonprofit Management and Leadership* 2, no. 4 (1992): 403 (quoted in Mason, *Leading and Managing the Expressive Dimension,* p. 52). See also Thomas H. Jeavons, *When the Bottom Line Is Faithfulness: Management of Christian Service Organizations* (Indianapolis: Indiana University Press, 1994).

35. Dorothy M. Brown and Elizabeth McKeown, *The Poor Belong to Us: Catholic Charities and American Welfare* (Cambridge, Mass.: Harvard University Press, 1997).

36. For a good discussion of the range of religious activity undertaken under the nonprofit umbrella, see Mark Chaves, "The Religious Ethic and the Spirit of Nonprofit Entrepreneurship," in Walter W. Powell and Elisabeth Clemens, eds., *Private Action and the Public Good* (New Haven: Yale University Press, 1998); Max L. Stackhouse, "Religion and the Social Space for Voluntary Institutions," in Wuthnow et al., eds., *Faith and Philanthropy in America,* pp. 22–37.

37. In recent years, financial problems have hit not just the small congregations but also the larger and more firmly established religious institutions. See Robert Wuthnow, *The Crisis in the Churches: Spiritual Malaise, Fiscal Woe* (New York: Oxford University Press, 1997).

38. Some argue that the expansive missions of religious hospitals and their commercialization have done a great deal to give them an unfair advantage. See James T. Bennett and Thomas J. DiLorenzo, "The Political Economy of Unfair Competition," in Bennett and DiLorenzo, *Unfair Competition: The Profits of Nonprofits* (New York: Hamilton Press, 1989), pp. 45–72.

39. Thomas Jeavons, "Identifying Characteristics of 'Religious' Organizations," in N. J. Demerath III et al., *Sacred Companies: Organizational Aspects of Reli-*

*gion and Religious Aspects of Organizations* (New York: Oxford University Press, 1998) pp. 79–95.

40. Further complicating the matter of assessing religious participation is the fact that surveys may well overstate actual church attendance. See C. Kirk Hadaway, Penny Long Mahler, and Mark Chaves, "What the Polls Don't Show: A Closer Look at U.S. Church Attendance," *American Sociological Review* 56 (1993): 741–752; and Stanley Presser and Linda Stinson, "Data Collection and Social Desirability Bias in Self-Reported Religious Attendance," *American Sociological Review* 63 (1998): 137–145.

41. Governor's Advisory Task Force on Faith-Based Community Service Groups (Austin, Tex.: Office of the Governor, 1996), p. 4.

42. See Mark Chaves, "Religious Congregations, Welfare, and 'Charitable Choice,'" *American Sociological Review* 64, no. 6 (December 1999): 836–846. Though the number of churches willing to consider applying for public funds is high, Chaves cautions that this number may exaggerate the number that actually will apply for funds under charitable choice.

43. Amy Sherman, "Implementing Charitable Choice," *Philanthropy* (January–February 1999): 14–19; idem, "Little Miracles," *American Enterprise* (January–February 1998): 64–68.

44. Tim Golden, "Opposition in San Francisco to Policy on Unmarried Partners," *New York Times,* February 6, 1997.

45. Michael Prince, "New York Eyes Partner Mandate: Councilman Seeks to Copy Controversial San Francisco Rule," *Business Insurance,* February 10, 1997.

46. Don Lattin, "S.F. Archbishop Insists He's Not Anti-Gay," *San Francisco Chronicle,* February 4, 1997.

47. Torri Minton, "S.F. Archbishop Agrees to Discuss Partners Policy," *San Francisco Chronicle,* February 4, 1997.

48. Steven Greenhouse, "Nonprofit and Religious Groups to Fight Workfare in New York," *New York Times,* July 24, 1997, p. 1.

49. Arthur Okun, *The Big Tradeoff: Equality and Efficiency* (Washington, D.C.: Brookings Institution, 1994).

50. Marvin Olasky, *The Tragedy of American Compassion* (Washington, D.C.: Regnery, 1992).

## 5. Social Entrepreneurship

1. For a series of profiles of young nonprofit entrepreneurs, working in fields as varied as environmental advocacy, AIDS prevention, child welfare, and literacy, see "A New Guard Emerges," *Chronicle of Philanthropy,* January 14, 1999.

2. See Jane Gallagher, "Peddling Products," in *Competing Visions: The Non-*

*profit Sector in the Twenty-First Century* (Washington, D.C.: Aspen Institute, 1997), pp. 49–72.

3. Howard H. Stevenson, Michael J. Roberts, and H. Irving Grousbeck, *New Business Ventures and the Entrepreneur* (Burr Ridge, Ill.: Irwin, 1994).

4. Karl Vesper, *New Venture Strategies* (Englewood Cliffs, N.J.: Prentice-Hall, 1980).

5. Joseph Schumpeter, *Can Capitalism Survive?* (New York: Harper and Row, 1952).

6. Ibid., p. 72.

7. Joseph Schumpeter, *The Theory of Economic Development* (New York: Harper and Row, 1947), p. 93.

8. See Robert D. Hisrich, "Entrepreneurship and Intrapreneurship: Methods for Creating New Companies That Have Impact on the Economic Renaissance of an Area," in Robert D. Hisrich, ed., *Entrepreneurship, Intrapreneurship, and Venture Capital* (Lexington, Mass.: Lexington Books, 1986).

9. Stevenson, Roberts, and Grousbeck, *New Business Ventures and the Entrepreneur.*

10. Dennis R. Young, "Entrepreneurship and the Behavior of Nonprofit Organizations: Elements of a Theory," in Susan Rose-Ackerman, ed., *The Economics of Nonprofit Institutions: Studies in Structure and Policy* (New York: Oxford University Press, 1986), pp. 161–184.

11. See J. Gregory Dees, *The Social Enterprise Spectrum: Philanthropy to Commerce,* Case no. 9-396-343 (Boston: Harvard Business School Press, 1996); and J. Gregory Dees, "Enterprising Nonprofits," in *Harvard Business Review on Nonprofits* (Boston: Harvard Business School Publishing, 1999), pp. 135–166.

12. For a good overview of the charter school movement and the challenges these organizations face, see Tom Loveless, "Starting from Scratch: Political and Organizational Challenges Facing Charter Schools," *Educational Administration Quarterly* 34, no. 1 (February 1998): 9–30.

13. Sarah Kass, "Boston's City on a Hill," *The Public Interest* (Fall 1996): 27–37.

14. Harvey Simon, "The Orange Hats of Fairlawn," Kennedy School of Government, Teaching Case no. 1034.0, Harvard University, 1991.

15. On the challenges of trusteeship, see Cyril Houle, *Governing Boards: Their Nature and Nurture* (San Francisco: Jossey-Bass, 1989); and David H. Smith, *Entrusted: The Moral Responsibilities of Trusteeship* (Bloomington: Indiana University Press, 1995).

16. For a good introduction to arts funding, see Margaret J. Wyszomirski, "Philanthropy and Culture: Patterns, Context, and Change," in Charles T. Clotfelter and Thomas Erlich, eds., *Philanthropy and the Nonprofit Sector in a Changing America* (Bloomington: Indiana University Press, 1999), pp. 461–480.

17. An account of the evolution of trusteeship can be found in Peter Dobkin Hall, "Resolving the Dilemmas of Democratic Governance: The Historical Development of Trusteeship in America, 1636–1996," in Ellen Condliffe Lagemann, ed., *Philanthropic Foundations: New Scholarship, New Possibilities* (Bloomington: Indiana University Press, 1999).

18. Jennifer Dunning, "The Joffrey Reorganizes as a Chicago Company," *New York Times*, September 8, 1995.

19. For a clear analysis of the factors driving nonprofit expansion, see Estelle James, "How Nonprofits Grow: A Model," in Rose-Ackerman, ed., *The Economics of Nonprofit Institutions*, pp. 185–195.

20. For a complete exposition of the historical growth of nonprofit organizations, see Peter Dobkin Hall and Colin B. Burke, "Voluntary, Nonprofit, and Religious Organizations and Activities," in *Historical Statistics of the United States: Millennial Edition* (New York: Cambridge University Press, 2002).

21. John Kreidler, "Leverage Lost: The Nonprofit Arts in the Post-Ford Era," *Journal of Arts Management, Law, and Society* 20, no. 2 (Summer 1996): 79–100.

22. A good discussion of the challenges facing arts organizations in the United States can be found in Gary O. Larson, *American Canvas: An Arts Legacy for Our Communities* (Washington, D.C.: National Endowment for the Arts, 1997).

23. In the arts, the move toward earned income has been very pronounced. For a discussion of the changing financial strategy of arts organizations, see Louise Stevens, "The Earnings Shift: The New Bottom-Line Paradigm for the Arts Industry in a Market-Driven Era," *Journal of Arts Management, Law, and Society* (Summer 1996): 101–113.

24. Bruce R. Hopkins, "Legal Issues in Fund Raising and Philanthropy," in Jon Van Til et al., eds., *Critical Issues in American Philanthropy: Strengthening Theory and Practice* (San Francisco: Jossey-Bass, 1990); Margaret A. Duronio, "The Fund Raising Profession," in Dwight F. Burlingame, ed., *Critical Issues in Fundraising* (New York: Wiley, 1997), pp. 37–57; Michael O'Neill, "The Ethical Dimensions of Fund Raising," in Burlingame, ed., *Critical Issues in Fundraising*, pp. 58–64.

25. For a discussion of the issues raised by cause-related marketing, see Kathleen A. Krentler, "Cause-Related Marketing: Advantages and Pitfalls for Nonprofits," in Virginia A. Hodgkinson et al., eds., *The Future of the Nonprofit Sector* (San Francisco: Jossey-Bass, 1989), pp. 363–374. For a broader discussion of the conflicts and problems raised by corporate contributions to nonprofits, see Joseph Galaskiewicz, "Corporate Contribution to Charity: Nothing More than a Marketing Strategy?" in R. Magat, ed., *Philanthropic Giving* (New York: Oxford University Press, 1989); Jerome L. Himmelstein, *Looking Good and Doing Good: Corporate Philanthropy and Corporate Power*

(Indianapolis: Indiana University Press, 1997); Reynold Levy, *Give and Take: A Candid Account of Corporate Philanthropy* (Boston: Harvard Business School Press, 1999); John Hood, *The Heroic Enterprise: Business and the Common Good* (New York: Free Press, 1996); and Curt Weeden, *Corporate Social Investing: The Breakthrough Strategy for Giving and Getting Corporate Contributions* (San Francisco: Berrett-Koehler, 1998).

26. See Glenn Collins, "AMA Seeks to Dismantle Sunbeam Deal," *New York Times,* August 22, 1997; Glenn Collins, "Cold Cash for the AMA: Look Who's Doing Endorsements," *New York Times,* August 17, 1997; Glenn Collins, "Sunbeam Sues the AMA on Voided Marketing Deal," *New York Times,* September 9, 1997.

27. For a discussion of the AMA and ACA deals, as well as accounts of numerous other endorsements by health charities, see James T. Bennett and Thomas J. DiLorenzo, "Commercialization of America's Health Charities," *Society* 34, no. 4 (1997): 67–72.

28. One recent report noted that more than a quarter of all nonprofits receiving $500,000 or more in private contributions reported no fundraising expenses on their tax forms. See "Charities' Zero-Sum Filing Game," *Chronicle of Philanthropy,* May 18, 2000, p. 1.

29. See Margaret Riley, "Unrelated Business Income of Nonprofit Organizations: Highlights of 1995 and a Review of 1991–1995," *SOI Bulletin* (Spring 1999): 80–112; James R. Hines, Jr., "Non-Profit Business Activity and the Unrelated Business Income Tax," *Tax Policy and the Economy* 13 (1999): 57–84; Richard Sansing, "The Unrelated Business Income Tax, Cost Allocation, and Productive Efficiency," *National Tax Journal* 51, no. 2 (June 1998): 291–302.

30. One reason nonprofits are able to get away with cost shifting is that the IRS is able to audit only a very small number of 990 tax returns each year. See Jennifer Moore and Grant Williams, "Taxing Times for the Tax Agency," *Chronicle of Philanthropy,* October 17, 1996, p. 1. Another explanation for the rise in unrelated business income reported by nonprofits lies in the continued confusion over where the line between related and unrelated income lies. In the face of regulatory uncertainty, some organizations are probably erring on the side of caution and reporting as unrelated many sources of income that may simply lie near the borderline.

31. In the field of health services, the trend toward commercialism translates into lower rates of charity care. See Bennett and DiLorenzo, "Commercialization of America's Health Charities," pp. 66–72.

32. For a full account of both the Novartis deal and other examples of commercial activity within higher education, see Eyal Press and Jennifer Washburn, "The Kept University," *Atlantic Monthly* (March 2000): 39–53.

33. Gilbert M. Gaul and Neill A. Borowski, "The Profitable World of Non-

profits," in Gaul and Borowski, *Free Ride: The Tax Free Economy* (Kansas City, Mo.: Andrews and McMeel, 1993), pp. 1–31.

34. James T. Bennett and Thomas J. DiLorenzo, *Unfair Competition: The Profits of Nonprofits* (New York: Hamilton Press, 1989).

35. Robert A. Watson and Ben Brown, *The Most Effective Organization in the U.S.: Leadership Secrets of the Salvation Army* (New York: Crown Business, 2001).

36. Marion R. Fremont-Smith, "Trends in Accountability and Regulation of Nonprofits," in Hodgkinson et al., *The Future of the Nonprofit Sector,* pp. 75–88.

37. John Murawski, "Former United Way Chief Gets Seven Years in Jail; Sentence Praised by Charities," *Chronicle of Philanthropy,* July 13, 1995, pp. 37–38.

38. See Steve Stecklow, "New Era's Bennett Gets Twelve Years in Prison for Defrauding Charities," *Wall Street Journal,* September 23, 1997, p. B15.

39. See Elizabeth Greene, "Embezzlement at Episcopal Church Highlights Needs for Controls," *Chronicle of Philanthropy,* May 18, 1995, p. 39; Michael Fletcher, "Baptist Group President to Resign," *Washington Post,* March 16, 1999, p. A2.

40. Elizabeth Greene, "The NAACP: What Went Wrong?" *Chronicle of Philanthropy,* May 4, 1995, pp. 27–29.

41. Devin Thornburg, "Adelphi, Weathering Crisis, Will Endure," *Newsday,* March 13, 1997, p. A57.

42. Regina E. Herzlinger, "Can Public Trust in Nonprofits and Governments Be Restored?" in *Harvard Business Review on Nonprofits* (Boston: Harvard Business School Publishing, 1999), pp. 1–28.

43. The idea of using information to regulate nonprofits is appealing, given the inability of the IRS to enforce existing rules and regulations. Several observers have concluded that the IRS simply does not have the manpower to oversee the growing number of nonprofits. See Gilbert M. Gaul and Neill A. Borowski, "IRS: The Cops That Can't Keep Up," in Gaul and Borowski, *Free Ride,* pp. 91–113; and Elizabeth Greene and Grant Williams, "Asleep on the Watch?" *Chronicle of Philanthropy,* July 27, 1995, p. 1.

44. Esther Scott, "Zoning Restrictions on Social Services for the Poor: The Case of Hartford, Connecticut," Kennedy School of Government, Teaching Case no. 1453.0, Harvard University, 1998.

## 6. Balancing the Functions of Nonprofit and Voluntary Action

1. Some believe that there is not enough independent, private support for advocacy efforts within the philanthropic world and that the funders' prefer-

ence for service delivery has weakened the ability of the sector to shape public policy in a productive way. See Karen M. Paget, "The Big Chill," *The American Prospect* 44 (May–June 1999): 26–33.

2. In 1995, Representative Ernest G. Istook, Jr., of Oklahoma proposed an amendment which would have prohibited groups that receive federal grants from spending more than 5 percent of private dollars to lobby or communicate with the government. Though ultimately defeated, the bill received substantial support and even passed in the House of Representatives.

3. The case of the University of Bridgeport, in Connecticut, is instructive. Facing a major financial crisis and rising debt, the university accepted an offer of aid from an affiliate of the Unification Church. In exchange for a major infusion of funds, the church insisted on and secured representation on the university's board of trustees and a role in recruiting students. The deal was a last-ditch effort to save the school and exposed it to severe criticism for allowing a religious entity to gain undue influence over a secular institution. See George Judson, "Making the Choice at Bridgeport University: Opting to Stay Alive," *New York Times,* April 16, 1992, p. B5.

4. A classic example is the country club that serves only affluent patrons and charges fees for all its services. See James M. Mayo, *The American Country Club: Its Origins and Development* (New Brunswick, N.J.: Rutgers University Press, 1998).

5. See David Cay Johnson, "AARP Sets Up a Taxable Subsidiary," *New York Times,* July 15, 1999, p. C9.

6. On the policy and managerial obstacles to nonprofit consolidation and mergers, see Garry William Jenkins, "Supporting Nonprofit Mergers and Strategic Consolidation through Law and Public Policy," Policy Analysis Exercise, Kennedy School of Government, Harvard University, 1998.

7. Kathleen S. Kelly, "From Motivation to Mutual Understanding," in Dwight F. Burlingame, ed., *Critical Issues in Fundraising* (New York: Wiley, 1997), pp. 139–164.

8. While there is a danger of mission creep connected to broad and multi-dimensional nonprofit activity, many organizations have solved this dilemma by finding connections and synergies between programs and activities. Sometimes this takes the form of shared staff; other times it involves cross-subsidization.

# Index